# A-Z OF STAFFORDSHIRE DOGS

## A POTTED HISTORY

CLIVE MASON POPE

ANTIQUE COLLECTORS' CLUB

First published 1990 by Resego AG. SA., Switzerland
Reissued 1996 by Antique Collectors' Club Ltd.

ISBN 1 85149 258 5



British Library Cataloguing-in-Publication Data
A catalogue record for this book is available from the British Library

Designed by Andi Gisel
Photography by Michael Ryan

Printed in England on Consort Royal Satin paper
supplied by the Donside Paper Company, Aberdeen,
by Antique Collectors' Club Ltd., Woodbridge, Suffolk, IP12 1DS

*The two most popular dogs of the nineteenth century*

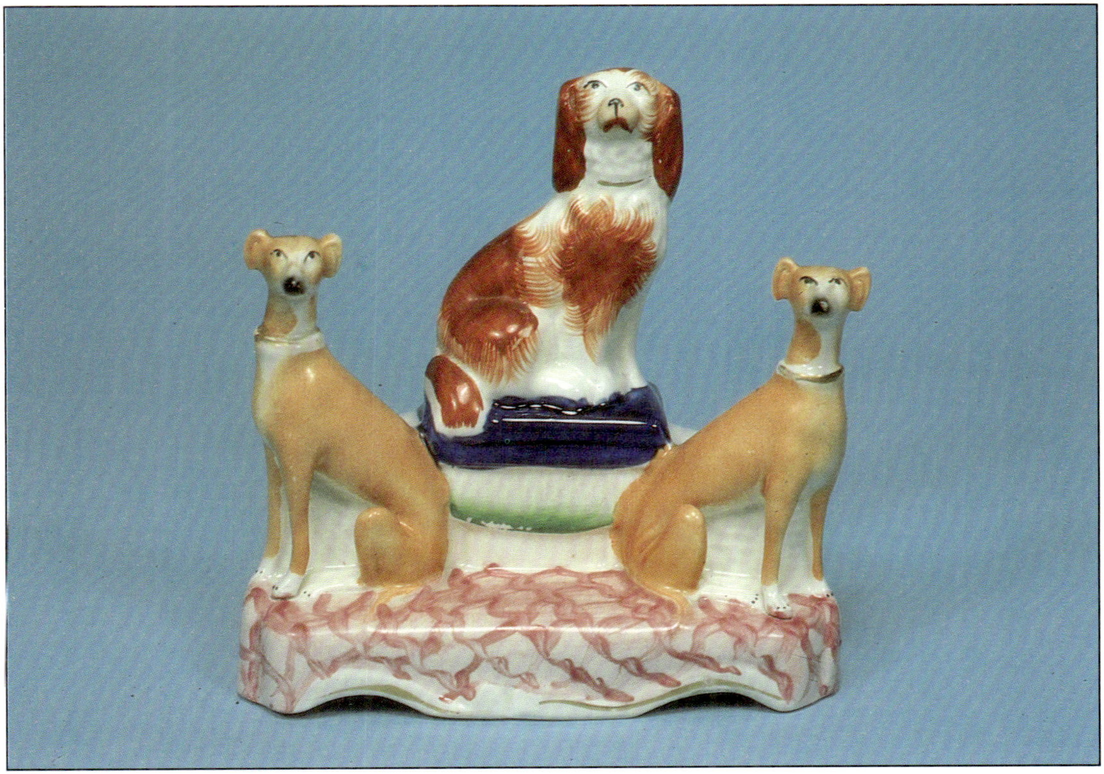

A centrepiece group of a King Charles Spaniel
sitting on a blue cushion with Italian Greyhound supporters
on a pink marblised serpentine base
Height 6¾ inches
Circa 1850

*"There is in every animal's eye a dim image and gleam of humanity, a flash of strange light through which their life looks out and up to our great mystery of command over them and claims the fellowship of the creature if not the soul".*

JOHN RUSKIN: 19th century Art Critic
(From his academy notes: 1858)

# Contents

# Foreword

*The human preoccupation of modelling dogs in clay stretches back well into the ancient world, reflecting the unique partnership man has achieved with this animal above all others.*

*Pottery dogs are frequently found amongst the Egyptian tomb companion figures and in China during the Han and Tang dynasties.*

*Pre-Columbian America has also revealed such examples with important early models found in Mexico and Peru.*

*It was not until the 18th century however that we notice a serious attempt to model identifiable breeds. This change brought about, it seems, by a wider interest in selective breeding, so as to ensure the more desirable qualities of particular sporting breeds, encouraged the artists and potters of the day to reflect this new canine enthusiasm in their art.*

*Meissen and other major European factories, echoed the sporting interest with several models of hounds and in France, the Royal Factory at Vincennes, its eye on the more domestic market, became famous for its delicate porcelain model of Madame de Pompadour's particular tiny pet, an appealing little Pug dog seated on its own tasselled cushion.*

*The English potters were quick to respond and the Chelsea factory produced a portrait of William Hogarth's famous Pug dog "Trump", again in porcelain.*

*Although there were very few Pugs in England at the beginning of the 18th century, this exotic breed appealed to the western taste for chinoiserie, fashionable at the time.*

*Numerous versions were produced by most of the English factories and with its total lack of usefulness for hunting or guarding, it was often portrayed sitting on a tasselled cushion.*

*The Derby and Bow factories remained true to the sporting instinct and also produced, alongside this pampered creature, several models of gun-dogs in action more appropriately set on oval bases of naturalistic scrub.*

*Around 1760 the London Delftware potters produced their handsome if somewhat undoglike models of hounds painted with blue patches and spots against a white background, revealing their Dutch inspiration and here we see the beginning of ideas in pottery rather than porcelain.*

*The Whieldon and Wood families of Burslem in Staffordshire, potted their colourful individual dog studies in a primitive and powerful style decorated in a combination of splashed yellow, green, brown and blue glazes. They modelled what they saw around them in the countryside, sporting dogs, usually on a raised rectangular base. No comfortable silk cushions for these hardy breeds to lie around on in the remaining days of the 18th century.*

*With the introduction of the new bone-china material in the early days of the 19th century the porcelain factories once again entered the race.*

*Minton produced models of Greyhounds, Sporting Spaniels and that persistent foreign Pug!*

*Similar models were made at Derby and the Alcock factory with the emphasis now on a rococo style base to sit better alongside the more flamboyant decorations of the period.*

*Queen Victoria's reign began in 1837 and with her marriage to Prince Albert in 1840 a new royal family began to grow.*

*The "family" began to include dogs of various breeds, who for a change did not have to earn their keep in the field but were loved and petted for their own sake. Dogs became "family" and nothing was more important to the Victorians than family. Their Queen's favourite, a King Charles Spaniel named "Dash" was taken to the nation's heart by means of paintings and prints which included him within the family setting.*

*The potters of Staffordshire saw their chance, they grasped popular thought by the collar, giving it life and form in pot.*

*Simplifying the modelling methods to satisfy this new demand, pairs of Spaniels were produced in great numbers, to decorate the mantelpieces of Britain. Jostling for attention in a great variety of colour and size they became popularly known as "comforters".*

*A nation of dog-lovers was born and almost every breed portrayed in clay, but the Spaniel reigned supreme finally dethroning the Pug.*

*Their makers were anonymous and their simple hand-painted decoration often carried out by children, achieving an individuality that remains perennially popular today.*

*We will never see their like again, as today's silent robot hands stamp out today's characterless imitations.*

# About the Author

*A schoolday essay, 'The 19th century Staffordshire Potteries', first prompted Clive's interest in Staffordshire figures.*

*He has been Staffordshire 'daft' ever since.*

*A successful and individual career as a Hair and Wig Designer in the world of show business allowed him to pursue his interest in Staffordshire whilst he continued to create a name for himself as one of the most sought after 'character-forming' designers with many of our leading actors insisting that Clive with his reputation for artistic line, an eye for colour and attention to detail, design the 'look' for their required characterisation.*

*Elizabeth Taylor, Rex Harrison, Ursula Andress and Sir Laurence Olivier have all added to their performances with Clive's help.*

*A Staffordshire collection finally encompassing his home and his heart and a desire to share this love and appreciation of the subject with others Clive (by this time a recognised authority on the subject), took the decision to leave his 'Star Names' behind and concentrate on the 'Star Quality' of Staffordshire.*

*The shop he established in Oxfordshire near Blenheim Palace, home of the Blenheim King Charles Spaniel, quickly became a mecca for discerning collectors from around the world.*

*Now retired and living in rural France, Clive's love of the animal world has certainly proved enduring (last count there were two dogs, three cats, two donkeys and several chickens).*

*The charming guest cottage furnished with Staffordshire (of course) is, it seems, almost permanently let, to past clients who have become firm friends.*

*There is even a penguin to greet you at cocktail time around the pool.*

*'It's a dog's life'*

*Bergerac, Dordogne*

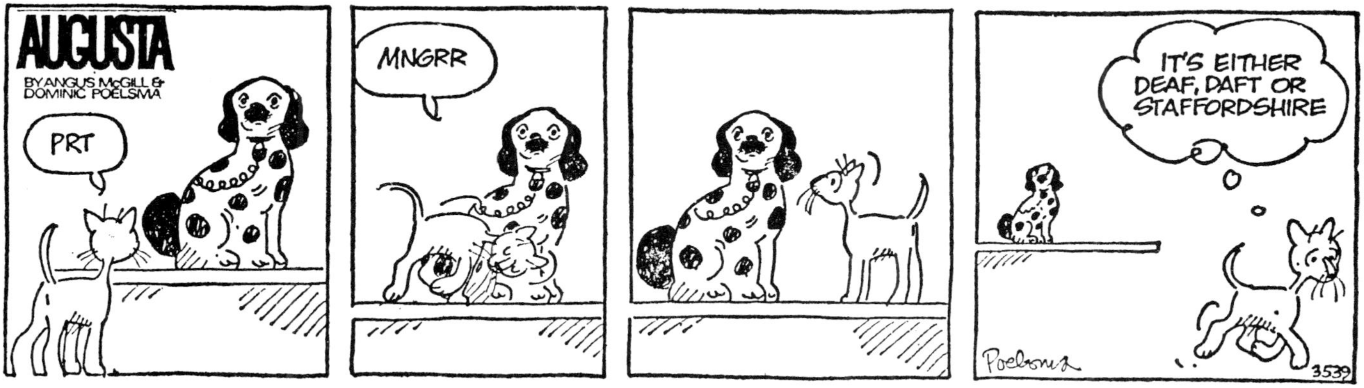


*Reproduced by kind permission of the* Evening Standard

# Preface

*Mention the word Staffordshire and dogs would seem to follow, yet in all the available reading concerning this quintessentially English folk art, although much has been said concerning its manufacture, its pageant of pottery personalities and menagerie of animals, the obvious oddly enough, has been almost entirely neglected. It was easy for me to understand the neglect whilst working on this study due to the enormous diversity of the subject and the extreme rarity of some models.*

*I made this task more difficult for myself by my determination to photograph only the finest examples to be found, preferring occasionally to photograph only a good single example rather than an inferior pair, thereby allowing the discerning collector further insight into the quality of modelling and painting that makes such a difference to appearance and therefore desirability.*

*My principal aim however was to record as many different breeds as possible dispelling the myth that, "A Staffordshire Dog must be a Spaniel".*

*There is no doubt Spaniels were everyone's favourite but they certainly did not have the field to themselves.*

# Introduction

*Although it is probable that a small percentage of the models presented may have been made at potteries in Wales or Scotland, the towns centred around the English county of Staffordshire offered the better location for their production due to the clays and an abundance of the coal necessary to fire the kilns.*

*Pottery after pottery set up in the area creating a cottage industry, pirate–ing each other's models to satisfy the demand.*

*Marketed collectively no individual factory mark was required, therefore, the generic term "Staffordshire" is accepted.*

*Never intended to languish behind the glass doors of china cabinets, Staffordshire dogs took "pride of place" in the home, reflecting around them warm feelings of homely attraction. They were modelled from prints and paintings and on many occasions almost certainly from life.*

*Often cast from simple two-piece plaster moulds, consisting of a front with blocked-in feet and a flat-back enabling them to be placed safely on a narrow mantelpiece, here they would sit and be admired from the front only.*

*However, many models were given considerably more attention, the subtle use of separate leg moulds for example, affording a more three-dimensional appeal. Other dogs were modelled and painted in the round.*

*The compelling, sometimes whimsical nature of the subject encouraged me whilst cataloguing to add my own personal titles to many of the figure numbers, such are the enduring qualities of love and affection this colourful pottery inspires.*

*Characteristics of dog breeds have of course changed over the last century, some potters interpretations may falter but thanks to surprisingly skilful modelling in many instances, most breeds are instantly recognisable. I have done my best to categorise them with the breeds listed in alphabetical order to allow the reader some points of reference.*

*Here then is my picture book of Staffordshire dogs.*

*I hope whilst adding to your appreciation of the subject it will become very "dog eared".*

# Afghan Hound

*Although the first recorded importation to Britain did not occur until the 1890s this ancient breed, a native of Afghanistan, was already well known enough through prints and paintings to have caught the potter's eye.*

*These hounds are good tempered and faithful, very good guards, and gentle with children.*

*Figure 1.* "The Power of Love"
The naive modelling lends these happy couples a special charm.
Circa 1875
Height 12½ inches

*Figure 2.* Dressed-up in full colour.
The dogs can also appear painted with rust patches.
Circa 1875
Height 12½ inches

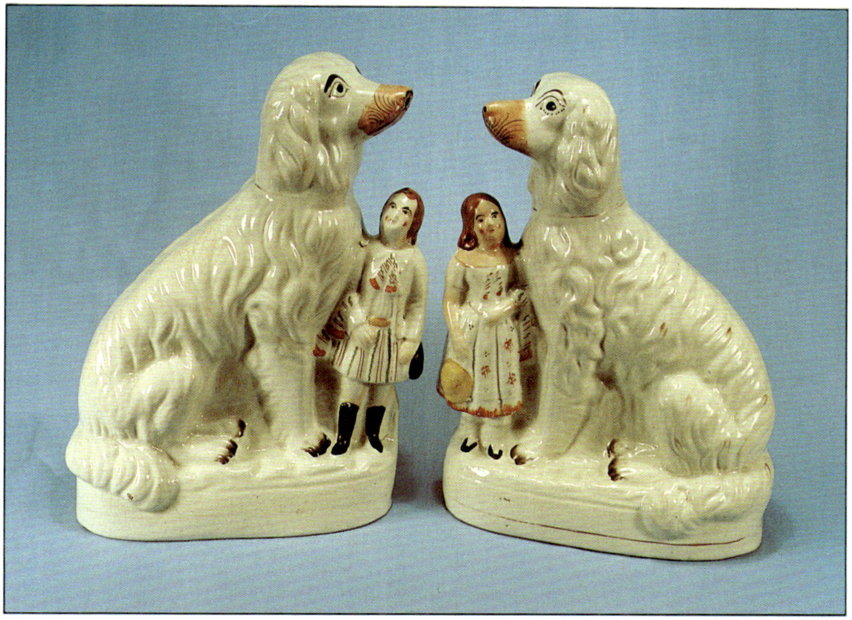

*Figure 1.*

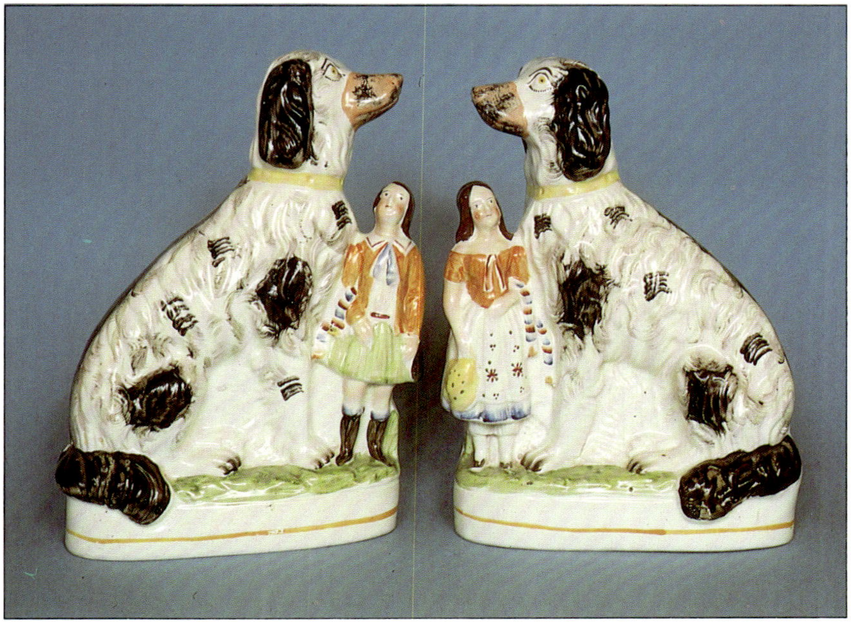

*Figure 2.*

# Bearded Collie

*When the Romans invaded in the first century this "ancient Briton" was already working cattle and sheep. Showing great sagacity, along with a charming character, its pleasant personality and lovable appearance has ensured its popularity to the present day.*

*Figure 1.* Reclining on shaped oval bases with especially attractive spill vases.
These dogs make a striking appearance.
Extremely rare.
Circa 1860
Height 10¼ inches

*Figure 2.* The same model as Figure 1 with differently painted spill vases.

*Figure 3.* Sitting against the farmyard fence.
The wide front leg positions affording them a commanding strength.
Circa 1860
Height 6½ inches

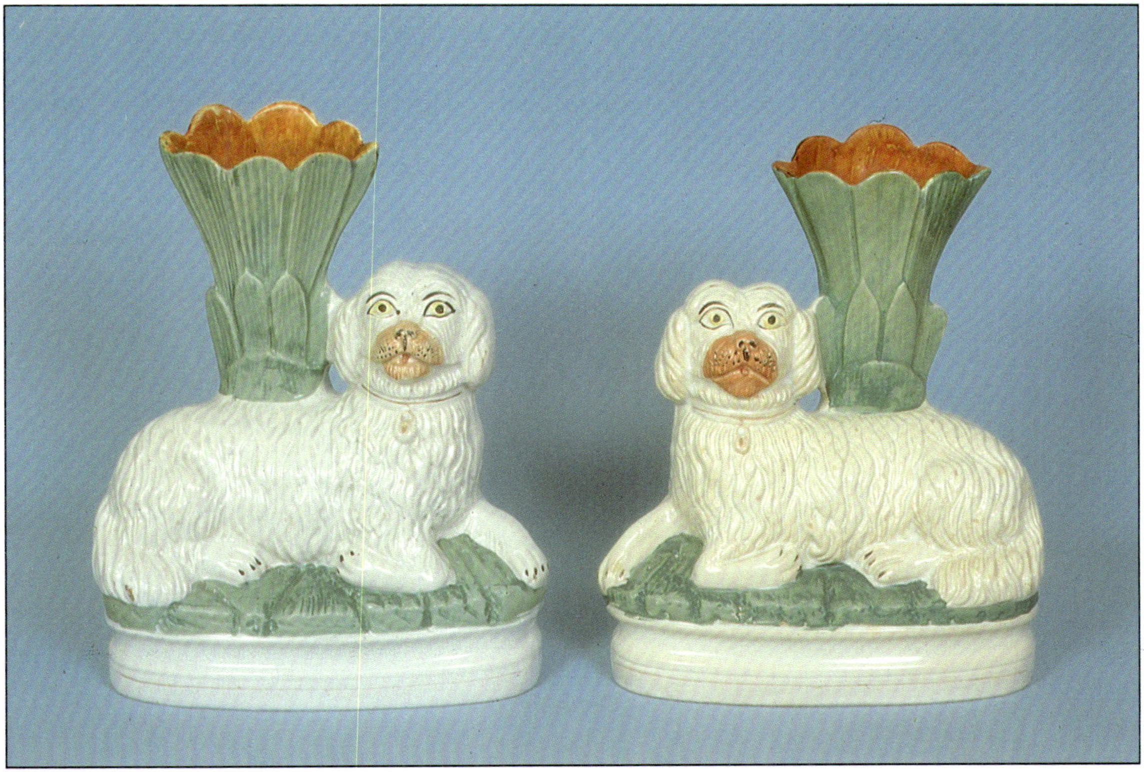

*Figure 1.*

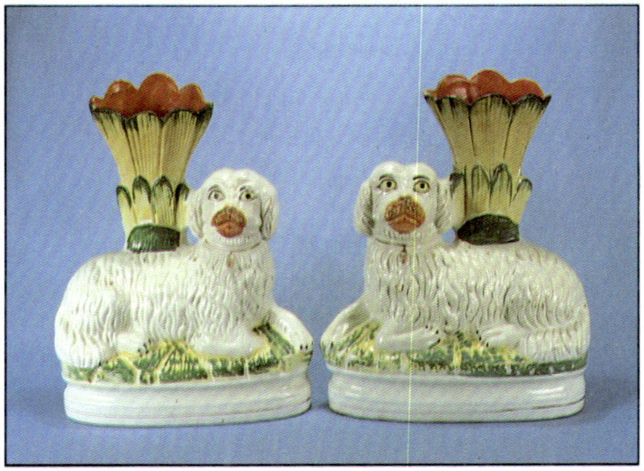

*Figure 2.*

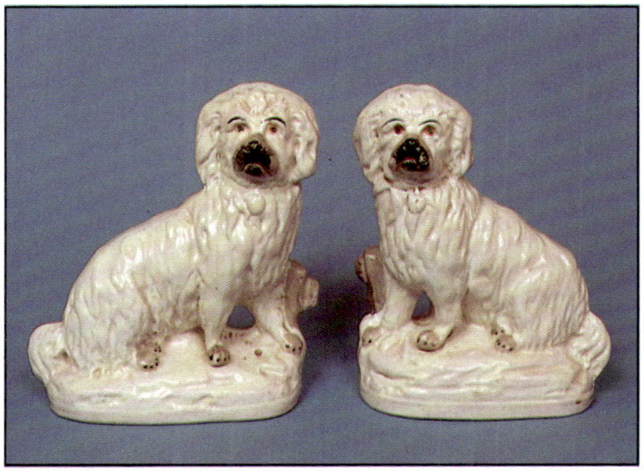

*Figure 3.*

# Bloodhound

*An old breed introduced into England from Normandy, known for its hunting and tracking abilities but not for its looks however, which may explain its lack of portraiture in pottery.*

*Figure 1.* "Gone to ground"
A spill vase group of a Bloodhound (and a Pointer) chasing a rabbit into its burrow.
The all around modelling and painting of this figure
allows a real feeling of movement to an attractive and rare group.
Circa 1845
Height 7½ inches

*Figure 2.* Back view of Figure 1.

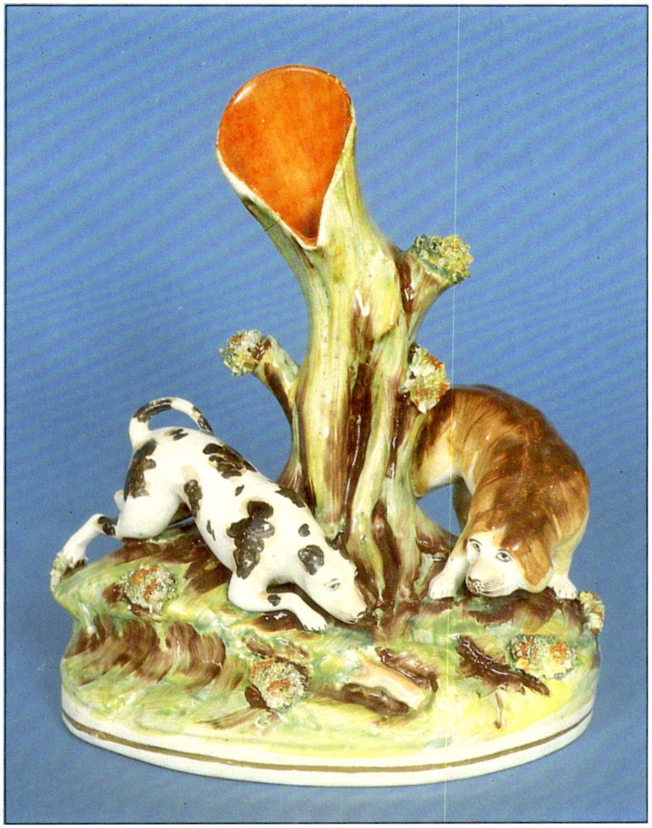

*Figure 1.*

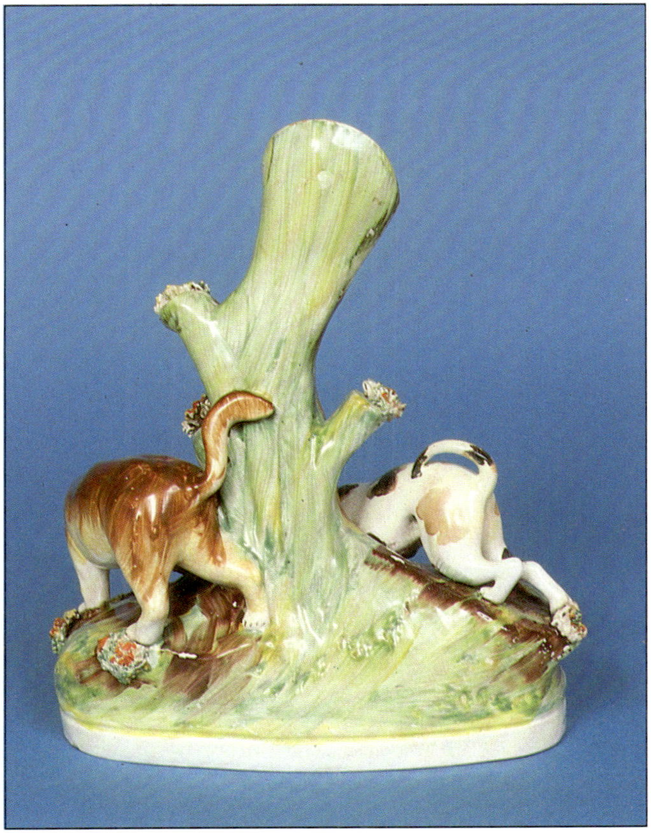

*Figure 2.*

# Border Collie

*Widely known for its great intelligence and sheep herding qualities. No farmer in the 19th century would have been without these handsome dogs.*

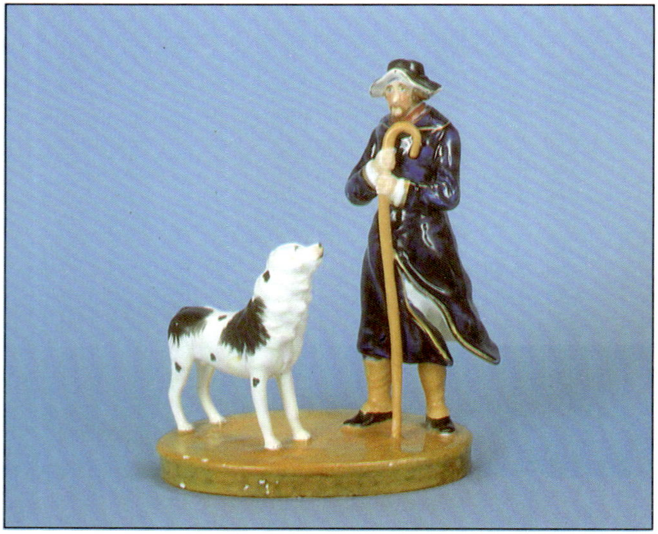

*Figure 1.*

*Figure 1.* "The Shepherd"
A porcellaneous figure unmarked but with definite characteristics of the Lloyd factory in Shelton. (Page 84).
Circa 1835
Height 6¾ inches

*Figure 2.* Beautifully modelled, standing on a cobalt blue rococo base, impressed with a leaf design and scrolled with gilt.
Circa 1845
Height 4¾ inches

*Figure 3.* "Little Girl Blue" with loving friend.
Circa 1845
Height 5½ inches

*Figure 4.* A superb study. The blue oblong base moulded with ferns.
Circa 1845
Height 3½ inches

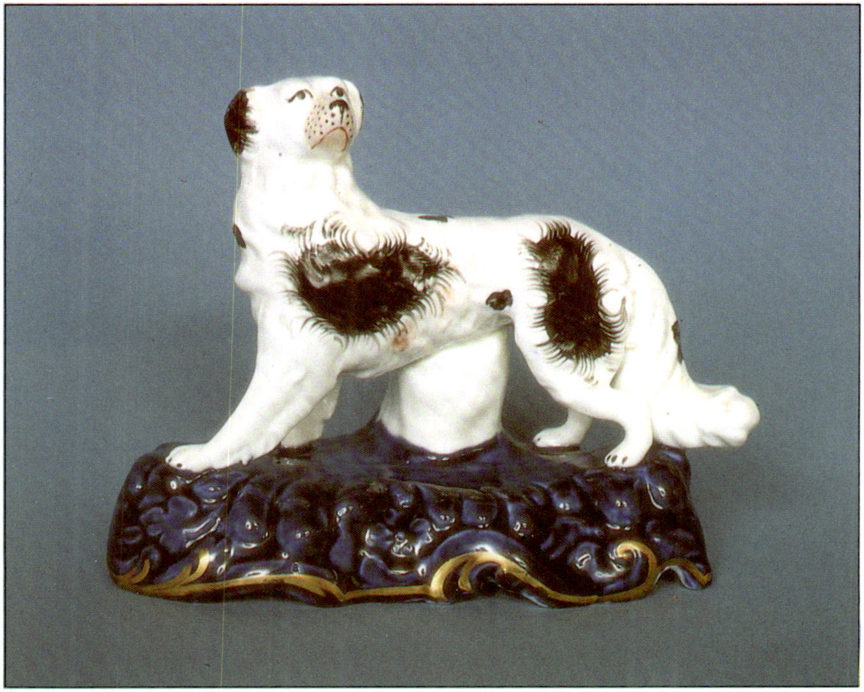

*Figure 2.*

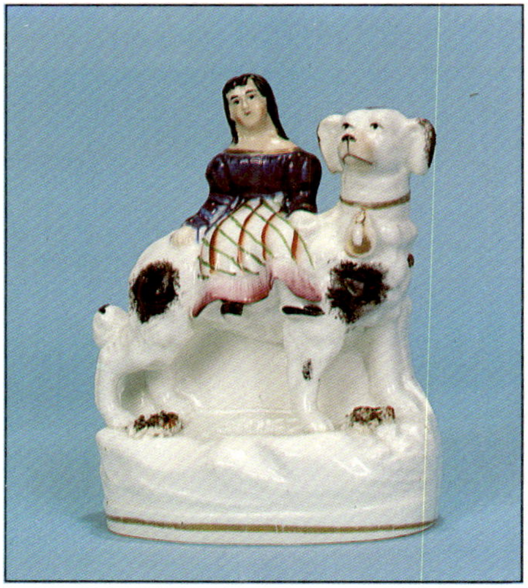

*Figure 3.*

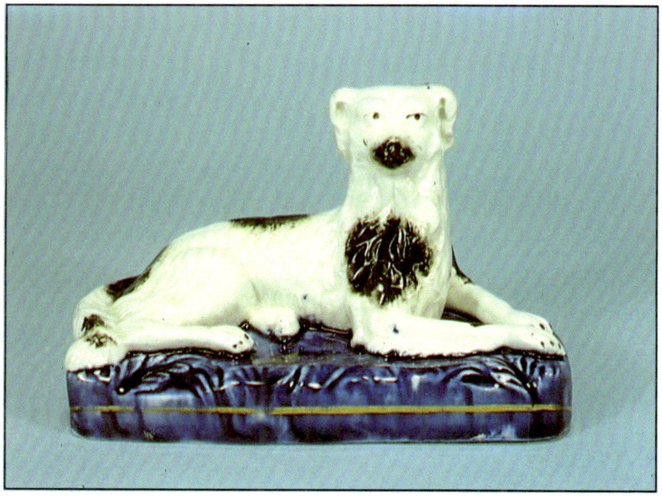

*Figure 4.*

# Collie

*The Collie's ancestors were probably an ancient breed of British dog and a breed of sheep-dog which arrived in Britain with the Roman invaders.*

*Sensitive and anxious to please he grows deeply attached to his owner and family and is specially affectionate with children.*

*His keen sense of belonging makes him an effective watch-dog.*

*Selective breeding has resulted in several distinct breeds.*

*Categorised under "C" to facilitate simpler reference, the Rough Collies pictured here are a result of a Borzoi cross around 1830.*

*For Bearded Collie see page 14.*
*For Border Collie see page 18.*

*Figure 1.* "Lassie come home!"
The careless sprayed paint effect dates them late into the century but their inset glass eyes appeal.
Circa 1890
Height 12¾ inches

*Figure 2.* Sitting on pink oval cushion bases with separately modelled front legs.
Circa 1865
Height 6 inches

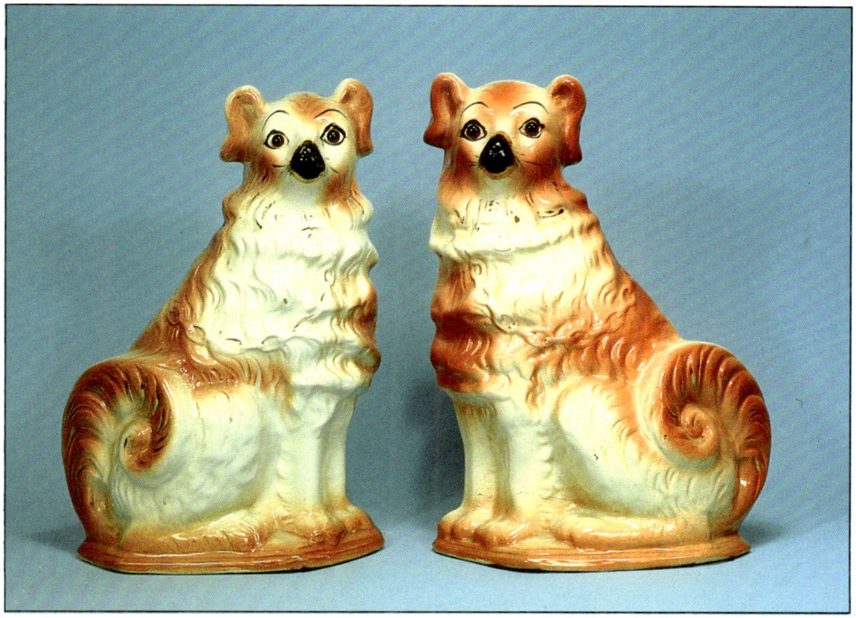

*Figure 1.*

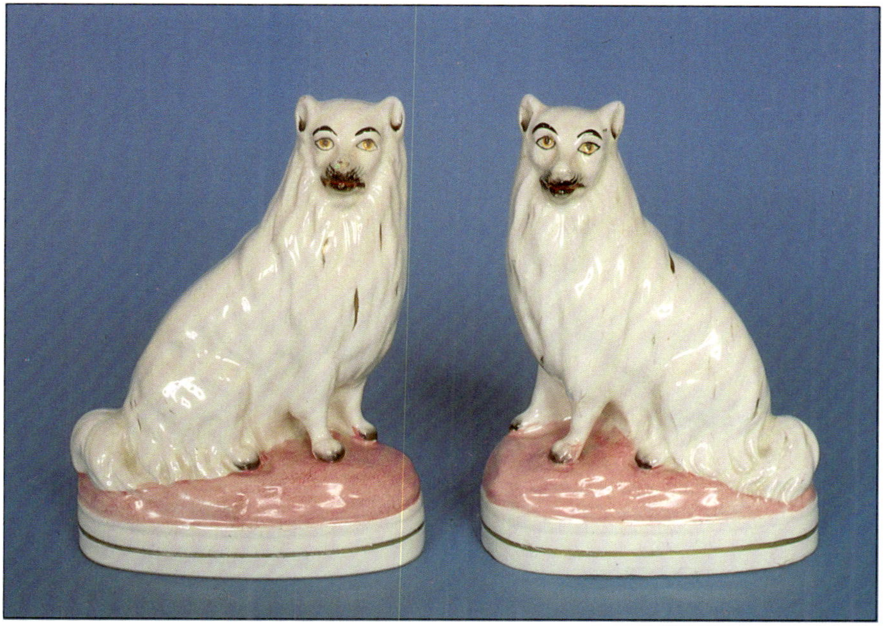

*Figure 2.*

# Dalmatian

*Deriving its name from Dalmatia, a region of Yugoslavia, the Dalmatians exact origins are uncertain. It arrived in England during the 18th century having already established itself as an excellent guard dog.*

*Totally compatible to the company of the horse, it loved to accompany carriages, trotting beside them and soon became the height of "chic" for every fashionable equipage.*

*As a symbol of elegance it retained its popularity throughout the 19th century even though its days of "Guarding the Carriage" were to be numbered.*

*Figure 1.* The decorative quality of the breed obviously inspired the potters to model several different versions.
This fine pair is a perfect example.
Circa 1845
Height 6½ inches

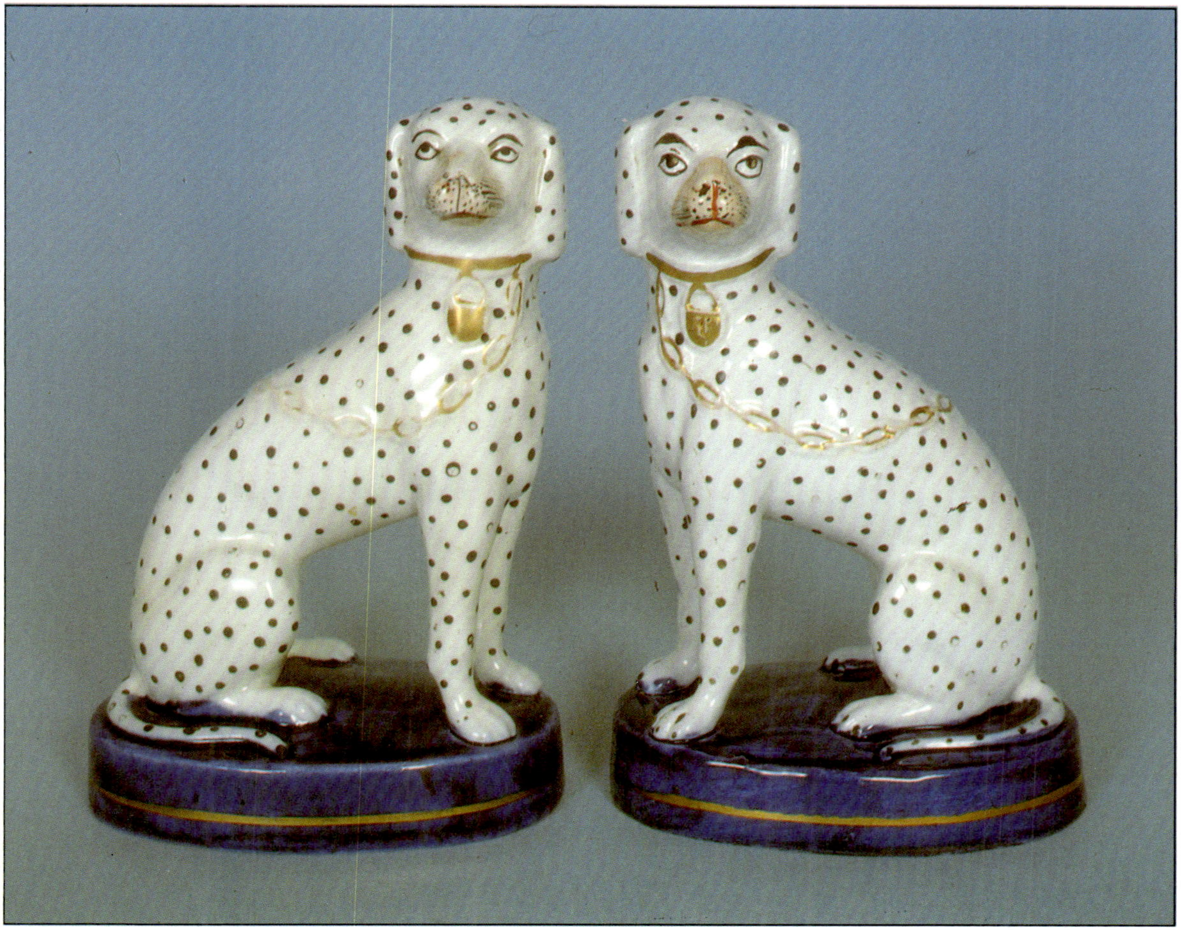

*Figure 1.*

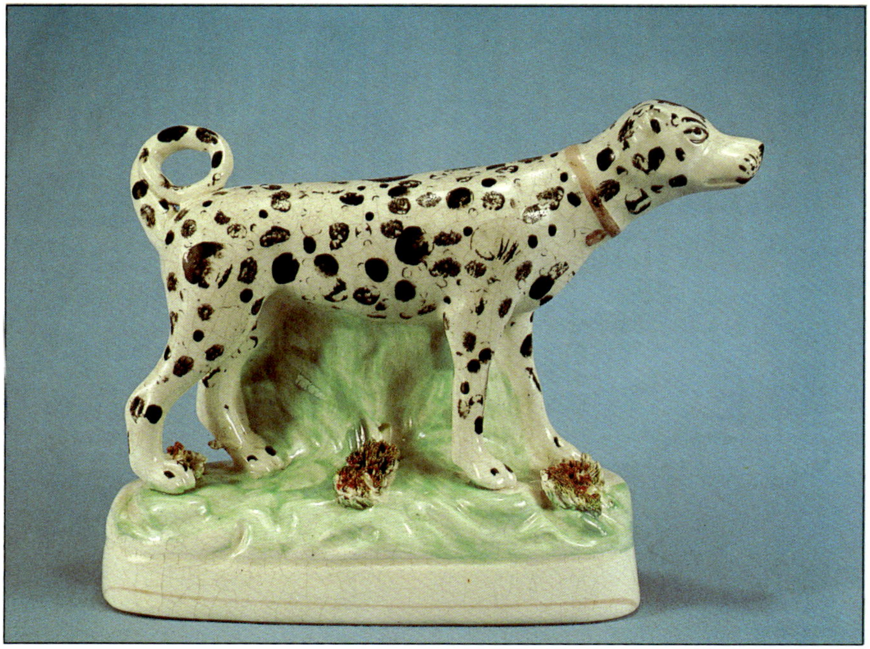

*Figure 2.*

*Figure 2.* One of a pair, but no less proud.
A very rare model.
Circa 1845
Height 5¼ inches

*Figure 3.* Finely painted with large and small spots, the painter surely must have had spots before his eyes!
But the result is quality at its best.
Circa 1850
Height 5¼ inches

*Figure 4.* Less lavishly painted, their simple clean lines save the day. Standing on mottled grassy mounds.
Circa 1875
Height 6¼ inches

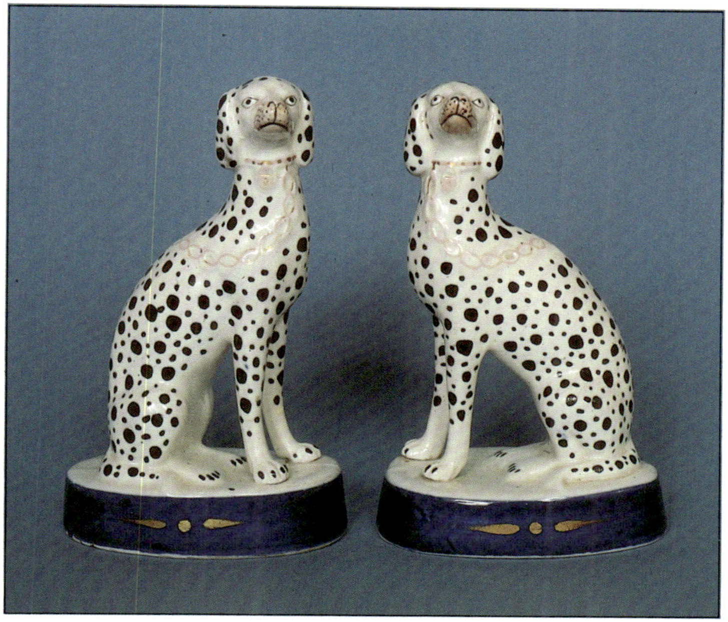

*Figure 3.*

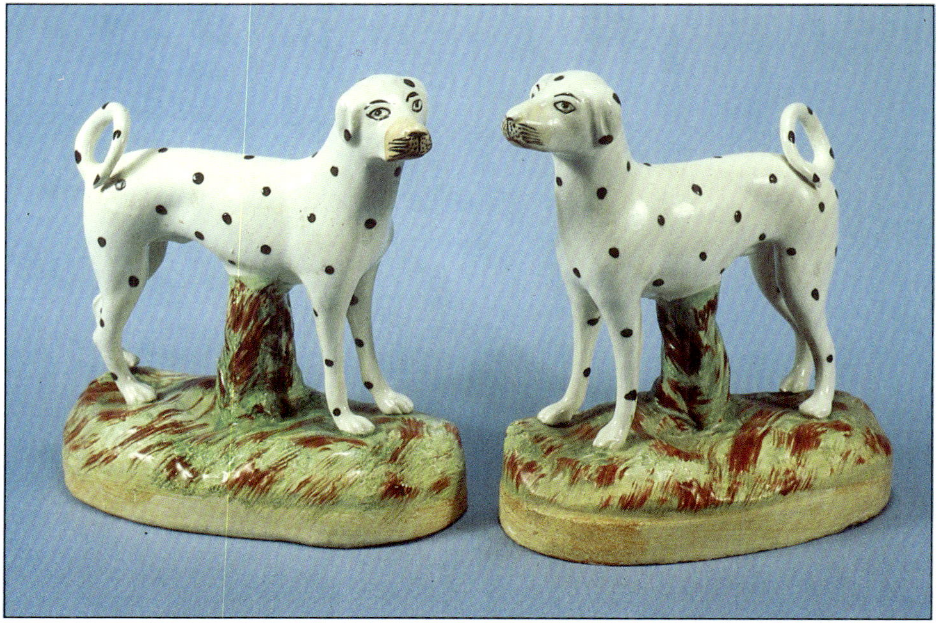

*Figure 4.*

# *Fin and Finesse*

*Although Staffordshire figures were generally cast from simple two-piece moulds it is worth noting that many of the dog models, due to the four-legged subject matter, are a greater work of art than a casual glance might suppose.*

*The fine legs (and tails) often required separate moulds and extra hand finishing.*

*Sometimes the same model would be afforded different treatment and could therefore be displayed from a vantage point other than the mantelpiece, to be viewed and admired from any angle, as can be seen on the opposite page.*

*Figure 5.* A haughty pair proud of their finely painted spots.
Painted in the round with separate front legs.
Circa 1850
Height 7¼ inches

*Figure 6.* The same model as Figure 5 but with back leg blocked in.
Circa 1855
Height 7 inches

*Figure 7.* Sitting on raised oval bases with both their front legs separate.
Circa 1860
Height 6½ inches

*Figure 8.* The same model as Figure 7 with back leg blocked in.
Circa 1855
Height 7 inches

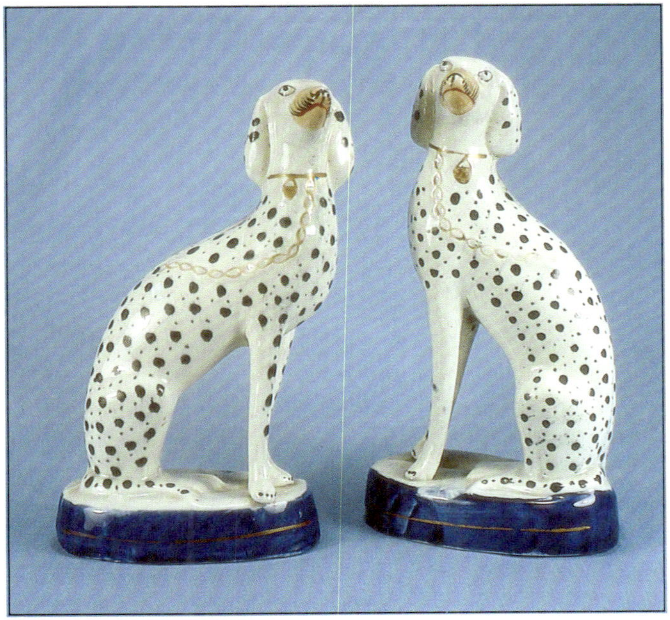

Figure 5.

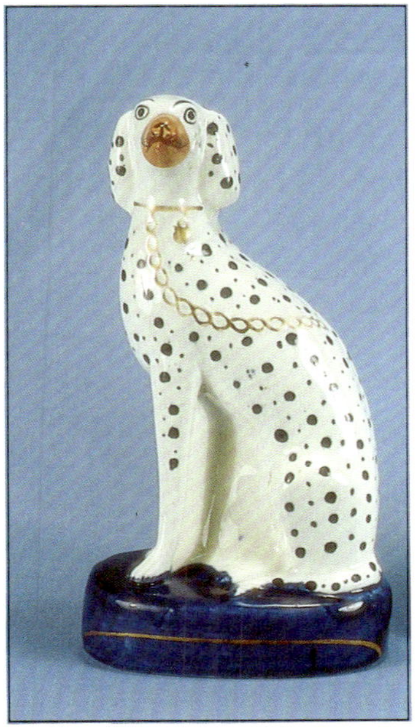

Figure 6.

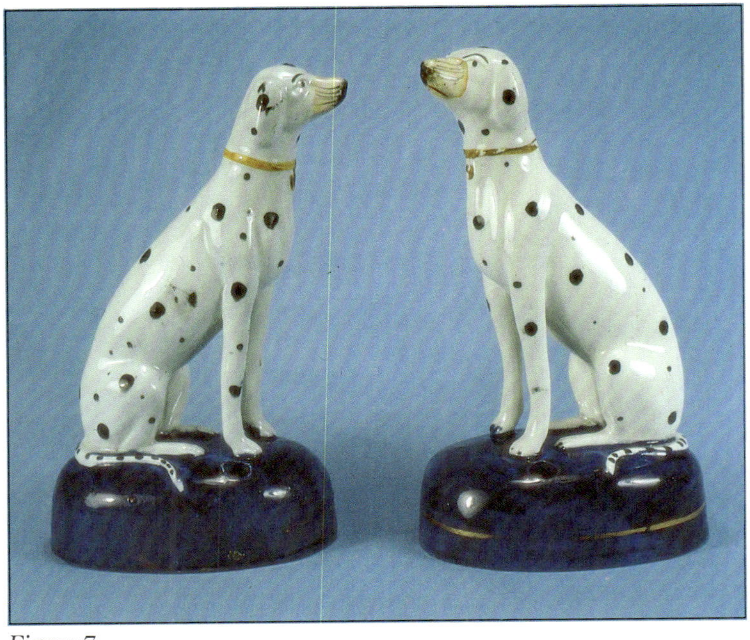

Figure 7.

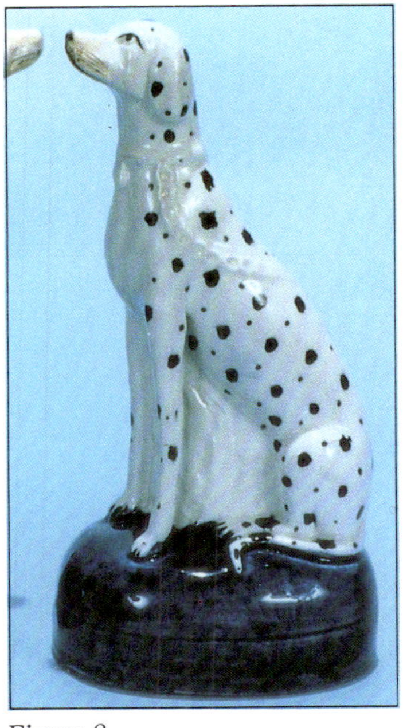

Figure 8.

# Economics

*Simple potters they may have been, but their artistry and scope must remain unsurpassed.*

*The economics of the modelling varies. The sizes vary, the painting and colours change, but in effect you are looking at the same model.*

*The model itself could even double-up for an alternative breed.*

*In this way the potters made the best use of their talents whilst catering to the differing tastes of the market–place.*

*Figure 9.* "The Three Faces of Eve"
The same model each one given a different personality with dextrous brushwork.
Circa 1850
Height 7¼ inches

*Figure 10.* Dalmatians or Whippets?
If you are confused, how do you think they feel!
These charmers have been treated to mossy clusters, an added decoration to their bases.
Circa 1845
Height 5 inches

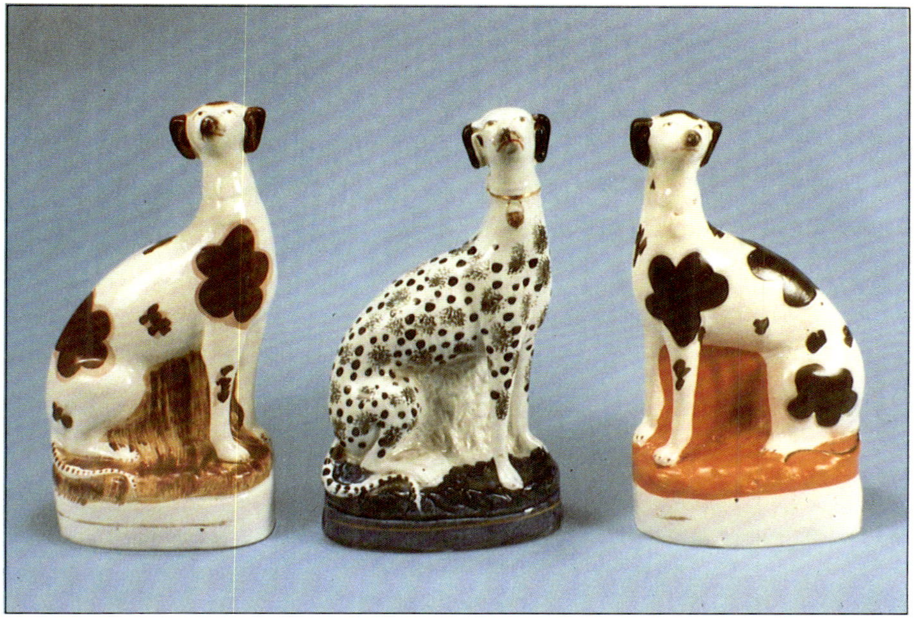

*Figure 9.*

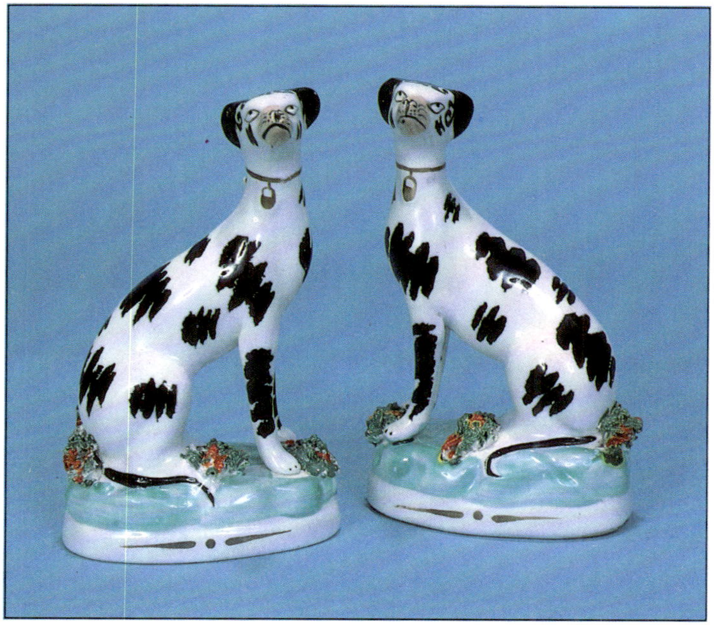

*Figure 10.*

# Deerhound

*The Deerhound could be described as a very large Greyhound wearing a rough shaggy coat. Its origins are lost in the mists of Scotland, certainly some authorities would claim he is descended from the Greyhound and developed a rough coat as a protection from the environment.*

*He was favoured by highland chieftains and known as the "Royal Dog of Scotland", anyone below the rank of Earl was forbidden to own one!*

*The breed was almost lost when the clan system collapsed in Scotland in the 18th century, but thanks to a band of famous enthusiasts including Sir Walter Scott and the royal painter Landseer, breeders once again turned their attention to this intelligent and surprisingly gentle dog.*

*Figure 1.* Sir Walter Scott and "Maida".
This beautiful porcellaneous figure is always untitled but is positively identified by the existence of titled earthenware versions.
A constant companion, Sir Walter's Deerhound "Maida" also appears with him on the Scott monument in Princess Street, Edinburgh.
Further immortalised by this famous novelist and in the paintings of his famous friend Landseer, "Maida" lives on in our hearts with this rare "dog" portrait.
Circa 1845
Height 14 inches

*Figure 2.* "Sense and Sensitivity"
This stunning three-dimensional group required no less than 6 separate moulds, proving the "simple" Staffordshire potters to be pure artists.
Circa 1850
Height 8¾ inches

*Figure 3.* Side detail of Figure 2.

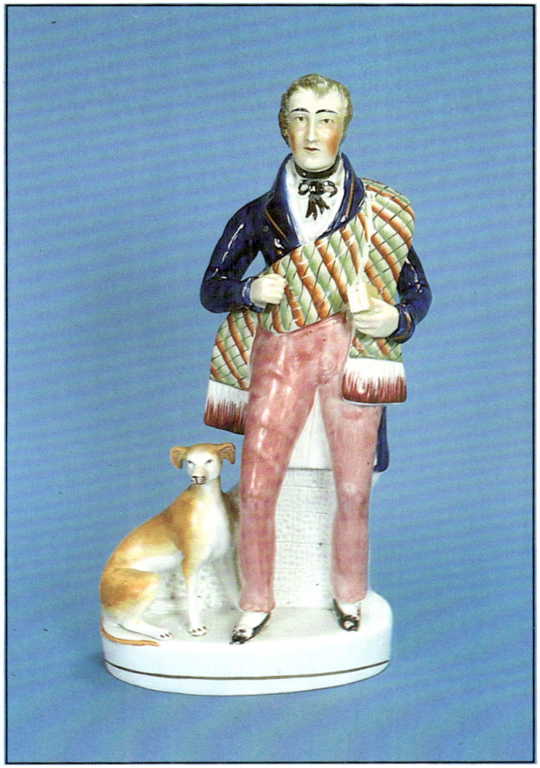

*Figure 1.*

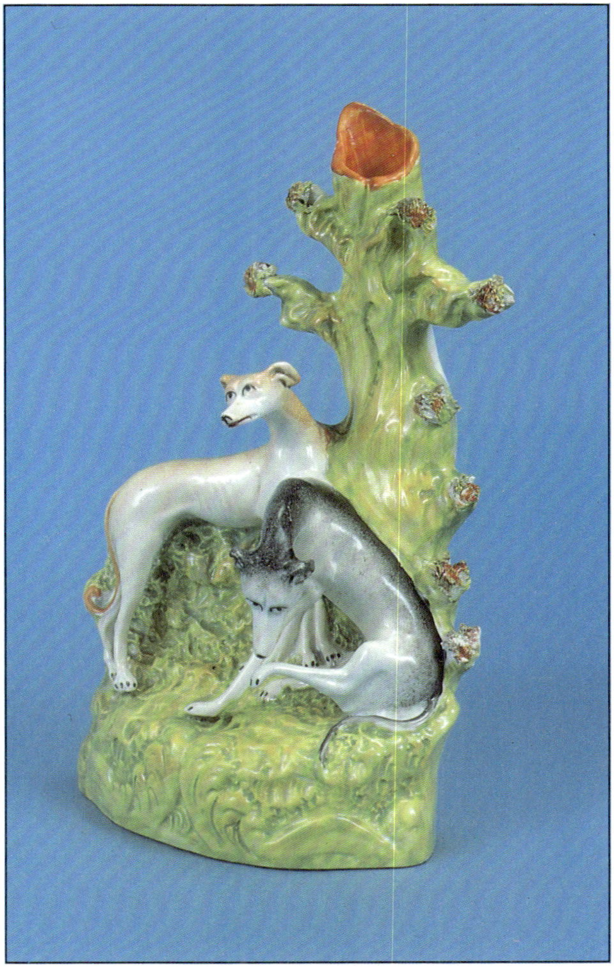

*Figure 2.*

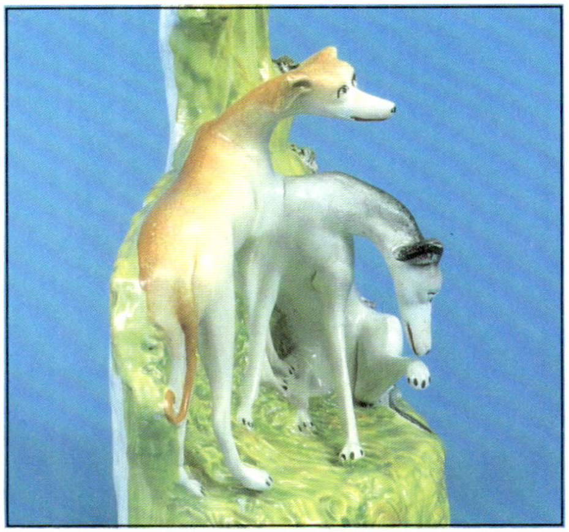

*Figure 3.*

# Dropper

*An old fashioned term for cross-bred Pointers and Setters.*
*A general all purpose sort of fellow!*

*Figure 1.* "The Woodcutter"
Many fine figure groups depicting rural life often included "man's best friend".
This particular group appears in two sizes.
Both are rare.
Circa 1855
Height 14 inches
Smaller version 12½ inches

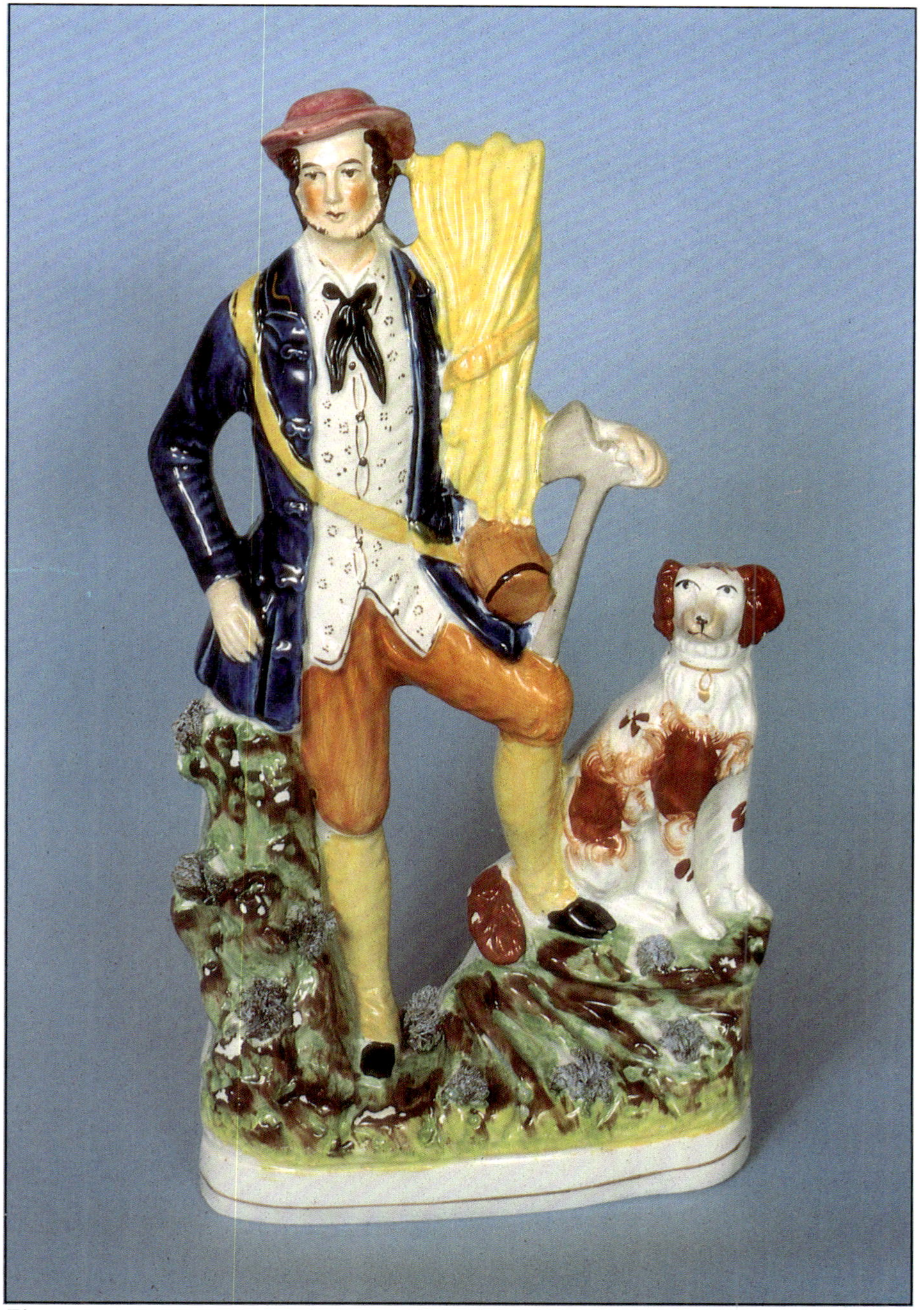

*Figure 1.*

# English Water Spaniel

*Now sadly extinct as a breed but once extremely popular.*
*It was probably the forebear of many of the sporting Spaniel breeds including the Springer Spaniel.*
*A water-repellent coat enabled him to plunge without hesitation into marshy waters to recover downed birds for his master.*

*Figure 1.* "The Dogfather"
Sitting on a blue oval base with a smart gilt line, inquisitively sniffing the air.
Circa 1850
Height 4¾ inches

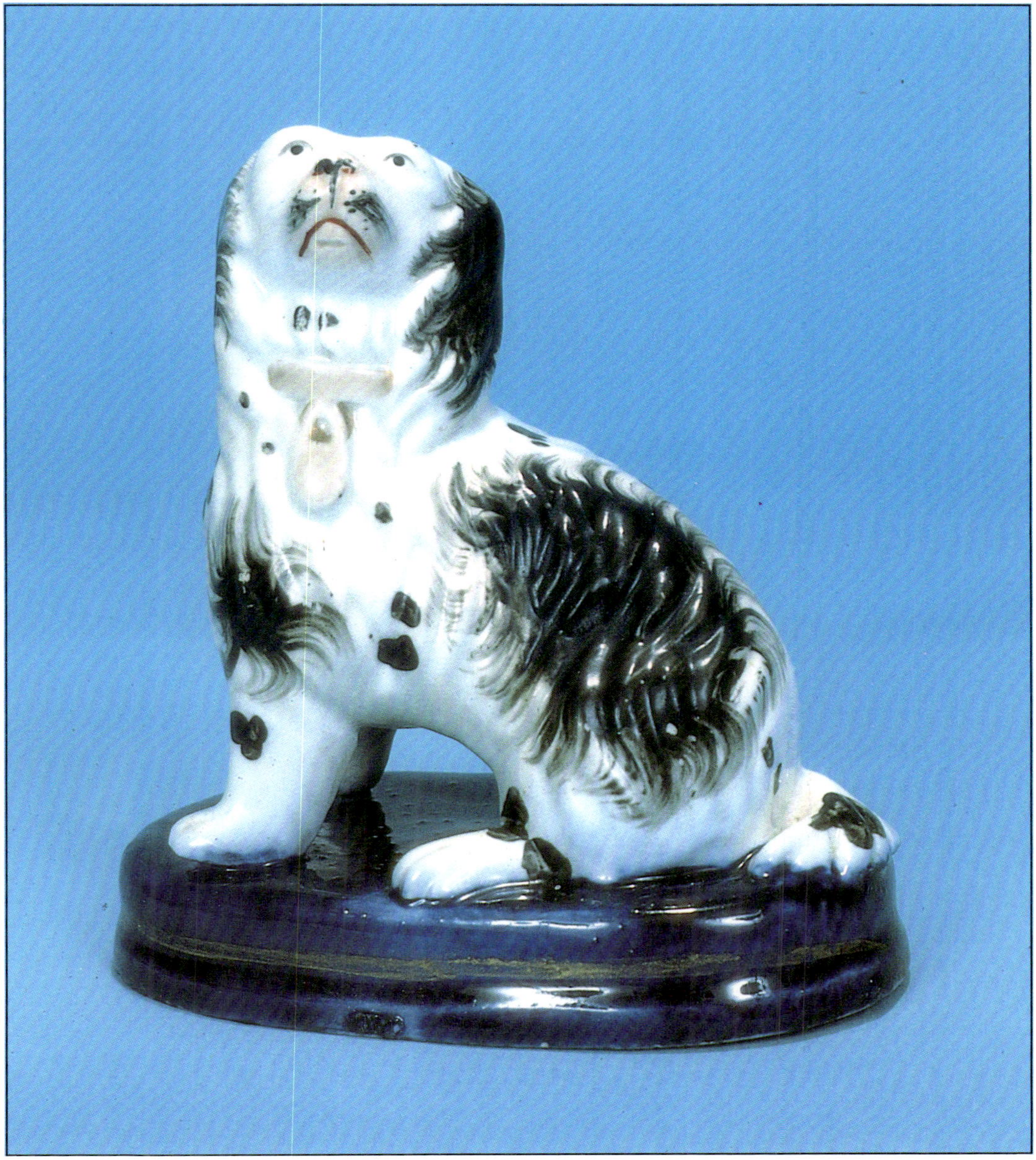

*Figure 1.*

# Foxhound

*Hounds have been used to hunt the fox since the 13th century and finally ousted stag-hunting, as the National sport of the English gentry during the 18th century.*

*To compete against the smaller more calculating quarry, the Foxhound evolved by crossing the larger Stag-hound with Bulldogs, Terriers and Greyhounds achieving determination and stamina along with greater speed.*

*Kept in packs and bred strictly for the hunt, he remained a pure working breed and a common sight throughout 19th century rural England.*

*Figure 1.* "On the Watch"
A beautifully modelled group with sureness of line and fine painting.
Circa 1850
Height 8¾ inches

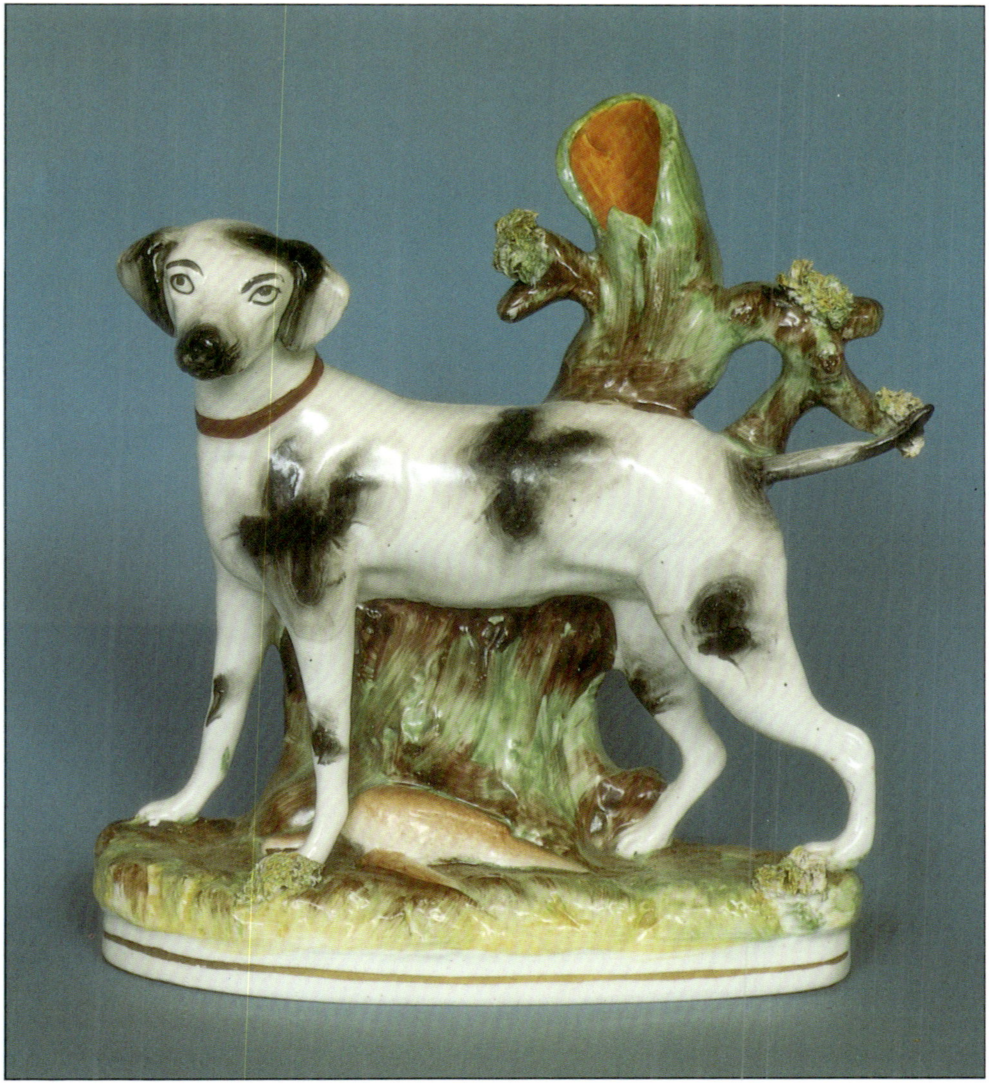

*Figure 1.*

# Great Dane

*A misleading name as he does not originate from Denmark at all, but was developed by German breeders where he is known as Deutsche Dogge (German Mastiff).*

*This gentle giant, courageous yet friendly, makes an excellent guard and gentle companion.*

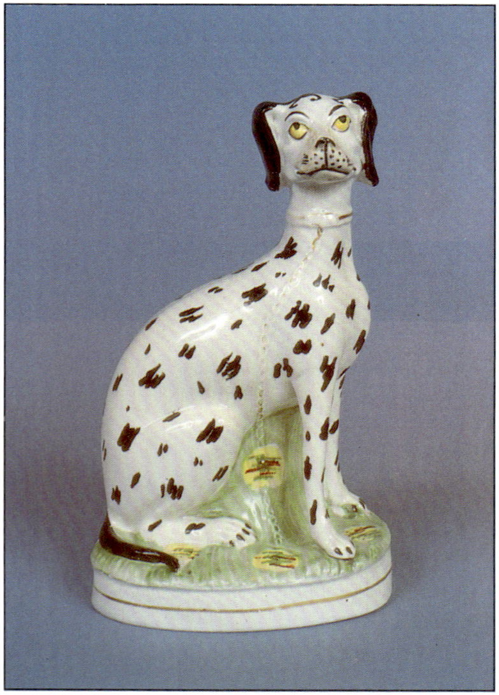

*Figure 1.*

*Figure 1.* A "Harlequin" Great Dane or potter's fancy?
This was one fellow difficult to categorise.
Perhaps the gypsies know the truth?
For the answer refer to the alphabet under L. (page 118).
Circa 1845
Height 8½ inches

*Figure 2.* This charming group modelled in the round, also appears with the dog painted a pale grey.
Extremely rare.
Circa 1850
Height 10¾ inches

*Figure 3.* Back view of Figure 2.

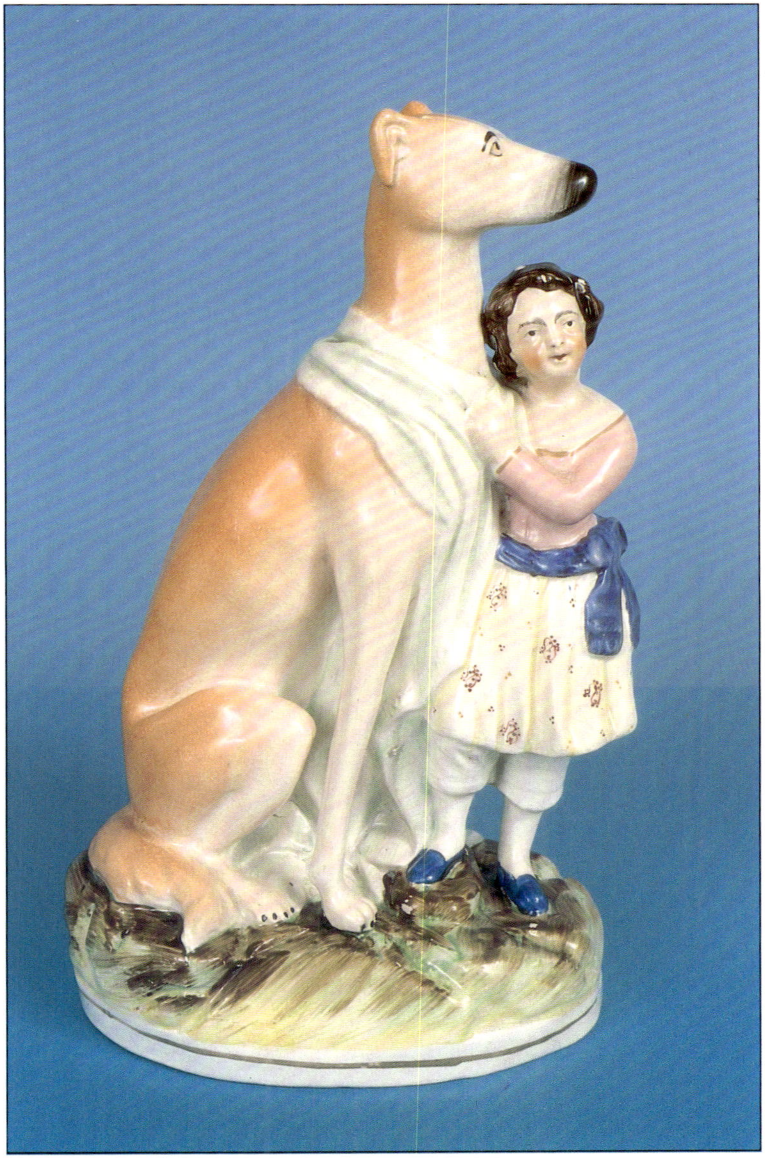

*Figure 2.*

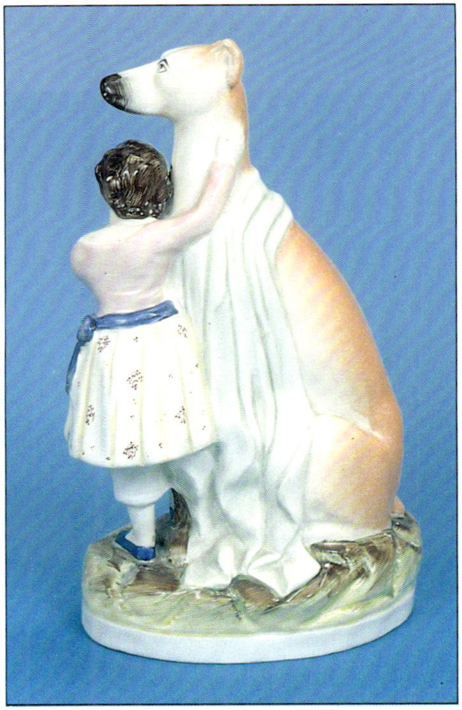

*Figure 3.*

# Greyhound

*A favourite of the ancient Egyptians, he is one of the oldest purest breeds in existence.*

*Prized as a hunting dog he is capable of outpacing such quarry as stag and fox. Down through the centuries he became the "chosen" dog for coursing (chasing live hare), but in the 19th century racing between dogs was introduced as a more humane alternative.*

*The fleetest dog in the world, the Greyhound can reach speeds of more than 40 miles an hour.*

*Many of the so-called "Whippet" models in Staffordshire are in fact Greyhounds or Italian Greyhounds. Both of these breeds were already well established and well known throughout the country.*

*Figure 1.* A much sought after pair of "Master M'Grath and Pretender".
The only named dog figures. "M'Grath" won the Waterloo cup in 1871 running against "Pretender".
Both dogs were already popular country-wide, it was odds-on who would win.
The result was so close it made both of them famous for posterity.
Circa 1871
Height 9¼ inches

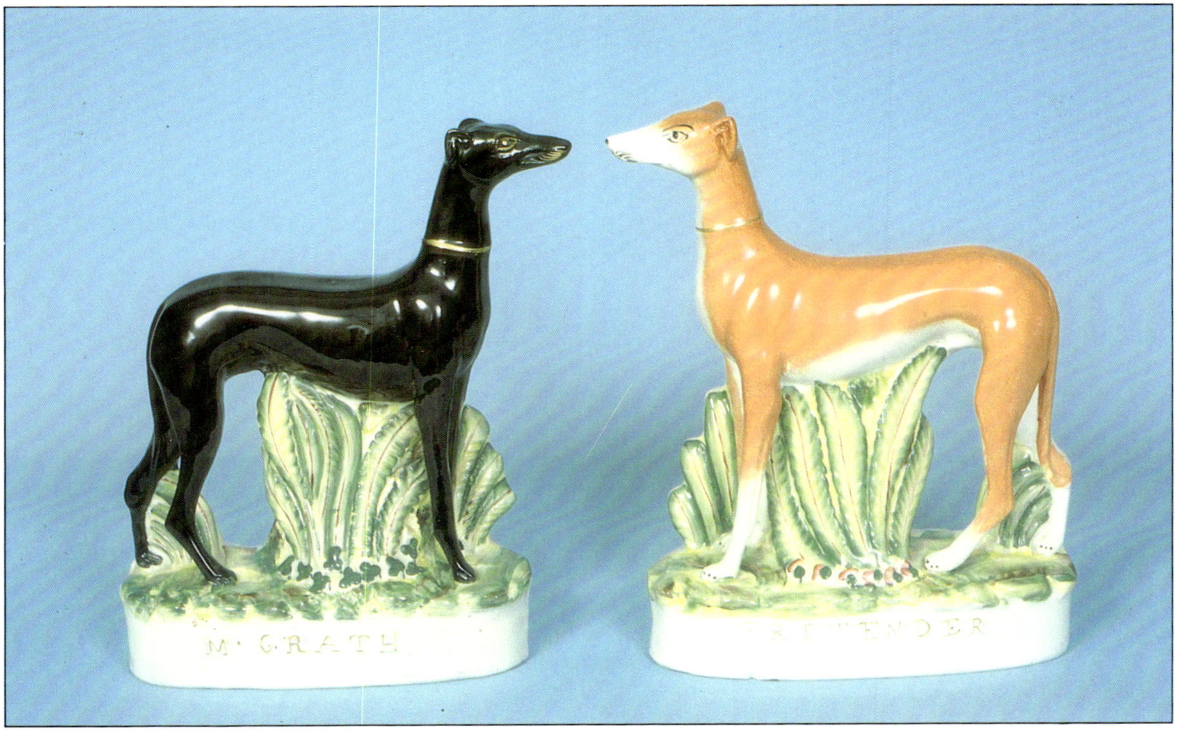


*Figure 1.*

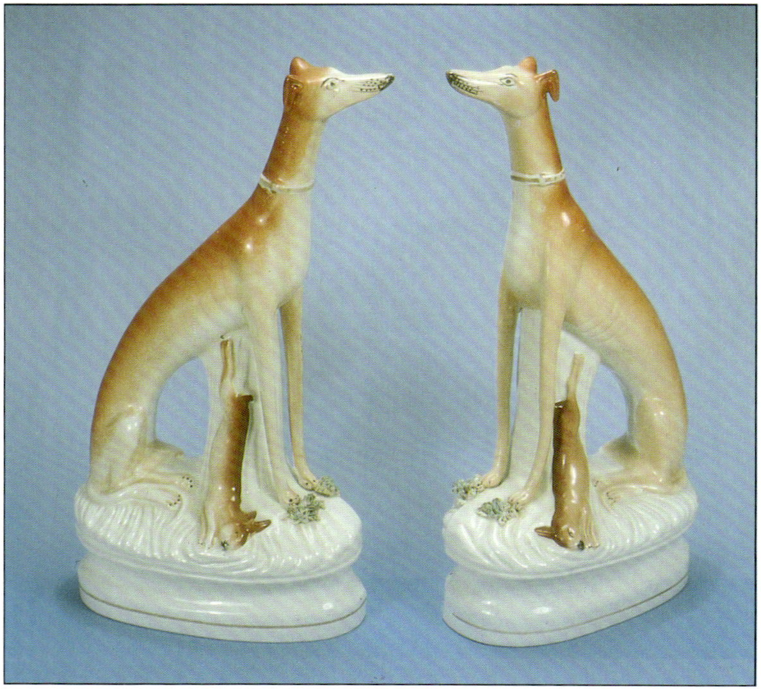

*Figure 2.*

*Figure 2.* "High and Mighty"
The tallest of the Greyhound models.
Circa 1860
Height 12½ inches

*Figure 3.* "Hares and Graces"
A pair of black and white Greyhounds, one carrying a hare in its mouth. Its pair with the hare on the base.
Circa 1850
Height 10¾ inches

*Figure 4.* The same model as Figure 3.
Note the ingenious use of blue, highlighting the lower part of the bases.
Circa 1850
Height 10 inches

*Figure 5.* Flowing and graceful lines. The faun-coloured hounds jumping a stream chasing after rabbits.
They have a particularly charming appeal.
Circa 1855
Height 11 inches

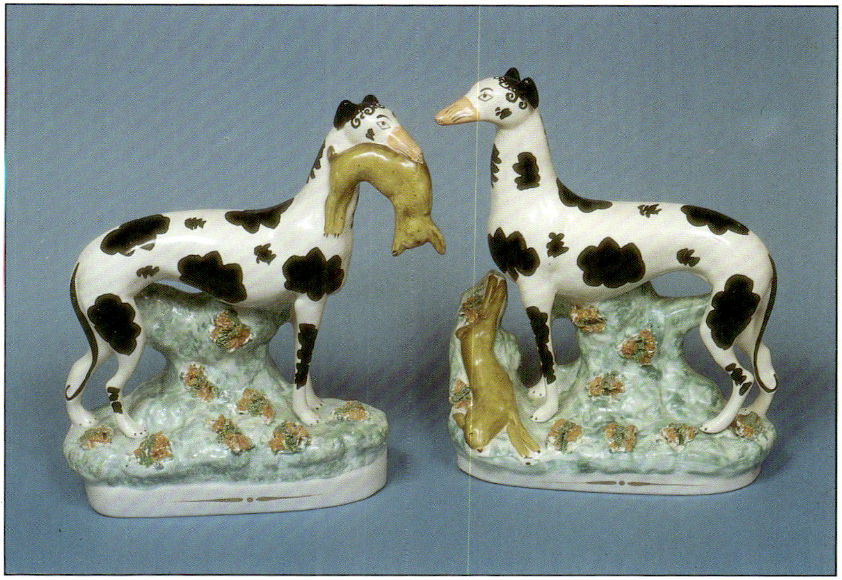

*Figure 3.*

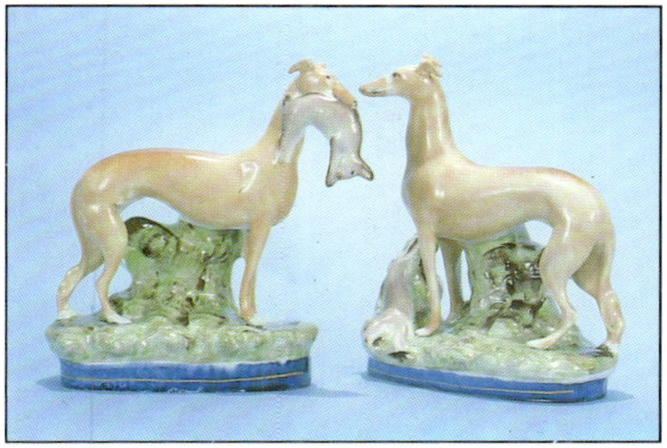

*Figure 4.*

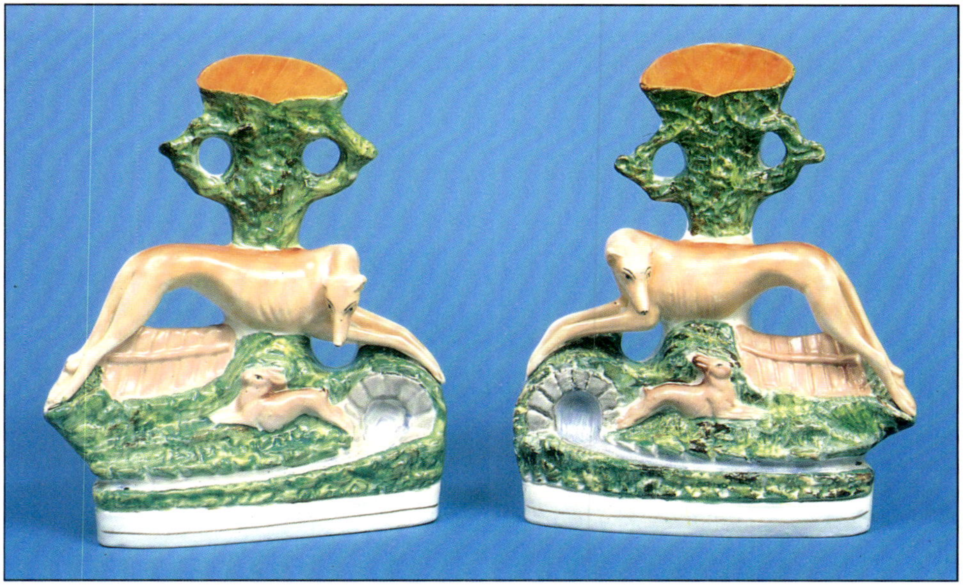

*Figure 5.*

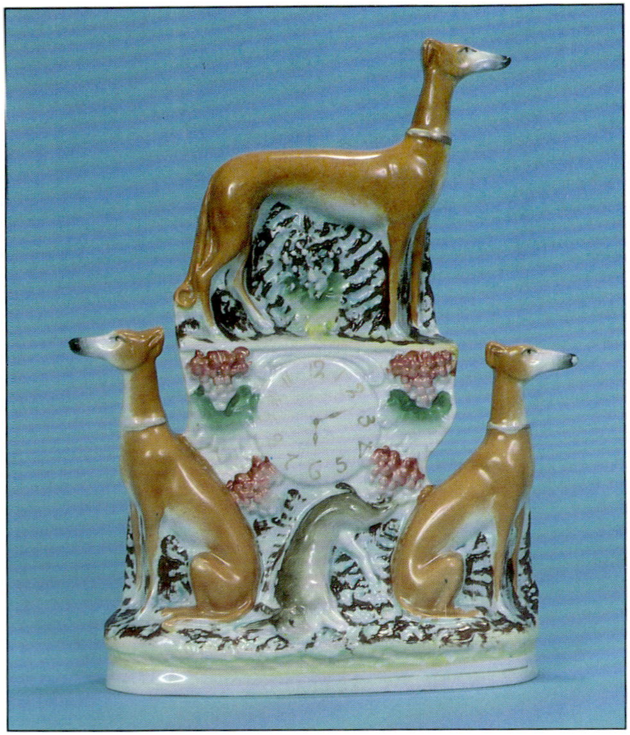

*Figure 6.*

*Figure 6.* "Time Standing Still"
A centrepiece clock group surmounted by a standing Greyhound with a seated Greyhound each side guarding a rabbit.
We all would like time to stand still occasionally.
This centrepiece makes it happen.
Circa 1860
Height 10¾ inches

*Figure 7.* An unusual and appealing group on a most attractive scrolled base.
Circa 1850
Height 7 inches

*Figure 8.* "Apollo and Daphne"
This spill vase group must have been quite popular as it was relatively easy to find until quite recently.
Finding one in perfect condition and well defined is now a quest for the discerning collector.
Circa 1860
Height 11¼ inches

*Figure 9.* "Run Rabbit Run"
An attractive variation of Figure 5, page 43.
Circa 1855
Height 11¼ inches

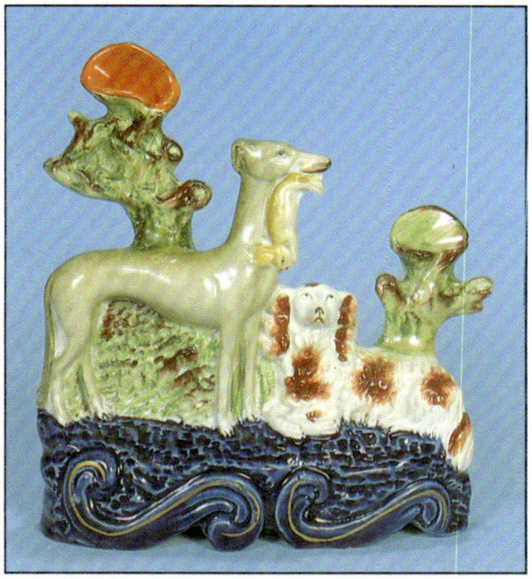

Figure 7.

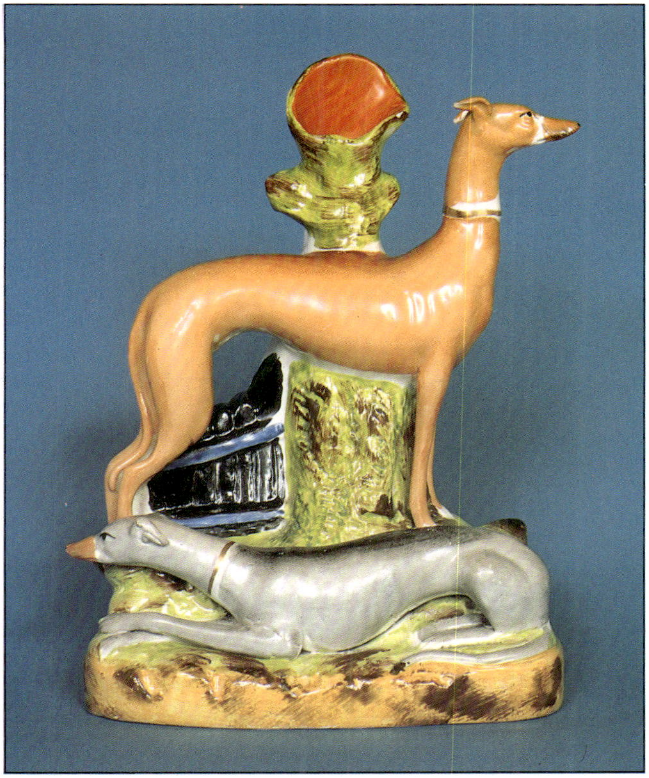

Figure 8.

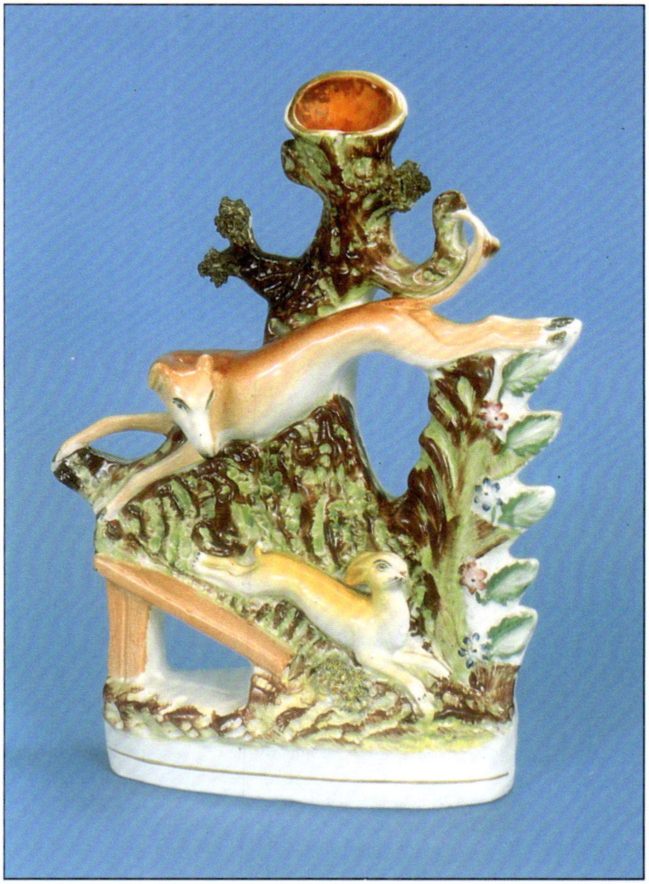

Figure 9.

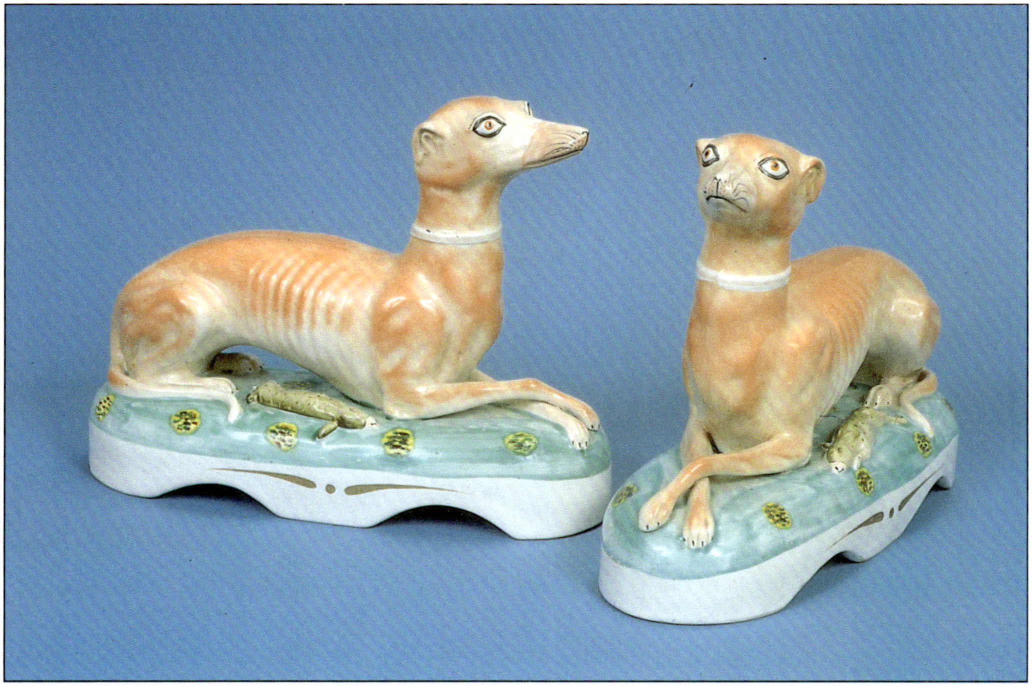

*Figure 10.*

*Figures 10/11/12.* These very large lying Greyhounds are always extremely finely modelled.
The three colour combinations presented are, as far as can be ascertained, their complete palette.
It may be probable however, that the black and white version may also appear on a cobalt blue base.
Circa 1845
Height 8¼ inches Length 10½ inches

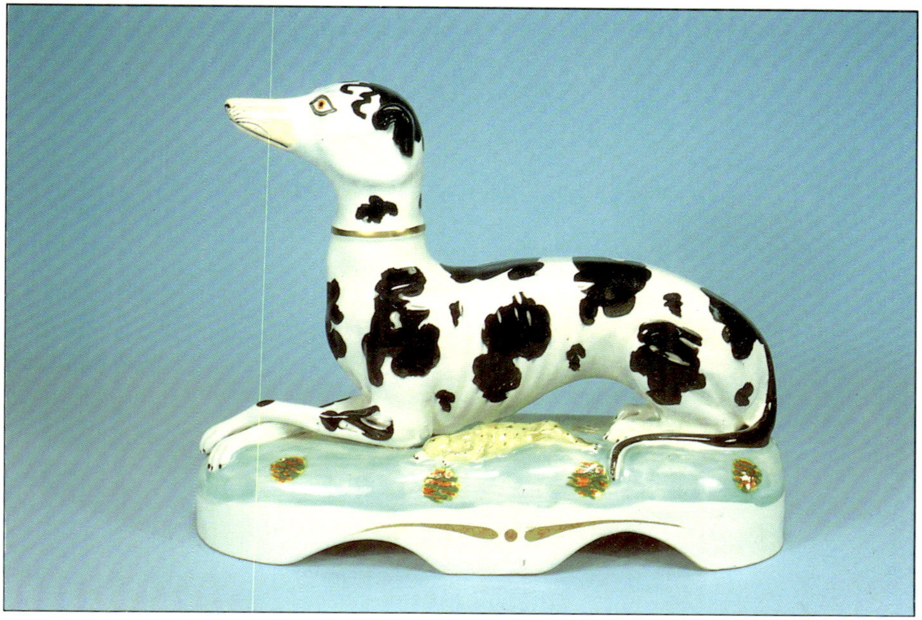

*Figure 11.*

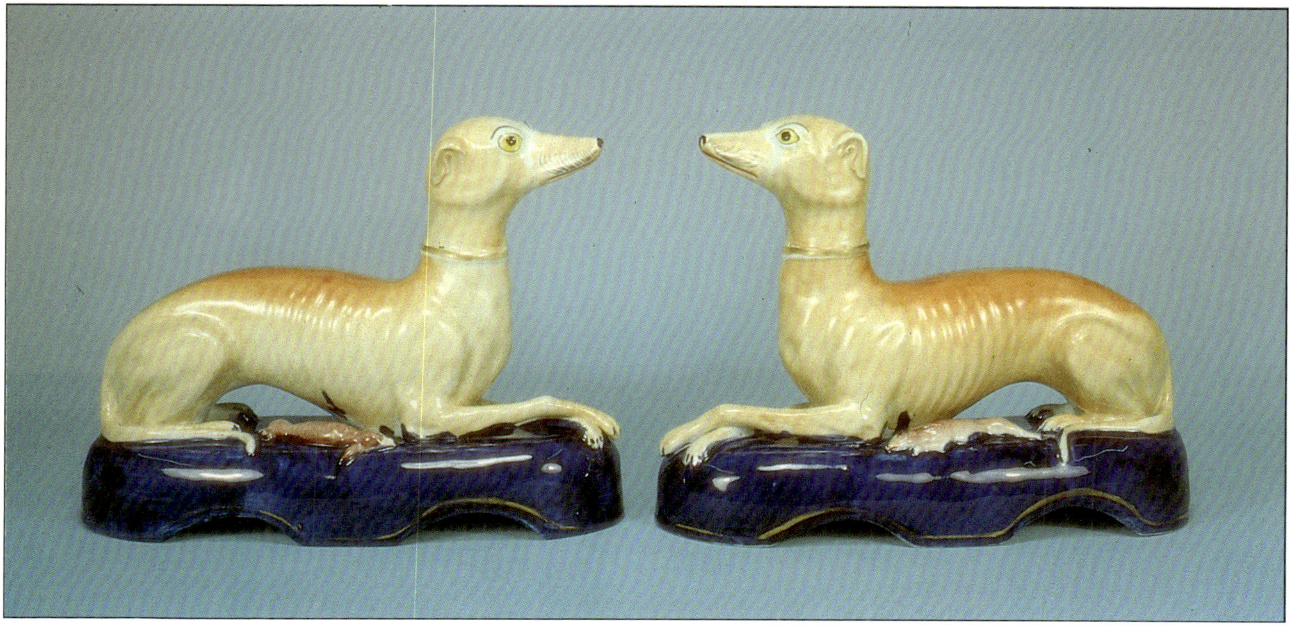

*Figure 12.*

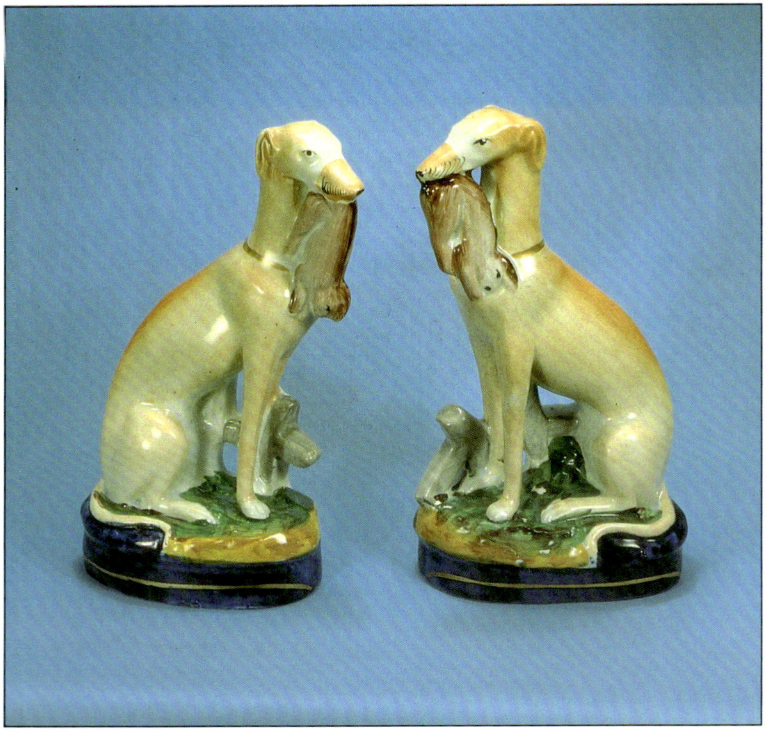

*Figure 13.*

*Figure 13.* Roast 'em mother, with all the trimmings.
Circa 1860
Height 10 inches

*Figure 14.* A pair of Greyhounds holding rabbits in their mouths with free-standing legs and cut-out tails, on oval bases.
Circa 1850
Height 11¼ inches

*Figure 15.* A pair of Greyhounds holding rabbits in their mouths on moulded oval bases.
Circa 1850
Height 11¼ inches

*At first glance they appear to be the same pair but take a closer look. The modelling on the bases is quite different allowing the hounds in Figure 14 to be completely free-standing with finer cut-out tails, also the rabbits have pricked-up ears.*

*A good example of small details that help to define quality.*

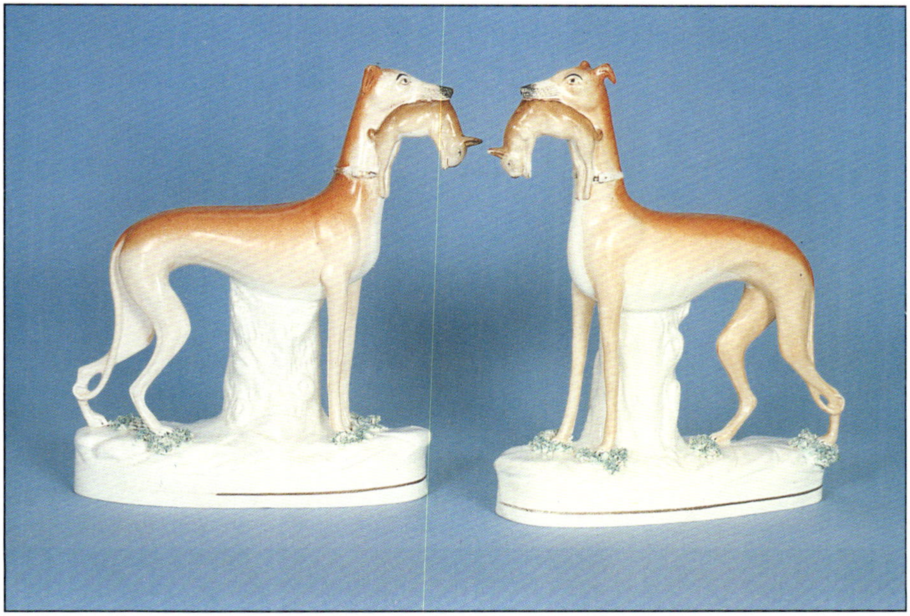

*Figure 14.*

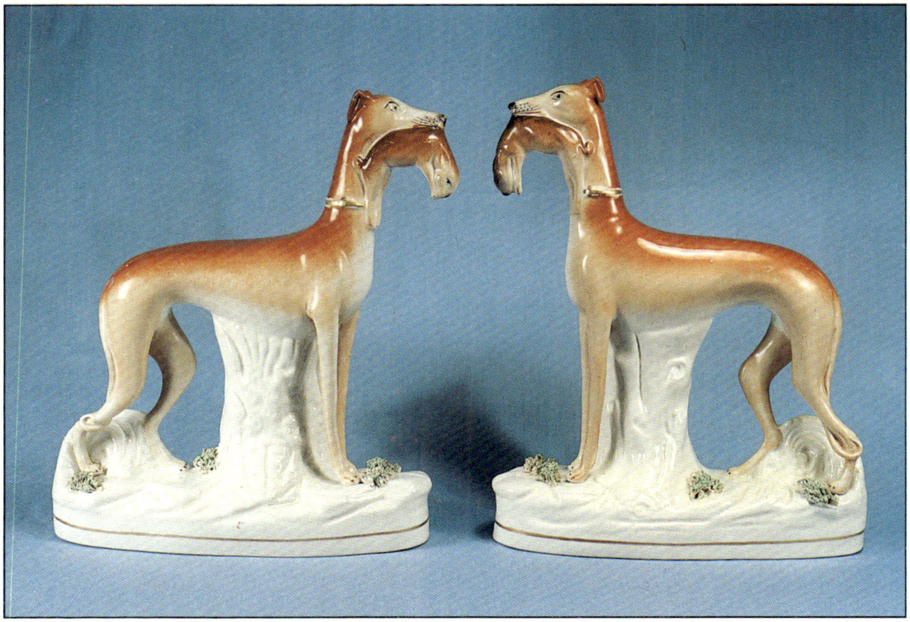

*Figure 15.*

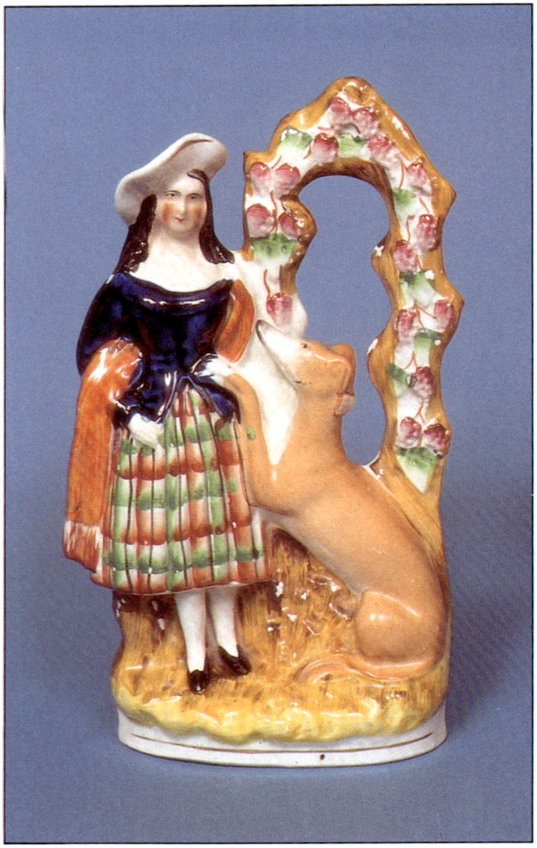

Figure 16.

*Figure 16.* "Waiting for Master"
Greyhound comforting his mistress
beside a grape arbour.
Circa 1855
Height 9¾ inches

*Figure 17.* An impressive pair of sitting-up rust-coloured
Greyhounds, with rabbits on the
grassy mound bases.
Circa 1875
Height 11¼ inches

*Figure 18.* An earlier version of Figure 17.
Displaying a finer colour palette and brushwork.
Circa 1850
Height 12 inches

*Figure 19.* A pair of hounds standing against flowering bush spill vases, with rabbits at their feet.
Circa 1860
Height 9½ inches

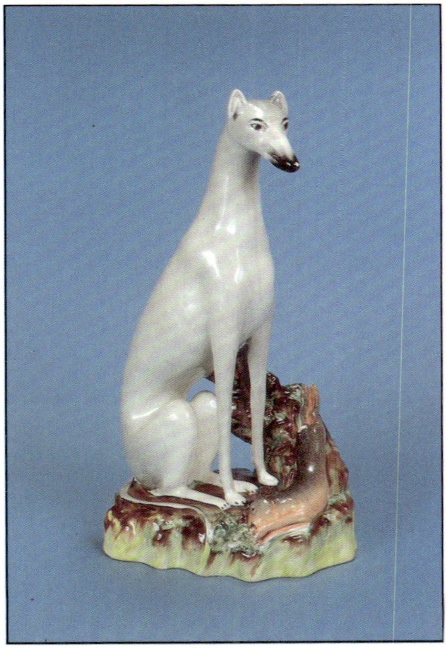

*Figure 18.*

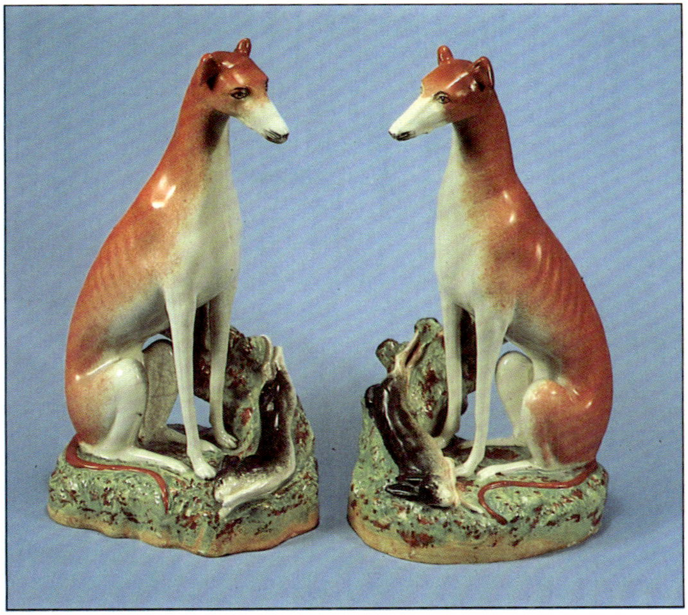

*Figure 17.*

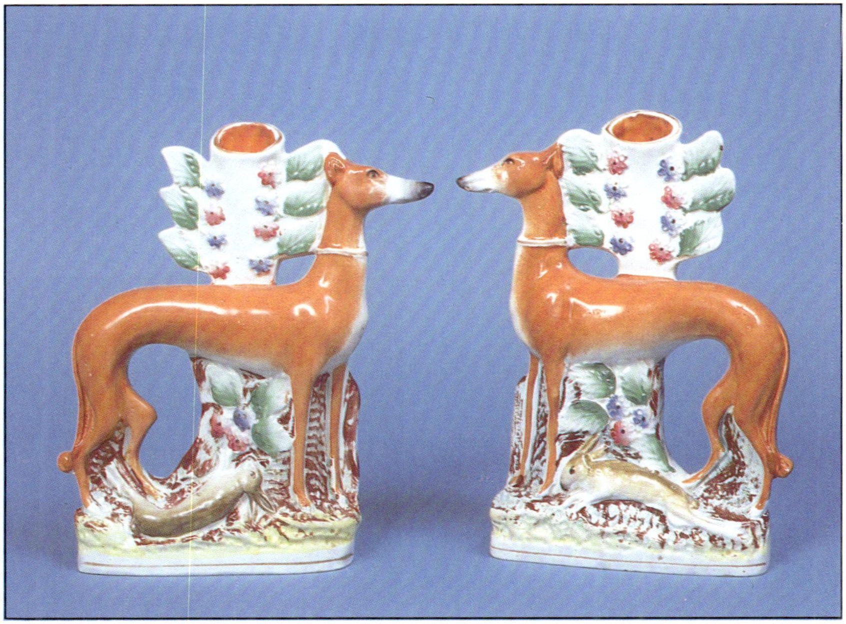

*Figure 19.*

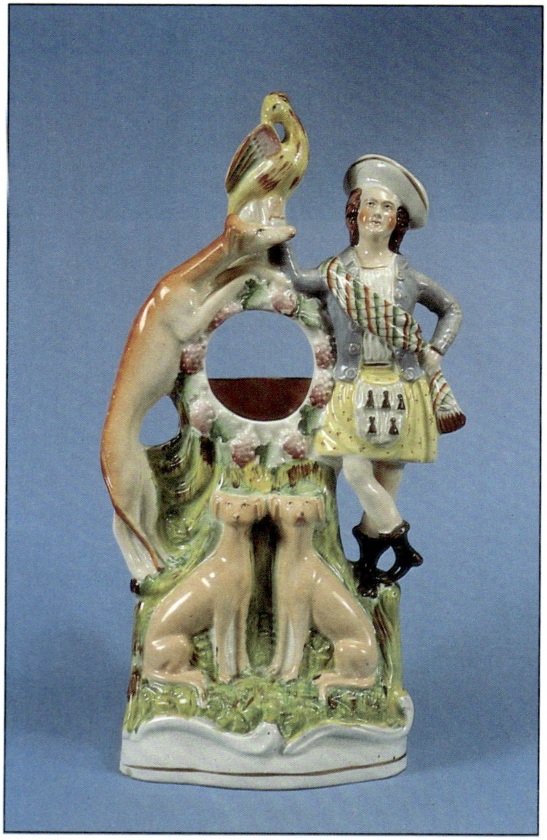

*Figure 20.*

*Figure 20.* A "Hunter" watch holder group.
Everyone knew when "Pa" was home,
when the clock on the mantelpiece had a face!
Circa 1850
Height 12¾ inches

*Figure 21.* The traditional quill holder as in Figure 22, here titled "A present from Ramsgate" in gilt script.
Reminding us somehow, of all our yesterdays.
Circa 1860
Height 4¾ inches

*Figure 22.* Quill holders.
The most popular and well known of the Greyhound models "usually" mistaken for Whippets!
Circa 1860
Height 6 inches

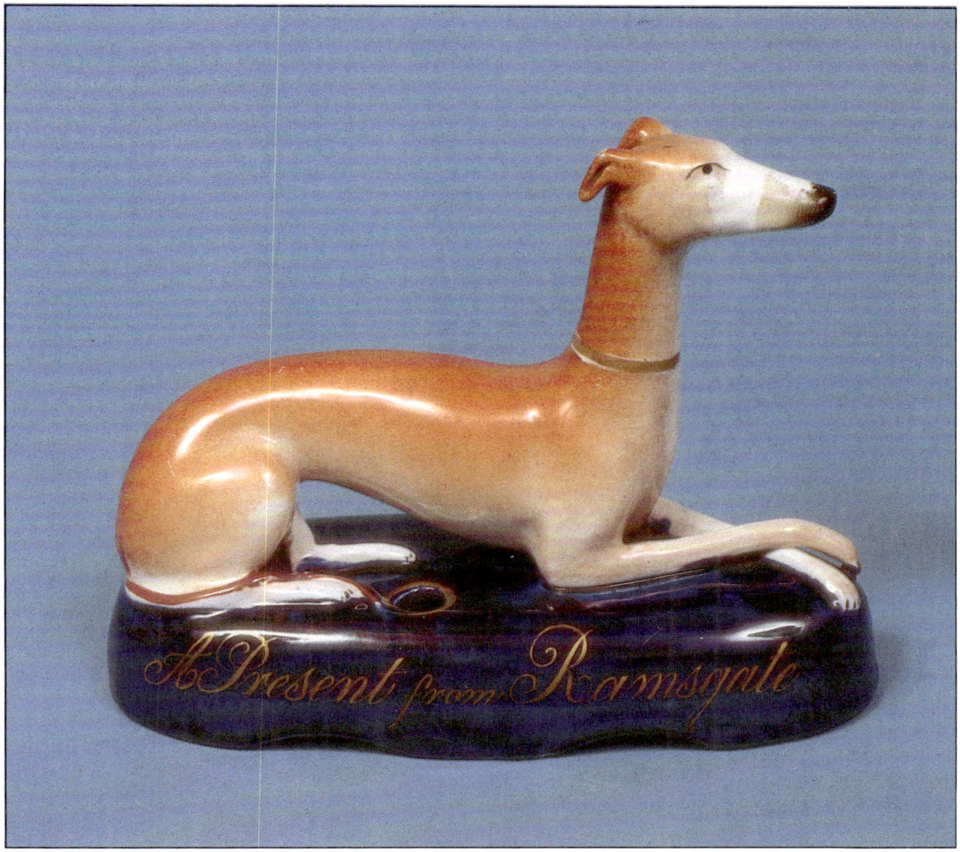


*Figure 21.*

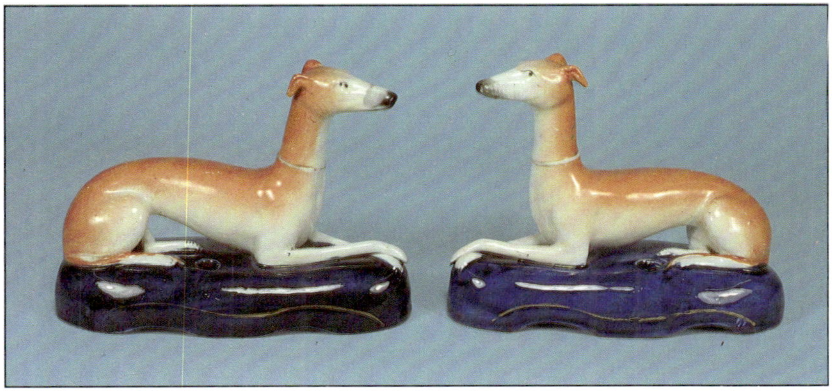

*Figure 22.*

# *Sampson Smith (1813 – 1878), Upper Hill Street, Longton, Staffordshire*

*Of our many anonymous Staffordshire potters producing Staffordshire dogs, Sampson Smith is the only maker apart from John Lloyd (see page 84) to use a factory mark.*

*Why both of these prolific potters only chose to use their mark so sparingly cannot be explained. We do know however that the Sampson Smith business continued after his death until 1963.*

*In 1948 old original moulds were discovered still bearing the Sampson Smith mark and well preserved enough to be re-used.*

*Therefore although the mark itself gives us a date of 1851 and is the date the mark came into existence, dogs bearing this mark can only be accurately dated by their colour palette, gilding and painting.*

*Figure 23.* "Spot the Deception"
There is just something "wrong" the colour palette is acceptable but its application and quality has a worrying look that no photograph can explain.
It requires a practised eye to disregard the "exciting find" of a factory mark.
Circa 1955
Height 10 inches

*Figure 24.* The re-introduced deceptive mark on base of Figure 23.

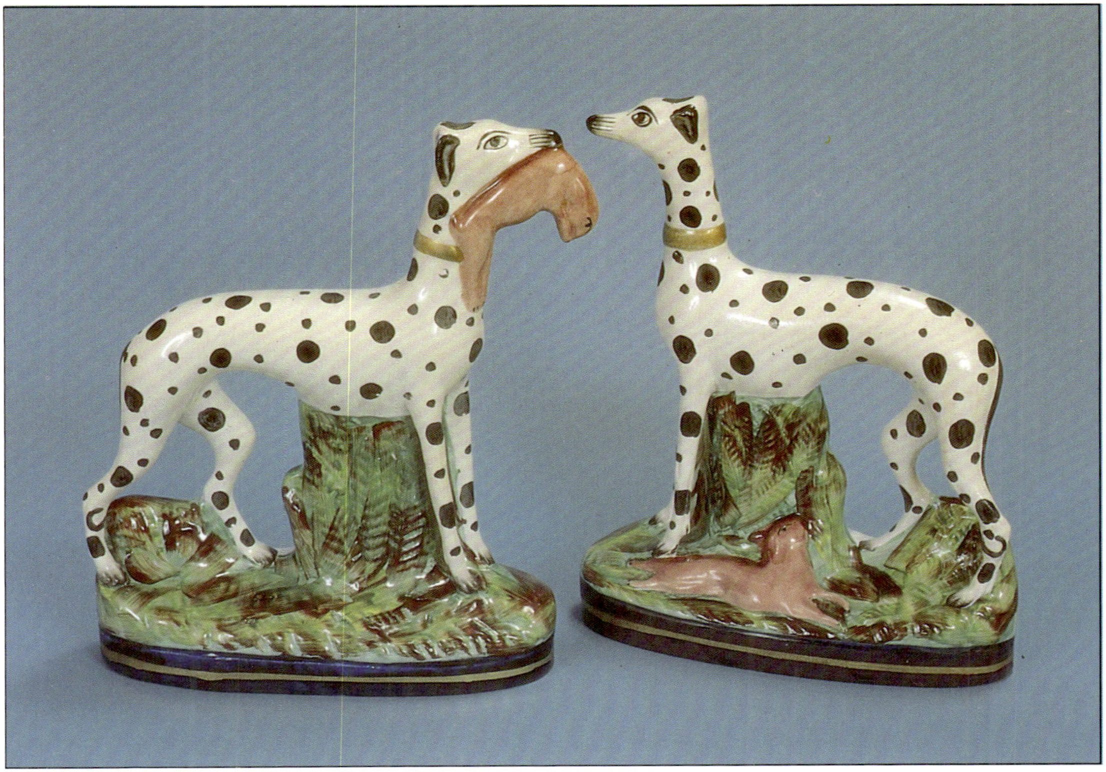

Figure 23.

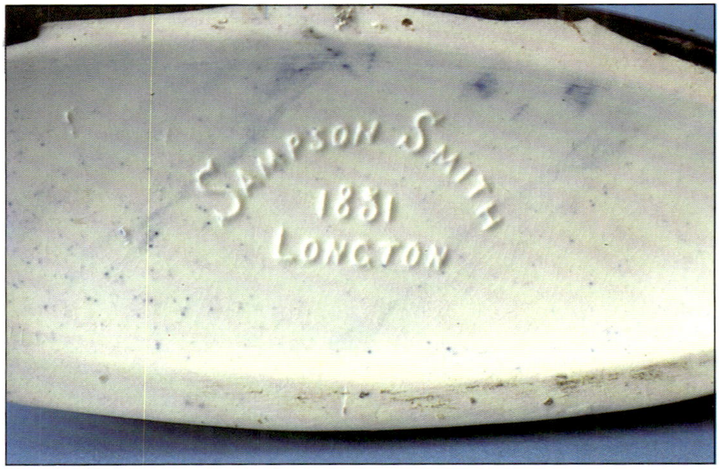


Figure 24.

# Harrier – Hare Hound

*The Harrier has been known in Britain since the middle-ages, bred specifically for the hunting of hares. It claims the French Basset and the Bloodhound amongst its ancestors, as well as the now extinct "Talbot" hound (derived from the Norman family name).*

*The oldest English pack dates back to the 18th century, although hare-hunting is rare today, it's an even older sport than fox-hunting.*

*Figure 1.* A quill holder group on a raised elaborate blue base.
The little fellow guarding a rather large hare.
This is a beautifully composed group but is not for the squeamish!
Circa 1845
Height 3½ inches

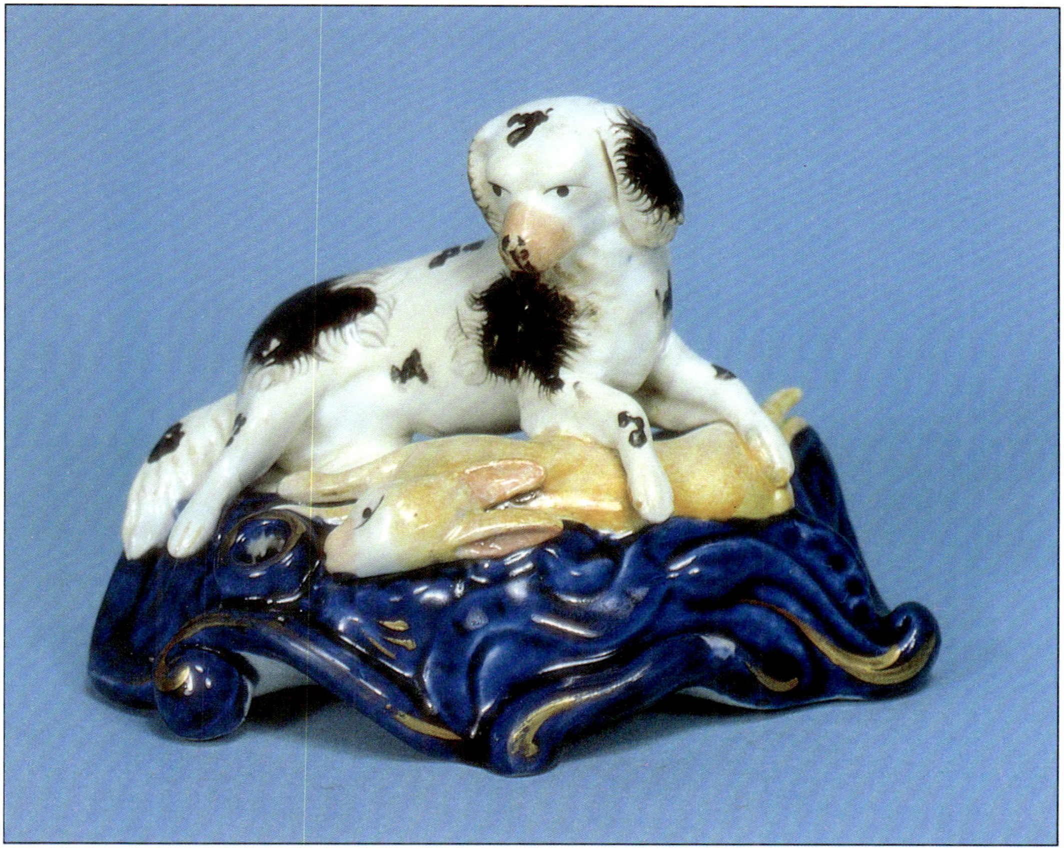

*Figure 1.*

# Irish Setter

*Though we think of them as deep rust in colour, these dogs were often red and white in the 19th century. A breed of physical beauty, elegance and charm. A good worker with retriever qualities as well as a gentle companion.*

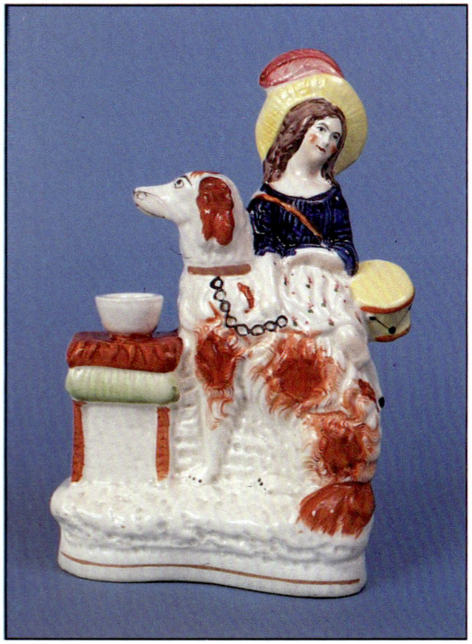

*Figure 1.*

*Figure 1.* "Dinner Time"
The similar subject matter suggests this group is probably from the same factory as Figure 2.
Circa 1850
Height 8 inches

*Figure 2.* "Good Friends"
A young boy playing his drum sitting on the back of his dog, whilst his sister is looking on.
This rare group is well composed and very pleasing to the eye.
Circa 1850
Height 10¼ inches

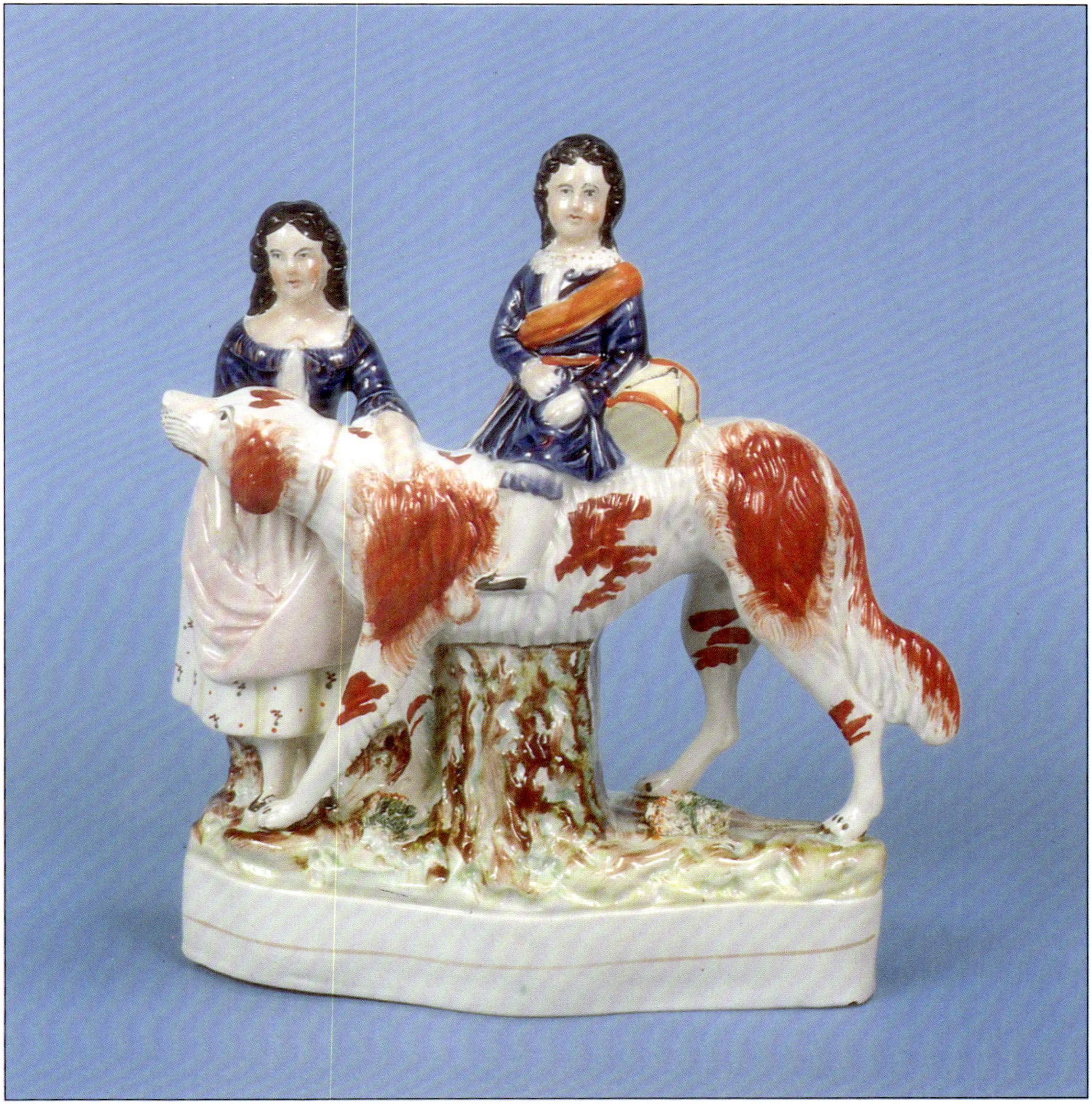

*Figure 2.*

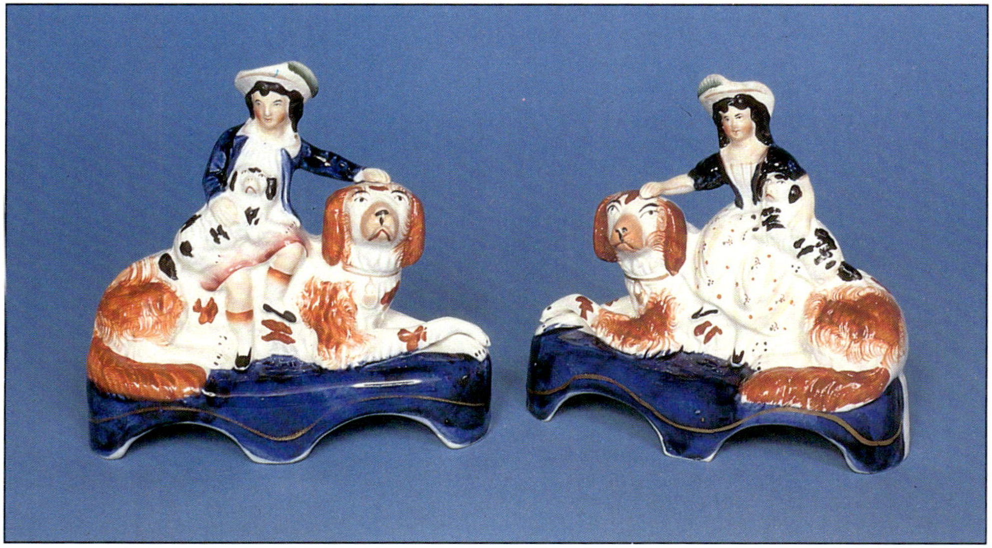

*Figure 3.*

*Figure 3.* Serpentine blue bases carry this pair of faithful Setters.
The children sitting on their backs
holding black and white puppies.
Circa 1850
Height 6¼ inches

*Figure 4.* A no-nonsense model of simple clean lines.
Circa 1865
Height 6 inches

*Figure 5.* Strong moulding, fine feathered painting and superior bases.
These fellows are quite satisfied with themselves.
Circa 1850
Height 11 inches

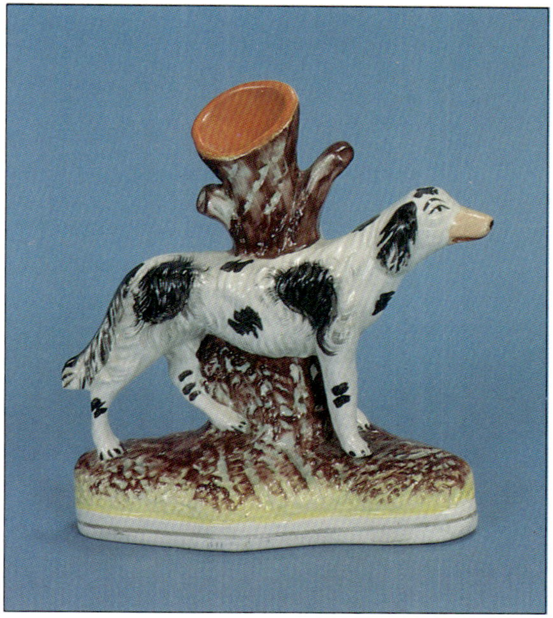

*Figure 4.*

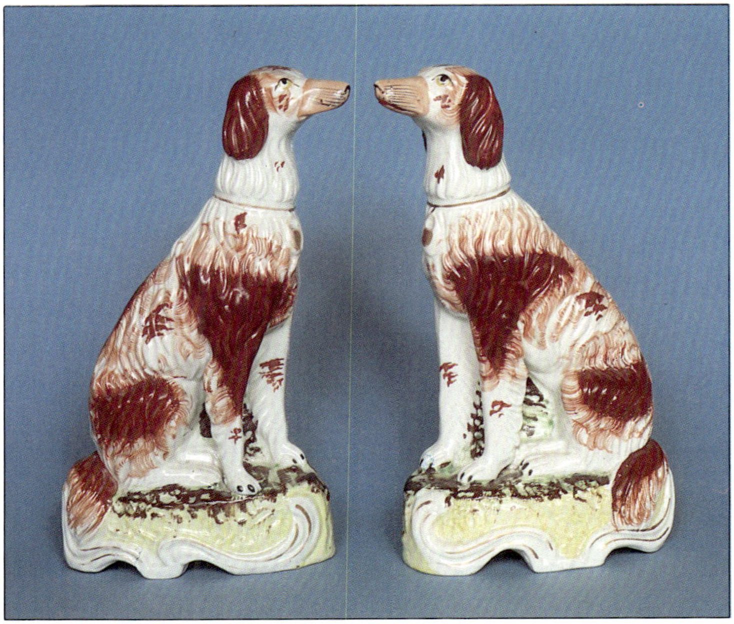

*Figure 5.*

*Figure 6.* An unusual pair of spill vase groups. The sleeping infants and their sheep being protected from snakes by their faithful dogs.
Circa 1850
Height 12 inches

*Figure 7.* Black and white puppies often seem to appear with red and white parents. The colour difference obviously helped to outline the puppies in cleaner detail.
Circa 1850
Height 8¾ inches

*Figure 8.* Victorian sentiment well represented. Pretty children sitting on large Setters (she is side-saddle of course). The dogs carrying home flower baskets in their mouths.
Circa 1855
Height 10 inches

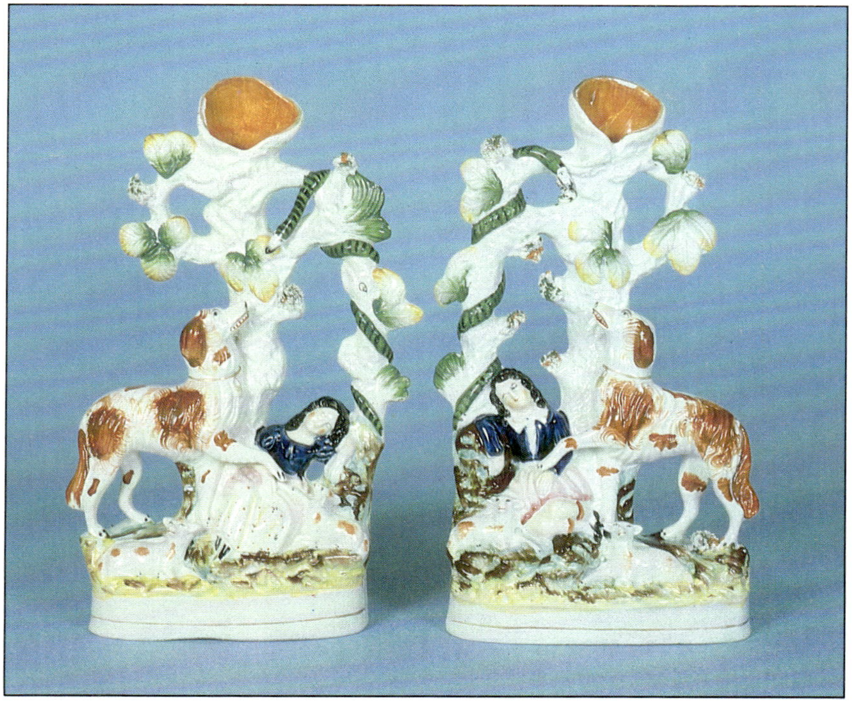

*Figure 6.*

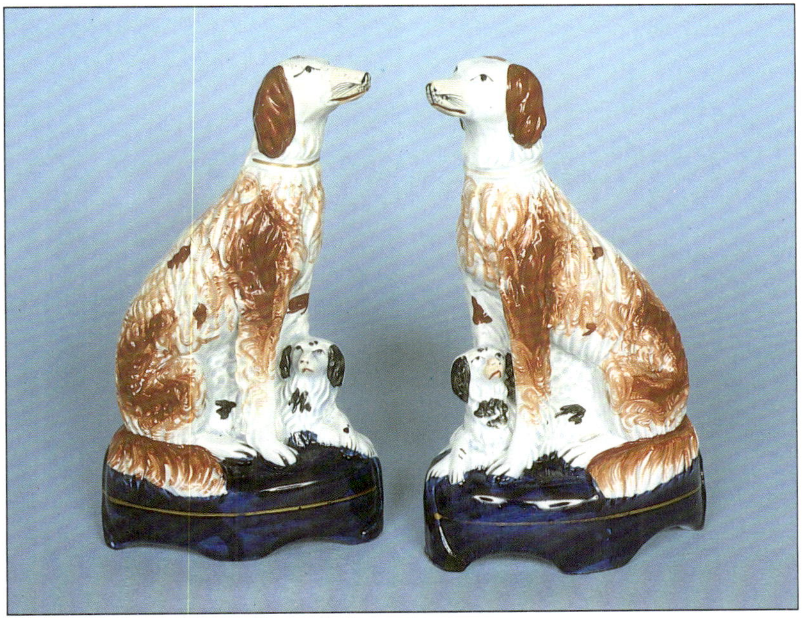

*Figure 7.*

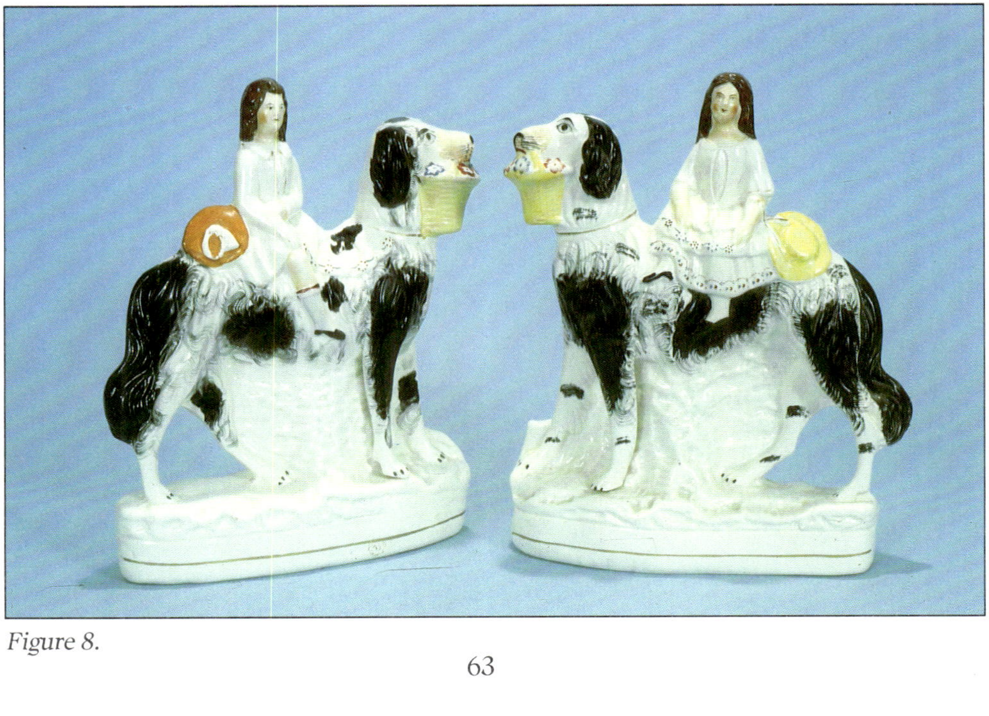

*Figure 8.*

# Italian Greyhound

*A miniature replica of the Greyhound, only their diminutive size and slight hump-back distinguishing them from their larger cousins. The breed as its name suggests, was developed in Italy.*

*A favourite of royal courts throughout Europe well back into the 16th century. It probably arrived in England with one of its royal "protectors". Certainly a portrait of Anne of Denmark dated 1617 (wife to the first monarch of a united Great Britain, James I) which hangs in Hampton Court Palace today, clearly shows several Italian Greyhounds. Up until the 19th century its tremendous popularity mainly as a "comforter" dog was only challenged by the re-emergence of the King Charles Spaniel.*

*The jury is still out.*

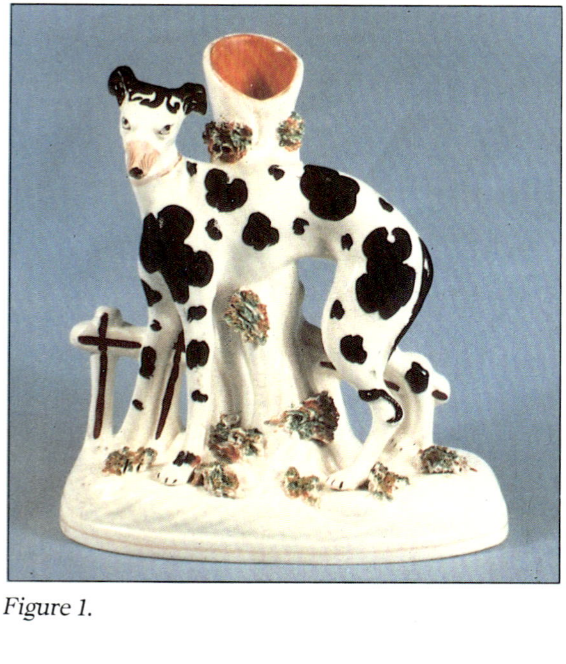

*Figure 1.*

*Figure 1.* Model as in Figure 2. With alternative colouring and the addition of moss clumps to the base and spill.
Circa 1850
Height 7 inches

*Figure 2.* "Elegance and Ecstasy"
A rare and sympathetically modelled couple, they appear to quiver with emotion.
Circa 1845
Height 7 inches

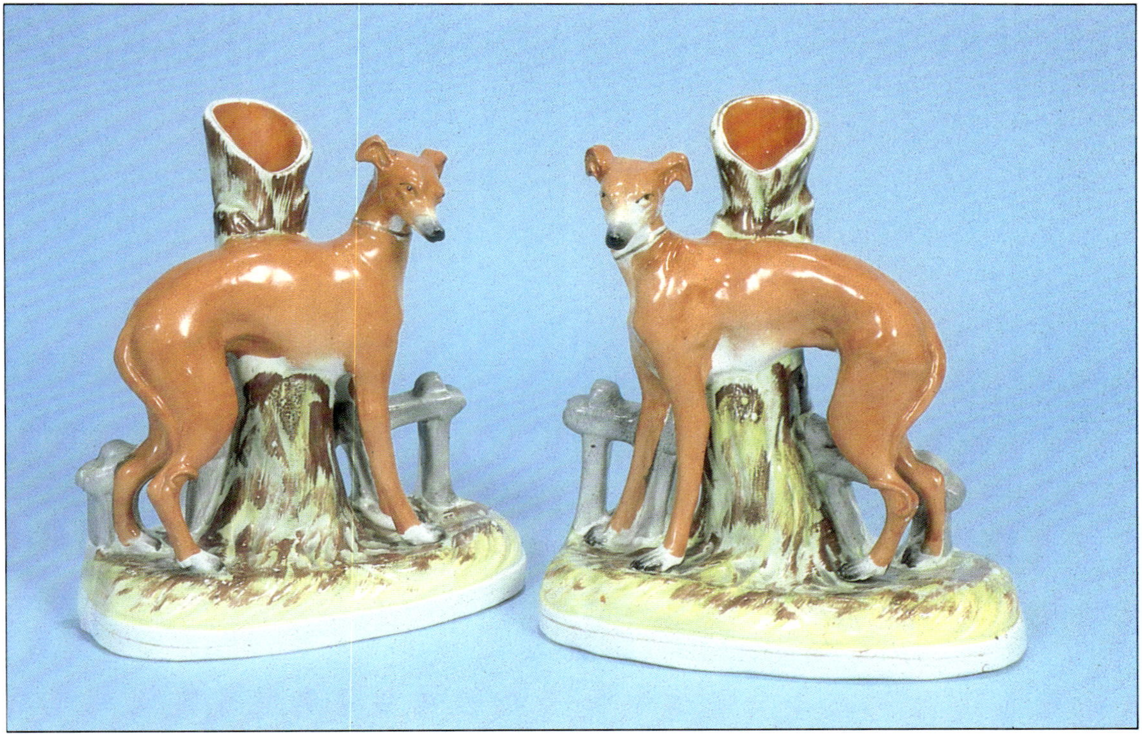

*Figure 2.*

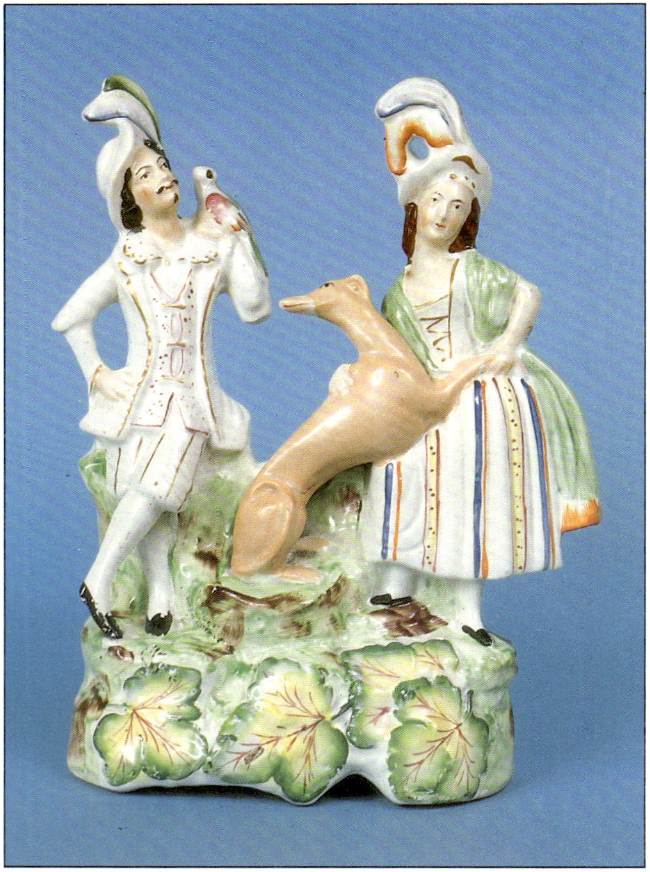

Figure 3.

*Figure 3.* A charming group of lovers with their hound and parrot on a delightful grassy-leafed base.
Circa 1850
Height 11 inches

*Figure 4.* "Come on play ball"
A most unusual group but poorly painted in this example, compared to the fine brushwork in Figure 2 of a similar model (minus friend).
Circa 1855
Height 7 inches

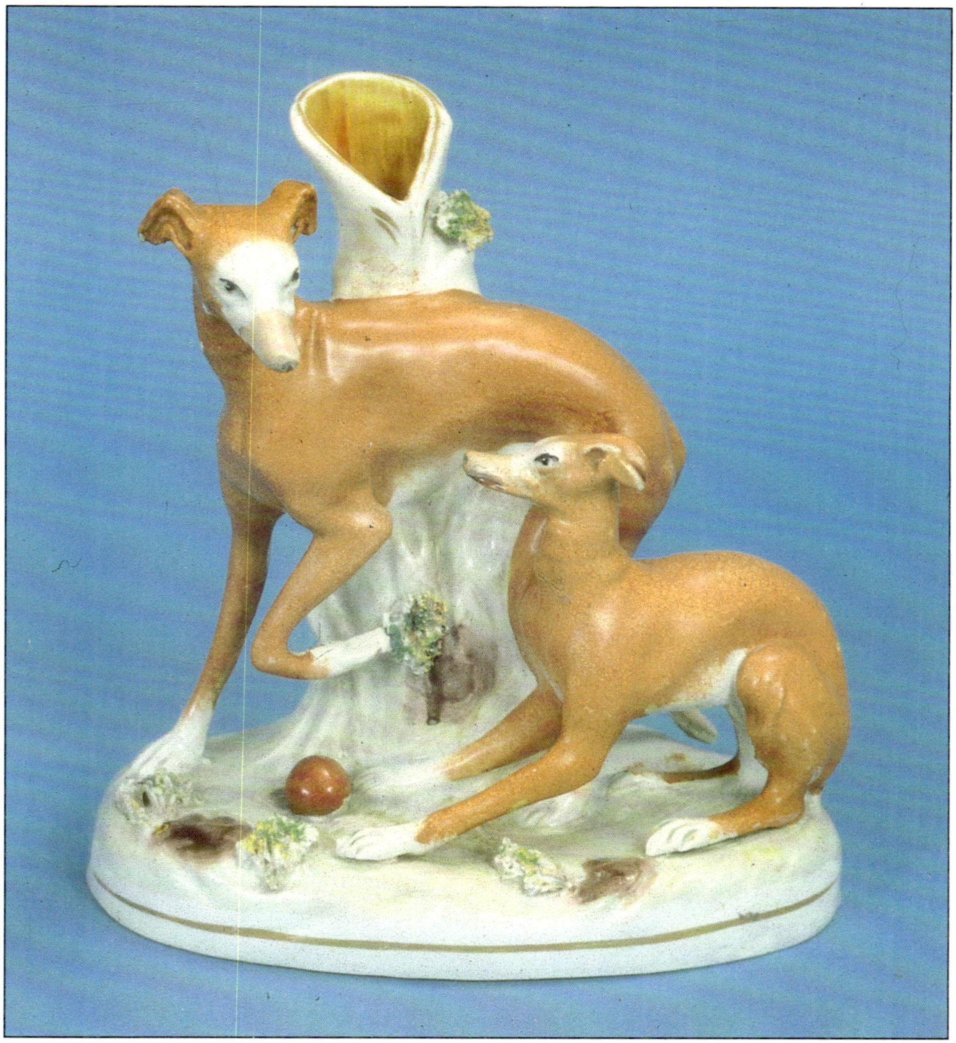

*Figure 4.*

*Figure 5.* Full of expression and self importance.
Circa 1850
Height 8 inches

*Figure 6.* "Elegance and Patience"
An attractive group simply but skilfully composed.
Circa 1845
Height 5½ inches

*Figure 7.* A good example of fine modelling and fine painting combined with attractiveness.
Circa 1845
Height 4¼ inches

*Figure 8.* "Delicacy in Motion"
Circa 1845
Height 2⅜ inches, Length 4¼ inches

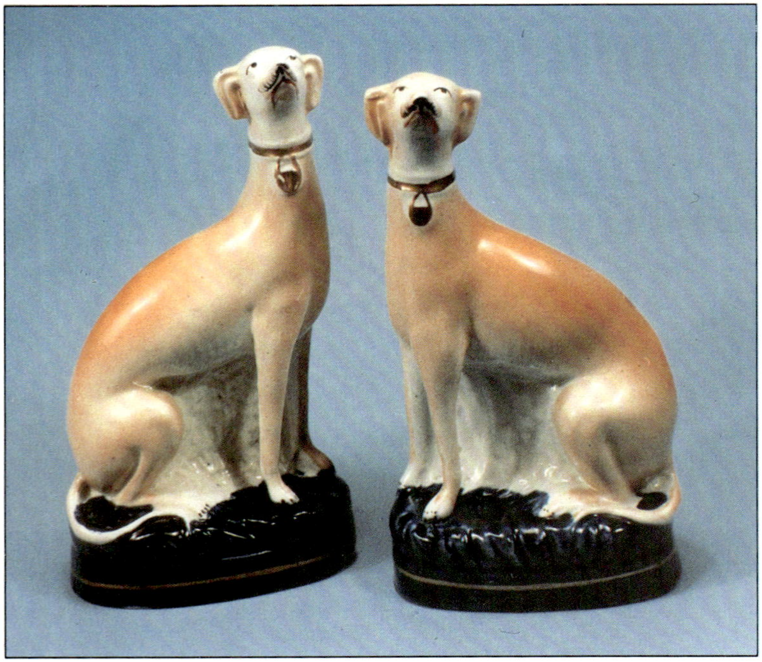

*Figure 5.*

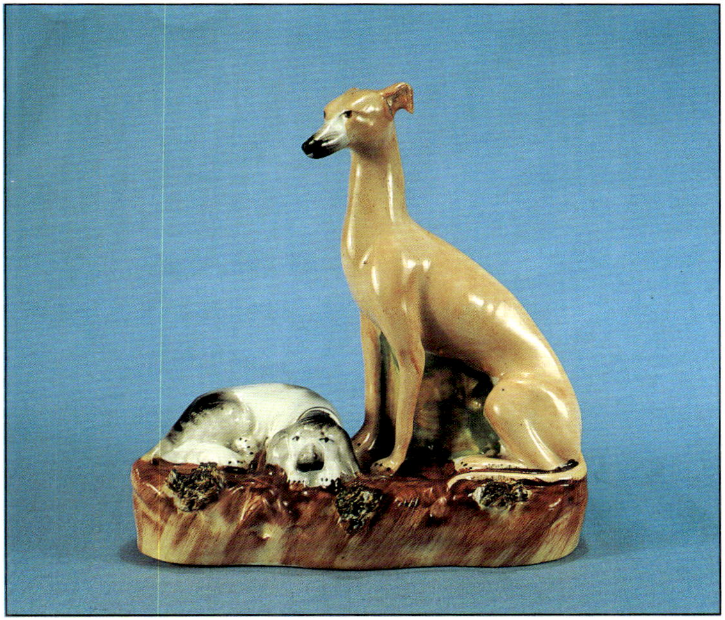

*Figure 6.*

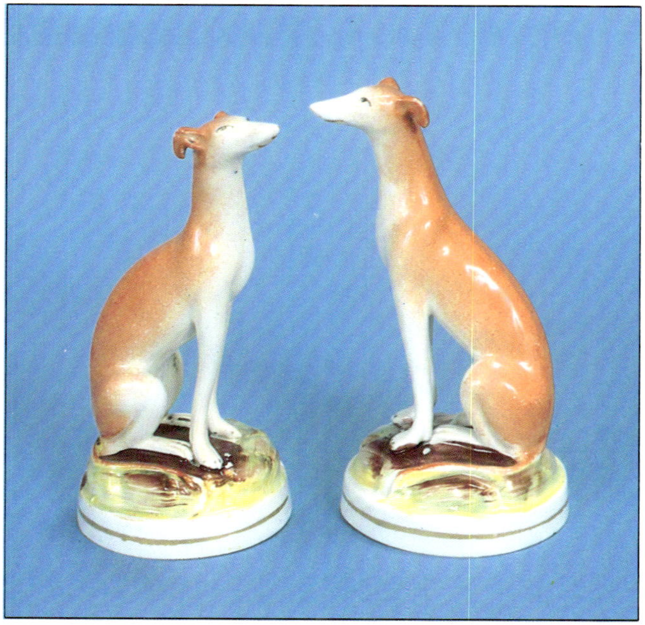

*Figure 7.*

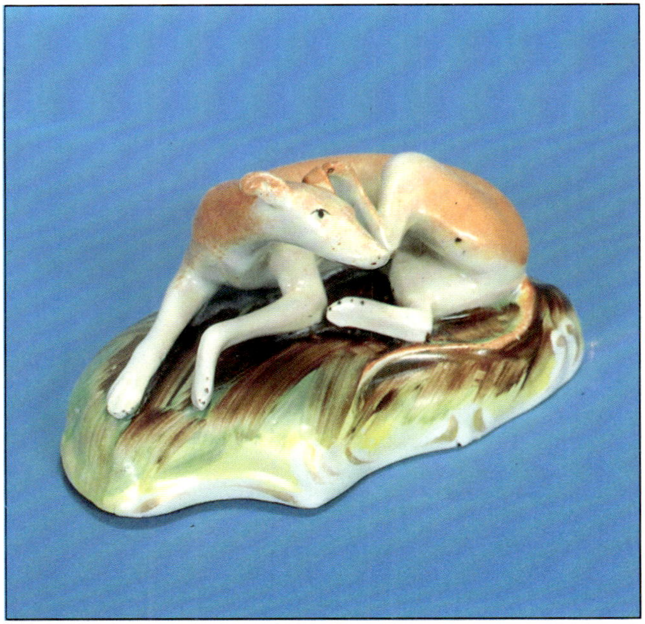

*Figure 8.*

# Japanese Chin

*The noble bearing of the Japanese Spaniel recalls an ancient past when it was the favourite of the Japanese imperial court.*

*With a sumptuous coat and a pom-pom tail held high, it moves with grace and elegance.*

*Queen Victoria was given one as a gift in 1853 as a playmate for the royal children.*

*Figure 1.* This exceptionally rare pair are completely free-standing, jauntily supporting the royal children.
Circa 1853
Height 5½ inches

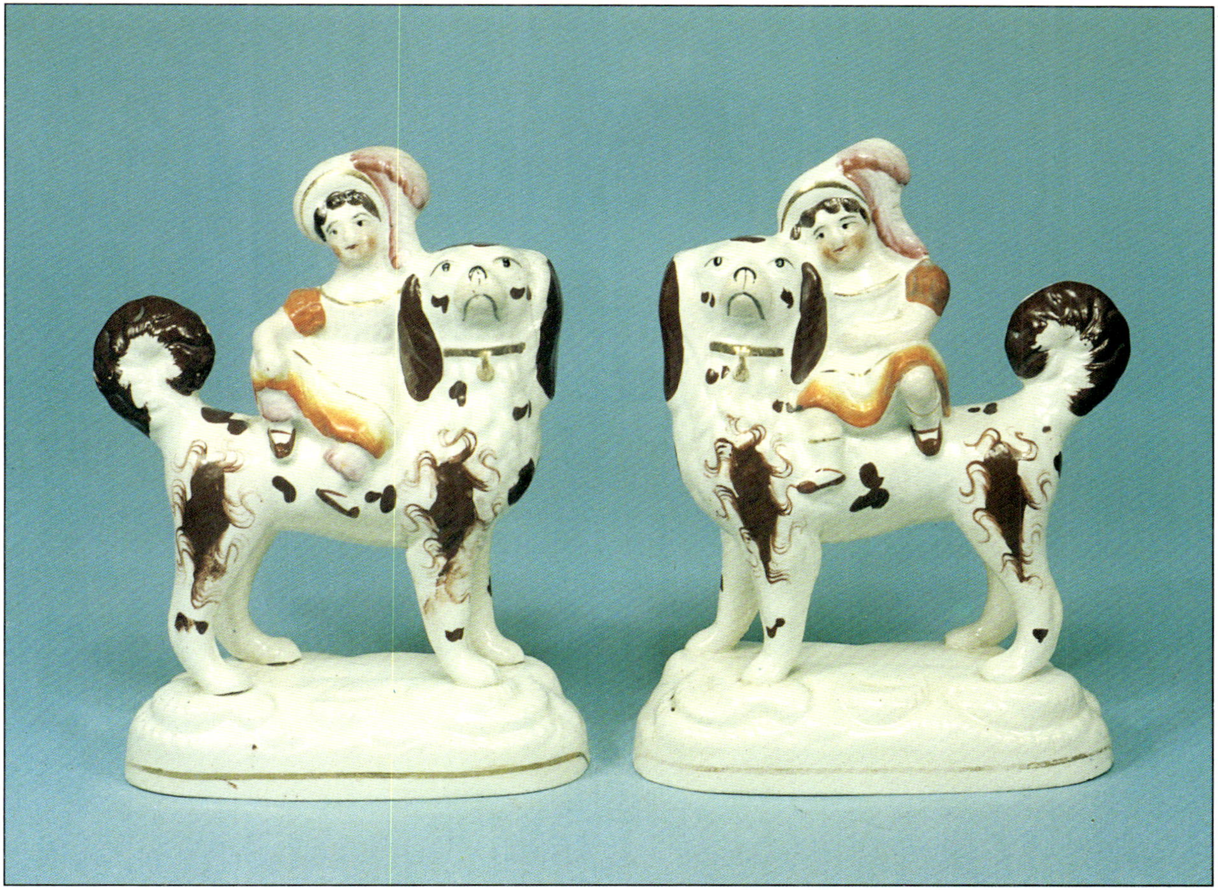

*Figure 1.*

# King Charles Spaniel

*Probably descended from the Japanese Chin this small spaniel has always been the true favourite of royality and even bears its name.*

*In the court of Queen Elizabeth I during the 1500s the ladies are said to have sought winter warmth by keeping them hidden under their enormous skirts.*

*Then known as* Spaniell Gentle *the term "Comforter Dog" was first used during this period. The name we use today is thanks to King Charles II, the King kept a large number as pets and were then known as the black and tans.*

*Three other varieties were developed later. Credit for one of these is ascribed to John Churchill who in 1702 became first Duke of Marlborough and made Blenheim Palace in Woodstock, Oxfordshire, his family seat. The chestnut red and white variety he produced is now known as the Blenheim.*

*Of all British Monarchs it was Queen Victoria who gave her canine subjects real respectability in the public eye when in 1840 the prefix* Royal *was added to the society for the prevention of cruelty to animals. The public knew her pets by name and saw them constantly in her company. Victoria's first true–love her beloved King Charles Spaniel "Dash" went everywhere with her (she had owned him since February 1833, before she met Prince Albert), he became famous in his own right, appearing in many embroideries and paintings of the period and explains the breed's tremendous popularity throughout the 19th century as a favourite comforter and lap dog.*

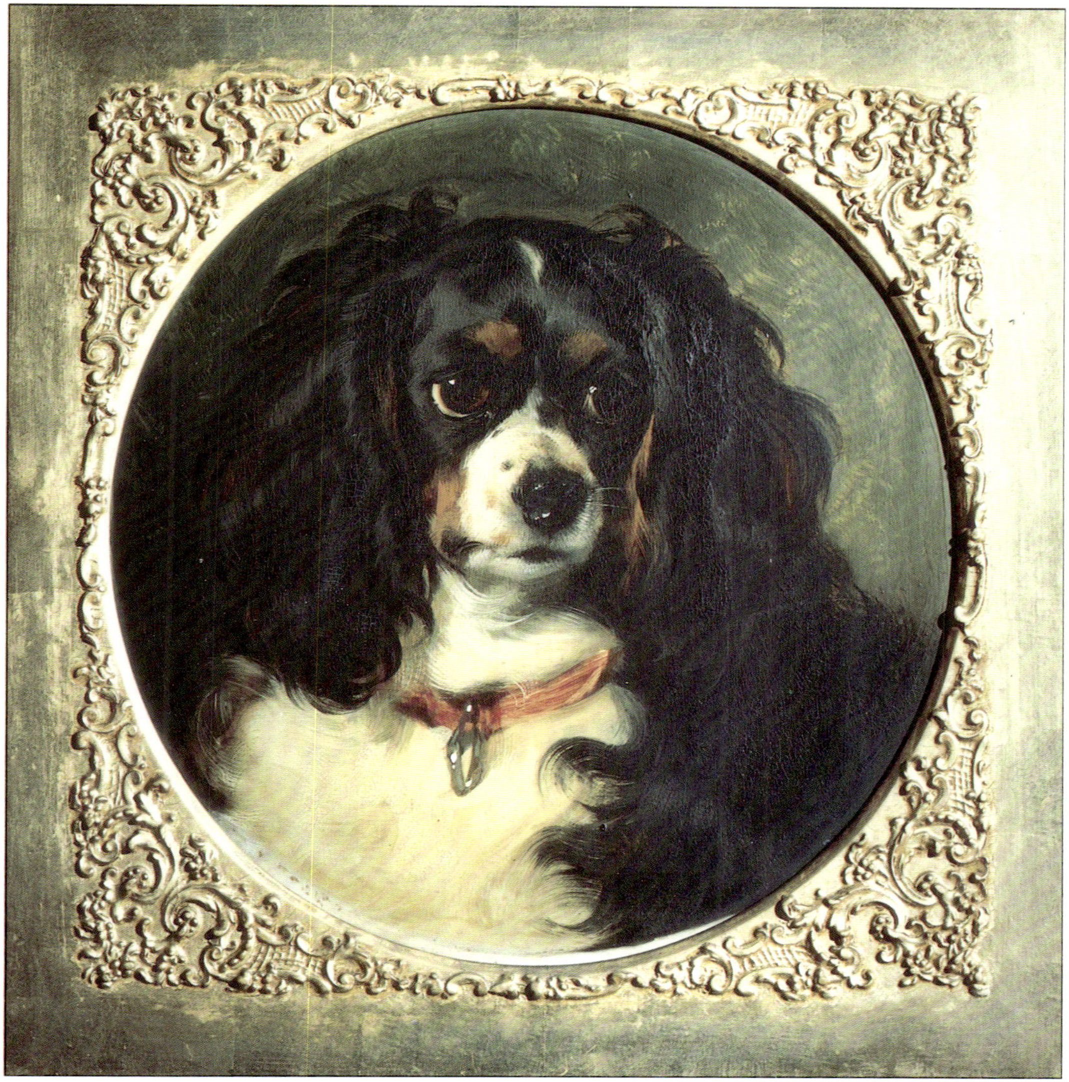

*Figure 1.* "Dash" Oil on panel, 1836, by Sir Edwin Landseer.
*Reproduced by gracious permission of* Her Majesty Queen Elizabeth II.

# *Spaniels on Bases*

*Many of the early models echo the flamboyant rococo scroll bases which are so apparent on 18th century porcelain figures.*

*Further study offers-up an infinite variety of alternative shapes and decorative effects from grassy covered mounds of naturalistic scrub, suggesting a sporting connection, right through to charmingly tasselled cushions for the favoured "comforter".*

*However, a smooth oval form governed by the economy of simple modelling appears to be the most characteristic of mid 19th century base shapes. Often painted in a rich cobalt blue with the sometimes added embellishment of a gilt line its occupant was highlighted to perfection.*

*Figure 2.* "Majesty and Grace"
With separate front legs and standing on pale pink bases, moulded with green leaves, this proud pair proclaim themselves the royal favourites.
Circa 1845
Height 7¾ inches

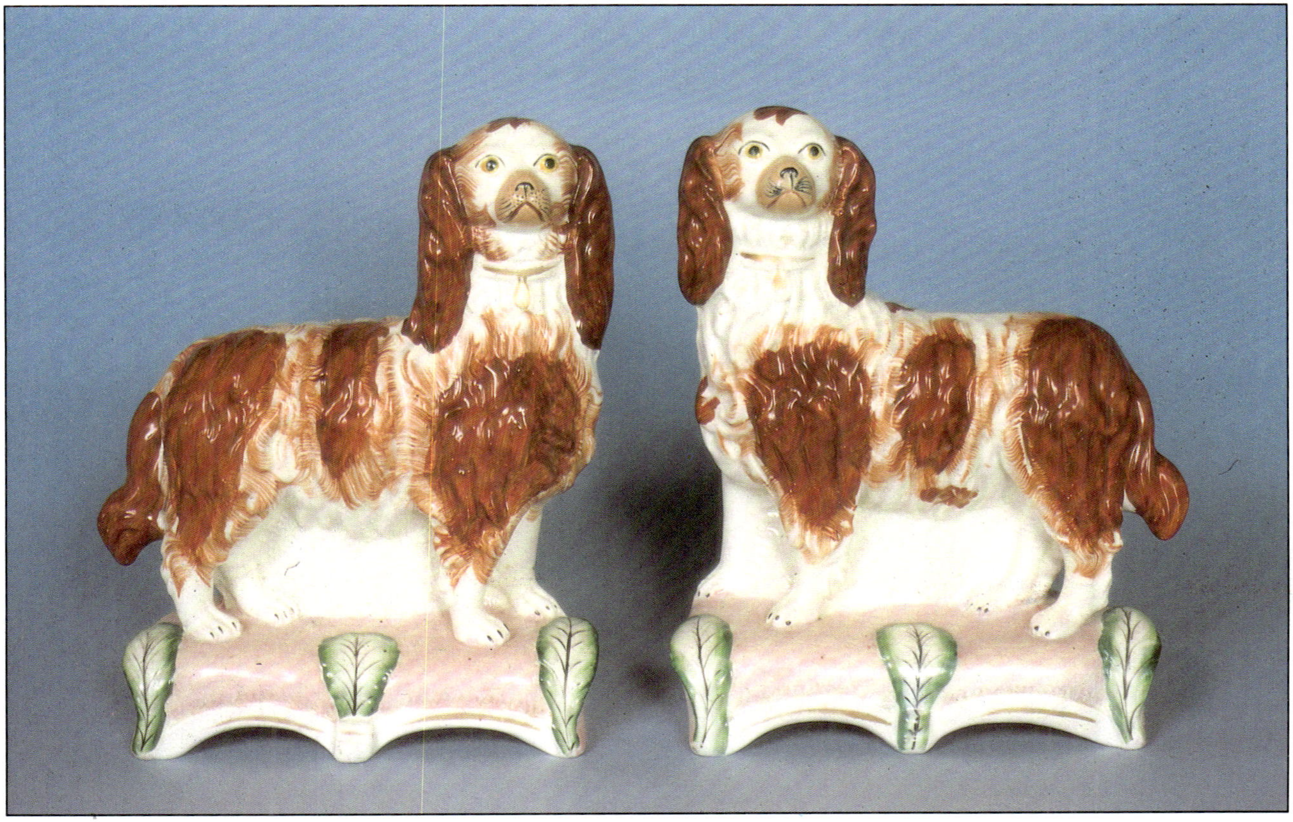

*Figure 2.*

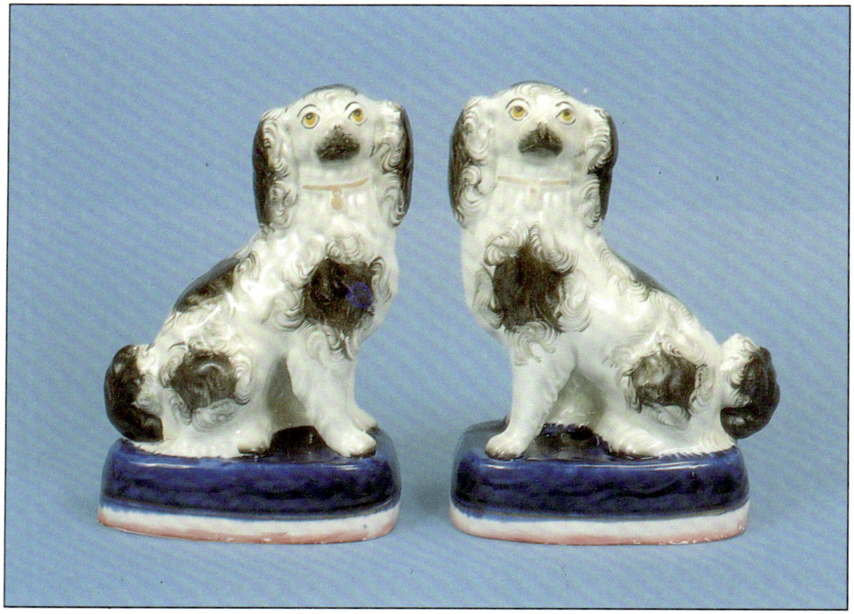

*Figure 3.*

*Figure 3.* "The Look of Love"
Sitting on blue bases fringed with pink.
Their front legs separate.
These charmers offer a full pedigree with quiet adoration.
Circa 1850
Height 8¾ inches

*Figure 4.* "Home Comfort"
A pair of Spaniels lying on pink fringed green cushions.
Quill holders.
Circa 1850
Height 4½ inches

*Figure 5.* Liver and white Spaniels sitting on unusually shaped bases with both legs separate.
Circa 1845
Height 8 inches

*Figure 6.* "Naughty and Haughty"
Red and white on oval blue bases with front legs separate.
Circa 1850
Height 7 inches

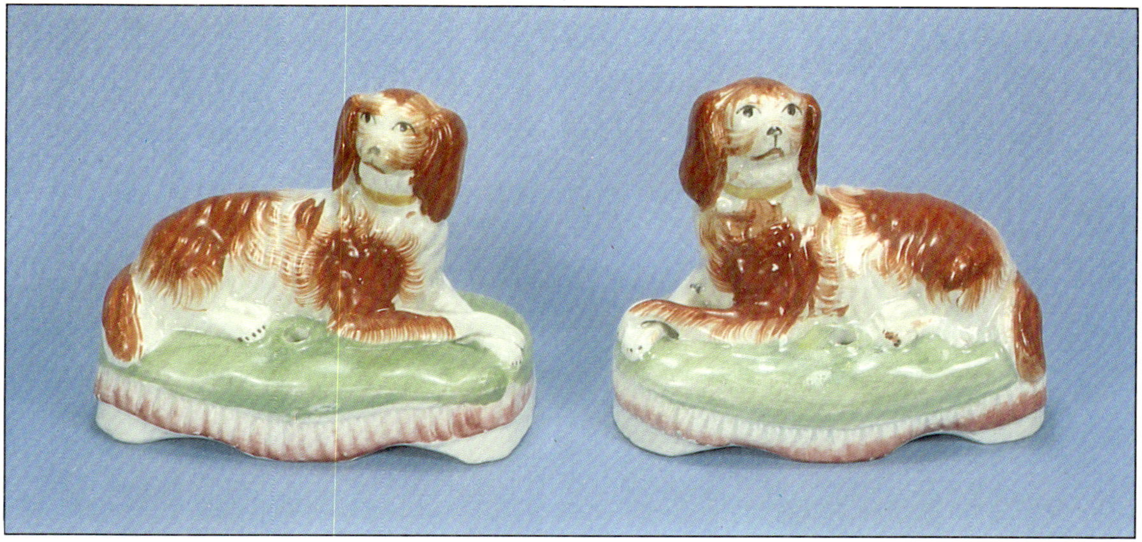

*Figure 4.*

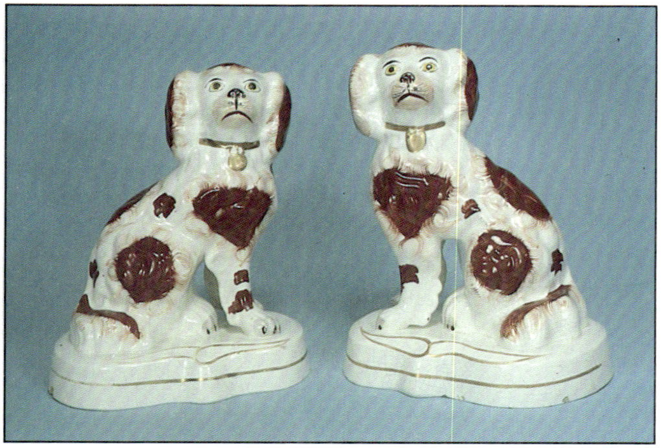

*Figure 5.*

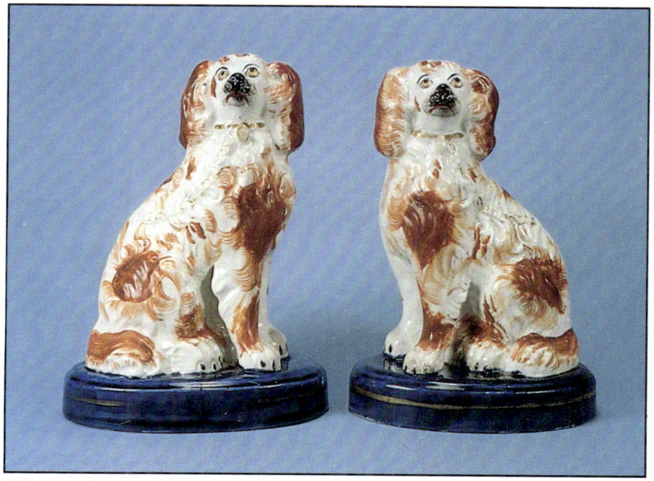

*Figure 6.*

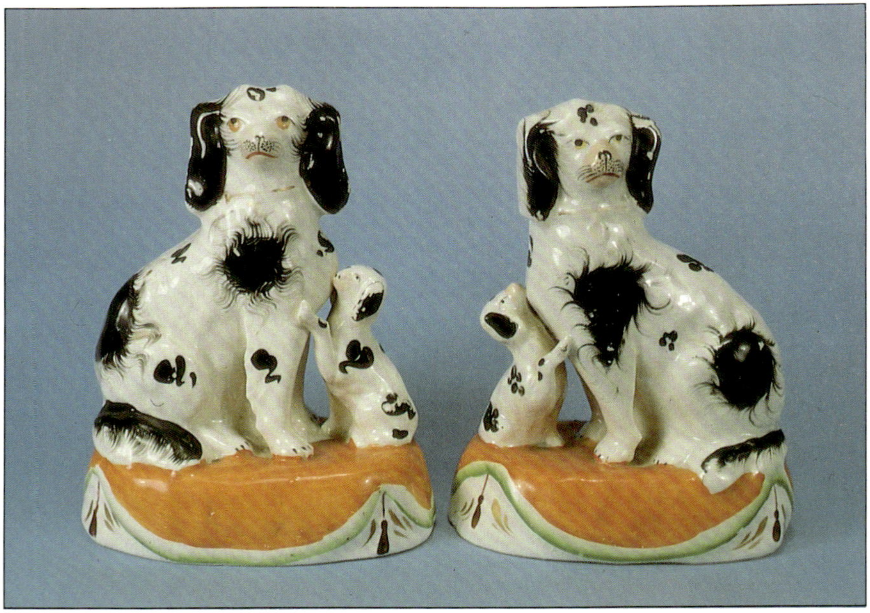

Figure 7.

*Figure 7.* An appealing pair of puppies with their parents, sitting on orange tasselled cushions.
Circa 1850
Height 6 inches

*Figure 8.* The porcellaneous body, fine modelling and appealing expressions, all set upon delightful tricoloured and tasselled cushions, pull at the heart strings of the hardest heart.
Circa 1850
Height 5 inches

*Figure 9.* Unusually elaborate acanthus leaf bases, support happy families.
Circa 1845
Height 3¼ inches

*Figure 10.* Chunky modelling, solid looking oval bases and strong painting offer this pair rather an aggressive air.
Circa 1845
Height 7¼ inches

*Figure 11.* This pair with puppies have blue eyes.
Blue eyes are quite rare throughout all the dog models.
Circa 1855
Height 7¾ inches

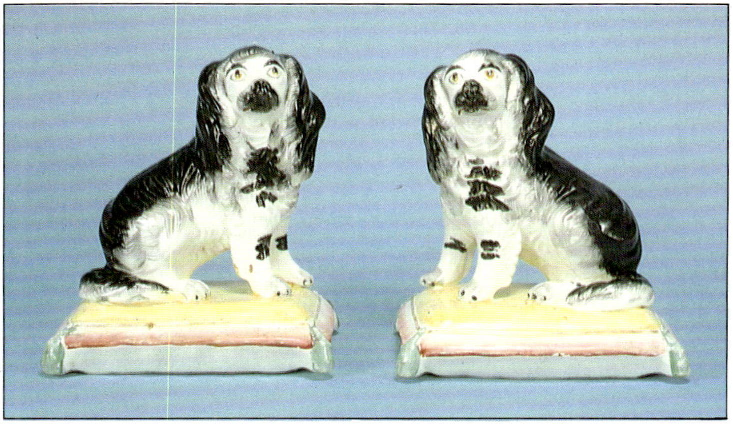

*Figure 8.*

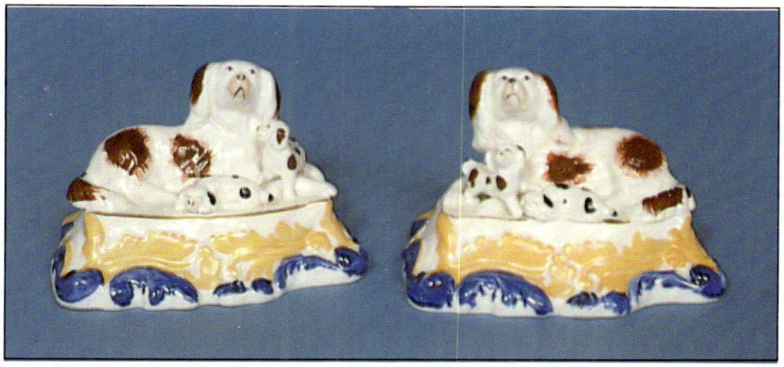

*Figure 9.*

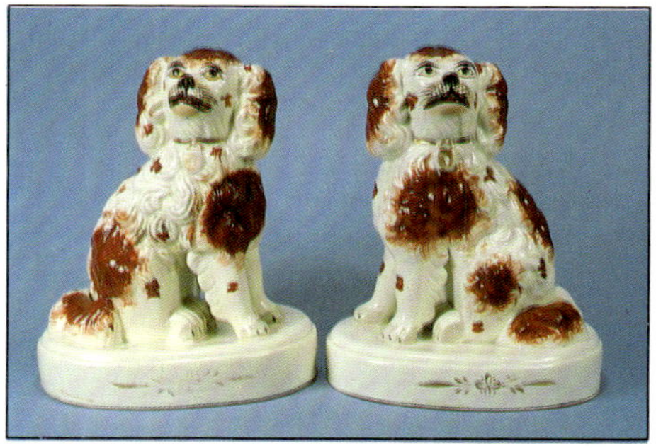

*Figure 10.*

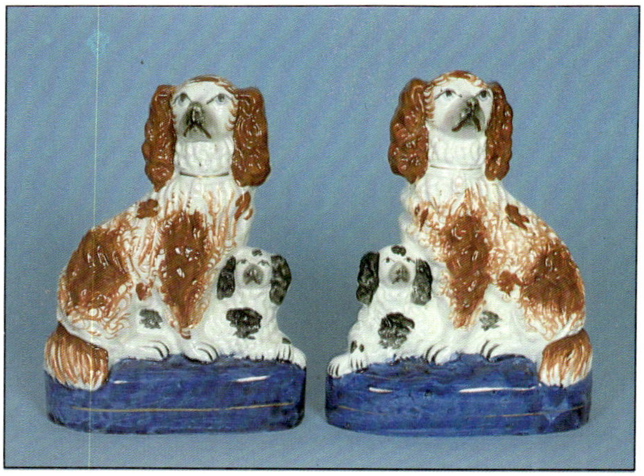

*Figure 11.*

# *Star Quality*

*The Great Exhibition opened its doors in May 1851. The huge glass and iron-framed building erected in Hyde Park to house all the exhibits, was immediately christened the Crystal Palace.*

*It celebrated the dawn of a new golden age of growing material prosperity, brought about by a high level of industrial production and expanding foreign trade.*

*The exhibiting manufacturers, large and small, were encouraged to show their superiority in art, design and manufacture, to the world. They were making every effort to be noticed (then as now!) against increasing competition and introduced new especially designed large impressive examples of their particular medium.*

*This very noticeable pair of Spaniels would certainly fit the criterion.*

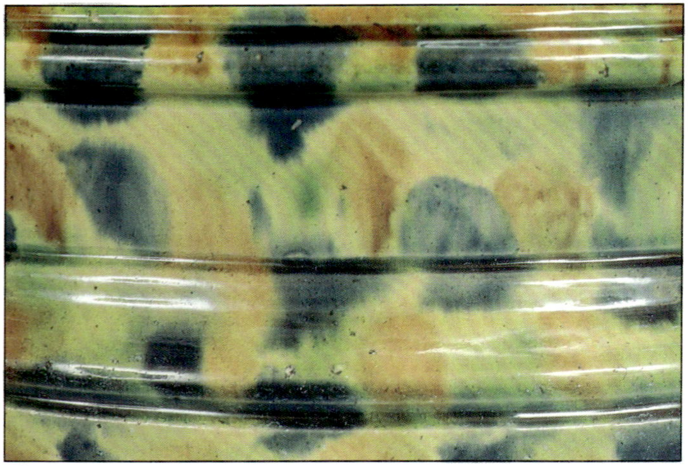

*Figure 12.*

*Figure 12.* Detail of base from Figure 13.

*Figure 13.* A pair of treacle-glazed stoneware Spaniels, sitting on remarkable colour splashed bases.
Circa 1851
Height 16½ inches

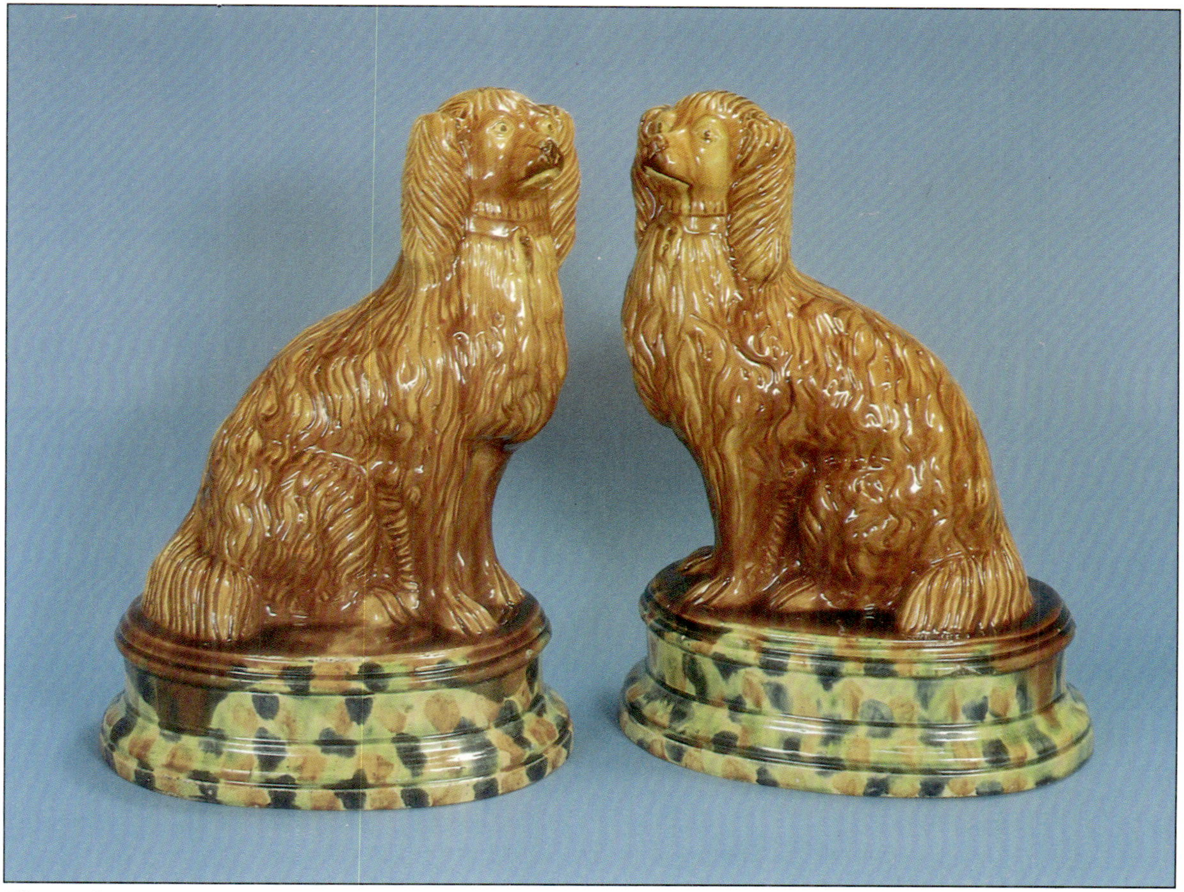

*Figure 13.*

*Figure 14.* "Be it ever so humble, there is no place like home"
Happy to find they have a kennel to live in.
These Spaniels are somewhat surprised at their good fortune, as kennel groups are rare.
Circa 1860
Height 5½ inches

*Figures 15/16/17.* A selection of family quill holder groups.
An amusing collecting theme, which may take a while however, as they are all quite rare.
Circa 1850/55
Height 5 inches – 6½ inches

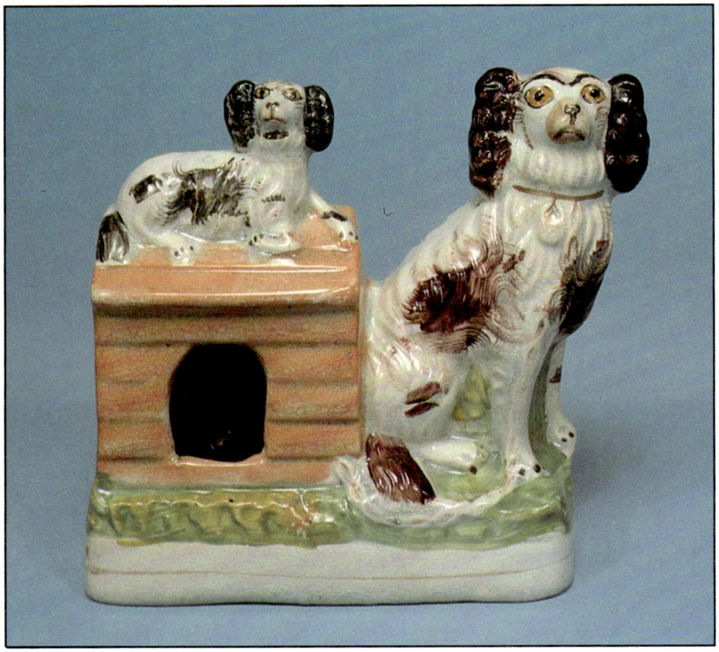

*Figure 14.*

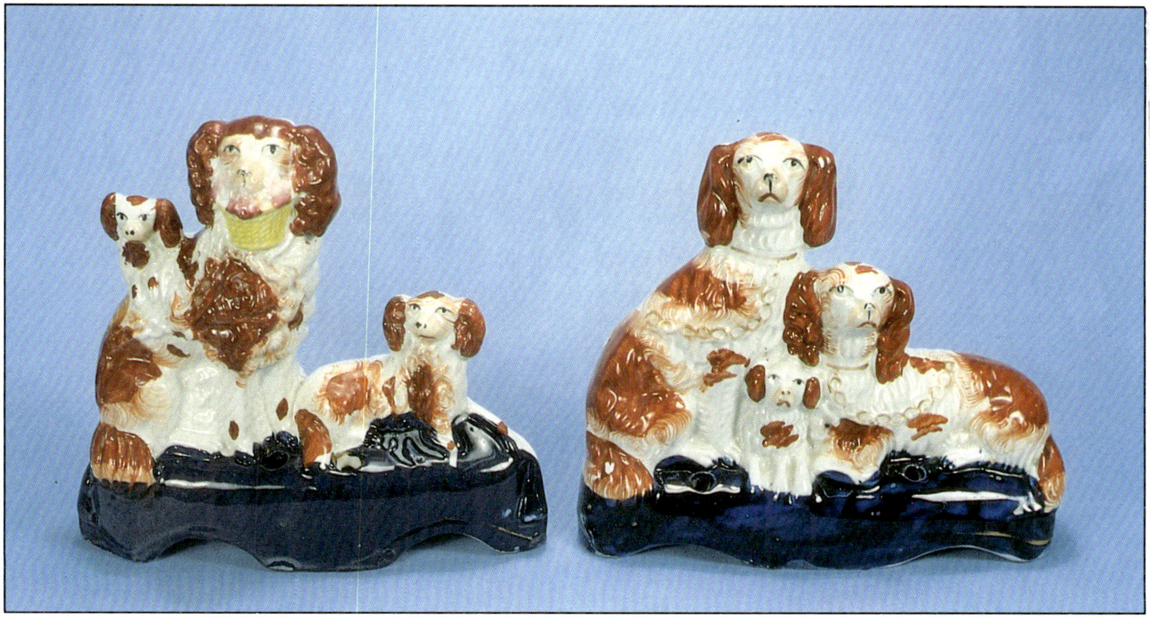

*Figure 15.*

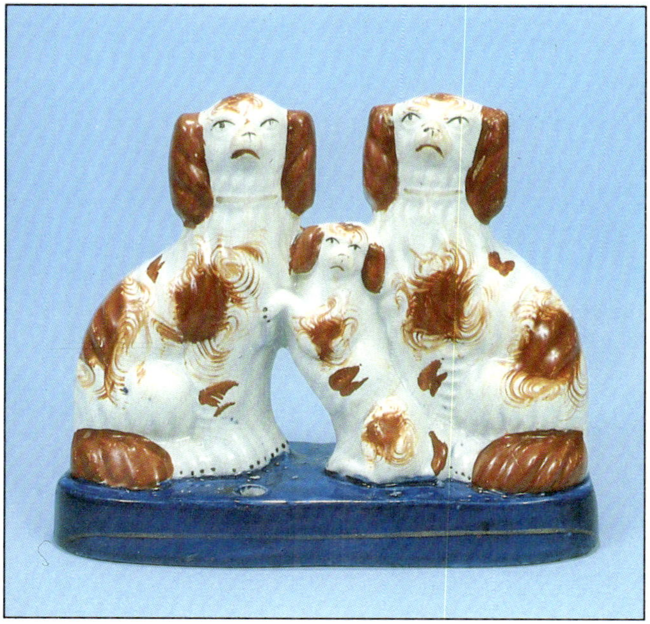

*Figure 16.*

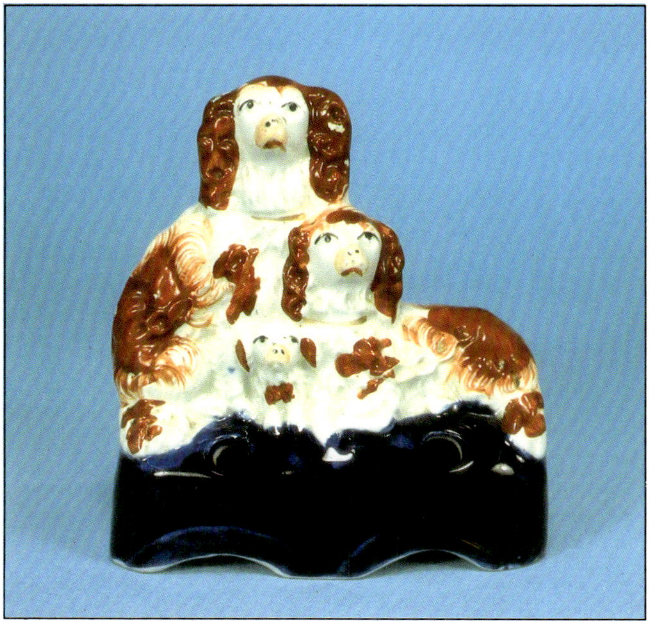

*Figure 17.*

# *John and Rebecca Lloyd, Shelton, Hanley, Staffordshire*

*John Lloyd (1805–1850) was known to be making pottery figures at the above address from 1834, his wife Rebecca continued for two years after his death.*

*Much of their work is unmarked.*

*The impressed Lloyd Shelton mark is in itself very rare. Here it allows us a valuable insight into this dog's pedigree.*

*It is the only mark I have ever seen on an early 19th century pottery dog and the only Lloyd Shelton mark recorded on an animal model.*

*Figure 18.* Liver and white Spaniel. Lloyd Shelton impressed base.
Circa 1840
Height 8¾ inches

*Figure 19.* Impressed mark on base of dog in Figure 18.

*Figure 20.* The Lloyd Shelton (unmarked) Spaniel.
The impressive scrolled base highlighted in gilt with a tulip and rose.
Circa 1840
Very rare
Height 9 inches

*Figure 21.* The Lloyd Shelton (unmarked) Spaniel in black and white.
The scrolled base painted in cobalt blue and lavishly gilded.
Circa 1840
Very rare
Height 9 inches

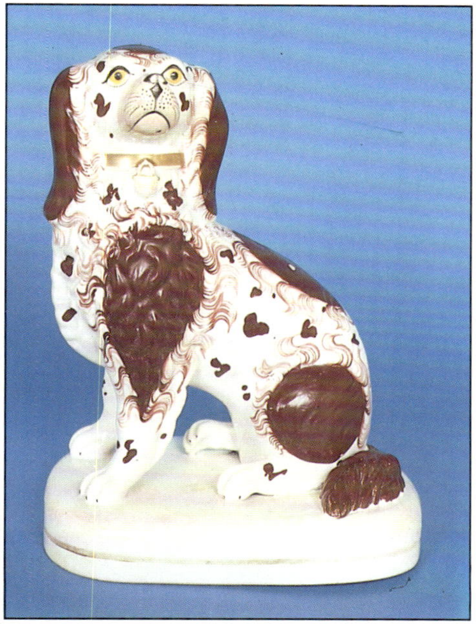
Figure 18.

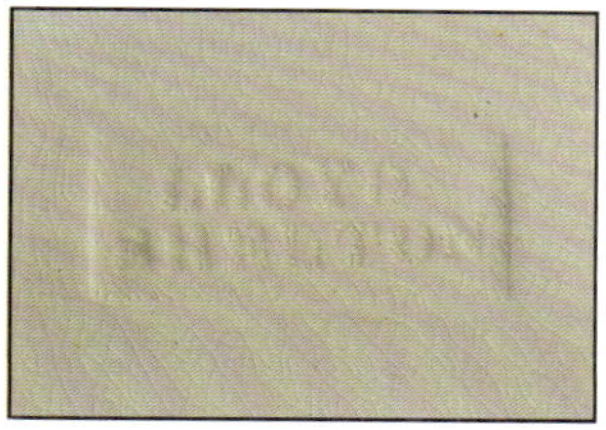
Figure 19.

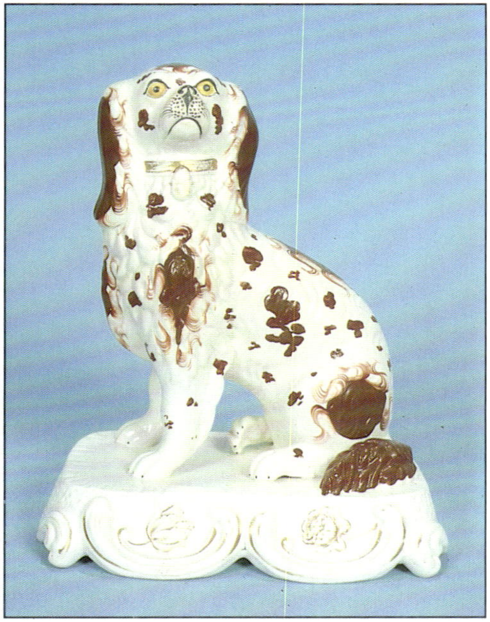
Figure 20.

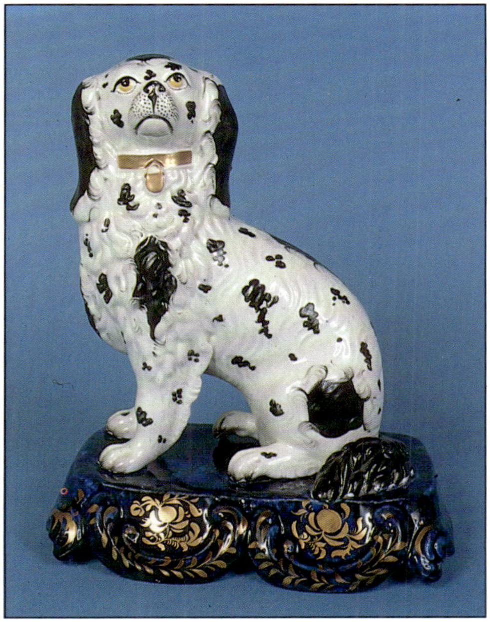
Figure 21.

# *Comforter Spaniel*

*This traditional title categorises the form of mantelpiece Spaniel that was potted from simple two-piece moulds.*

*Sold in pairs, comforter dogs were available in a variety of size and colour to suit all tastes and everyone's pocket.*

*The photographs on the following pages represent a cross-section of basic models.*

*The majority may be found in alternative coloration.*

*Figure 22.* Although unmarked in a "factory" sense, this model is afforded distinction by impressed size numbers on their bases ranging from No. 1 (the largest) to No. 6 (the smallest).
Obviously manufactured by the same pottery, the numbers helped to identify the model size required for buyers re-ordering.
Collecting the complete set can be rewarding, some numbers are relatively easy to find but No. 6 is rare.
The model is also available in black and white.
The whole set in good condition is very rare.
Circa 1850

| | | |
|---|---|---|
| Heights | No. 1 | 12¾ inches |
| | No. 2 | 10 inches |
| | No. 3 | 9 inches |
| | No. 4 | 7¾ inches |
| | No. 5 | 6½ inches |
| | No. 6 | 5½ inches |

*Figure 23.* Base of numbered model (size 2)

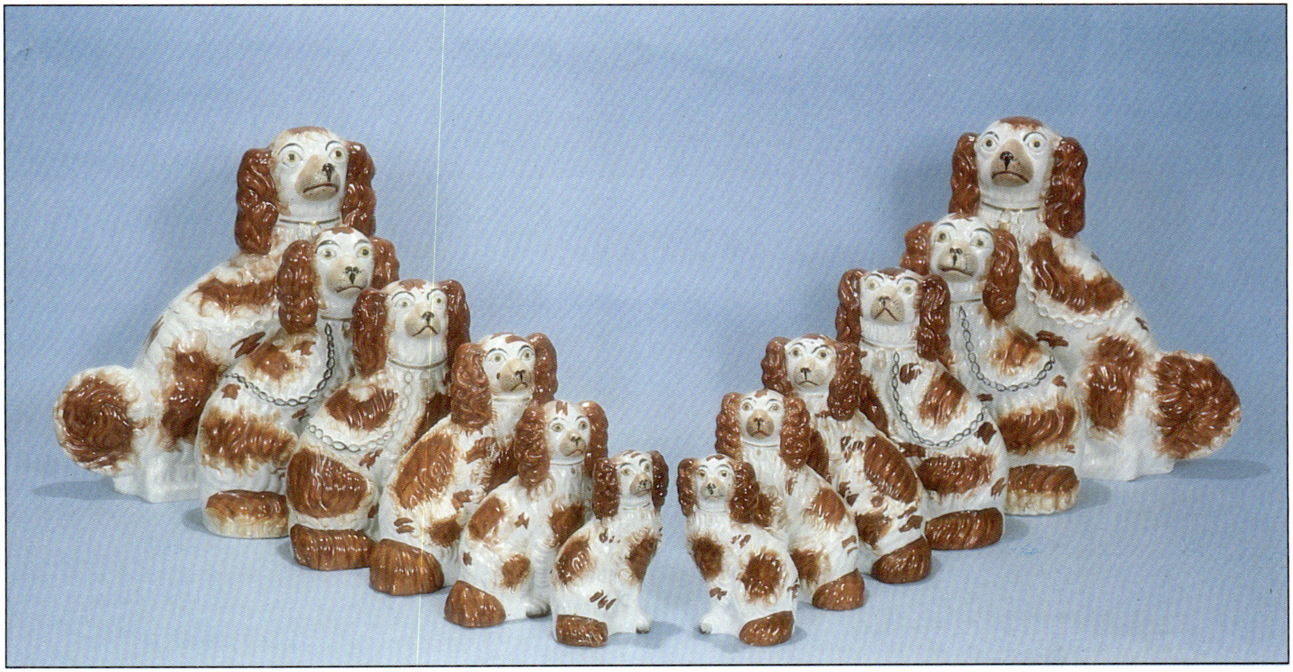

*Figure 22.*

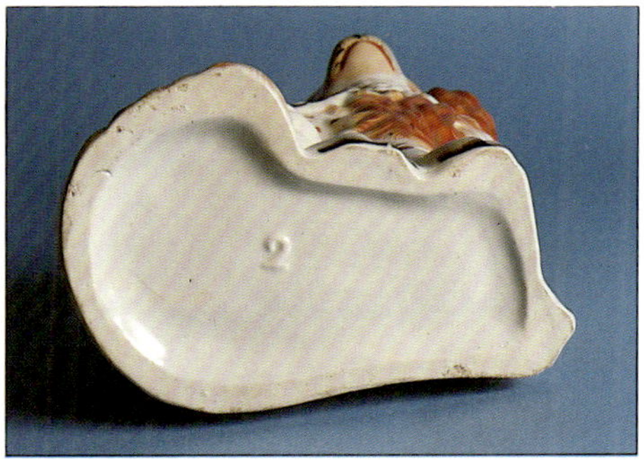


*Figure 23.*

*Figure 24.* "Top honours" go to this model along with Figure 43 page 98, for being the tallest of Staffordshire Spaniels!
Circa 1855
Height 15 inches

*Figure 25.* "Chunky bodied Spaniels" with a satisfied "after dinner" look.
Circa 1850
Height 10½ inches

*Figure 26.* This particular pair presents us with the opportunity to dismiss the old wives tale that pairs of differing size were put together in the pottery deliberately as male and female.
There are several reasons which explain this difference in height.
They may have been mismatched at the pottery, or the change-over to a new mould may not have exactly coincided.
The main reason, however, is that during their lifetime two singles have been "married" together.
Many models have some slight height difference which is normal but such a difference as in the pair illustrated, do not make them "Mr. and Mrs."
Circa 1855
Height Left 14¾ inches
Right 14 inches

*Figure 27.* A pair of No. 2 Spaniels in black and white, see page 86 Figure 22. Numbered set.
Circa 1850
Height 10 inches

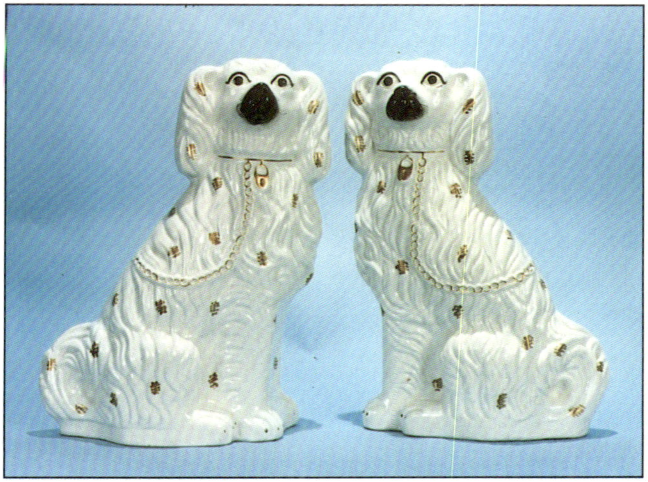

*Figure 24.*

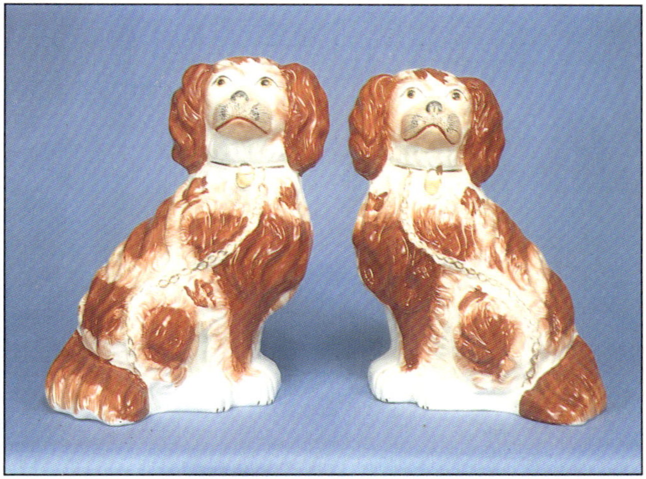

*Figure 25.*

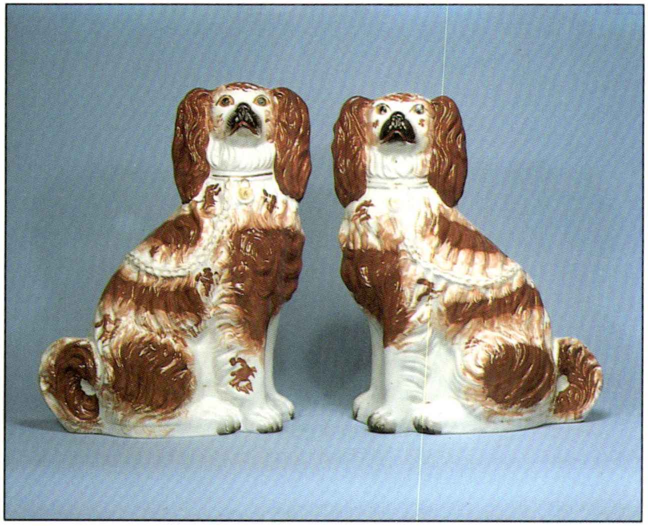

*Figure 26.*

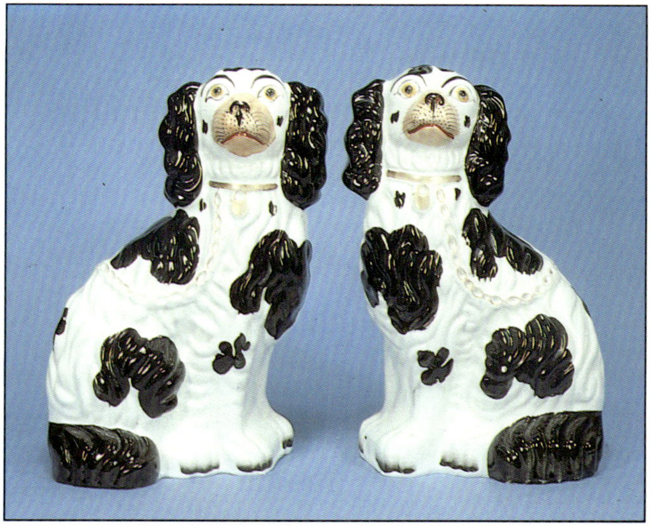

*Figure 27.*

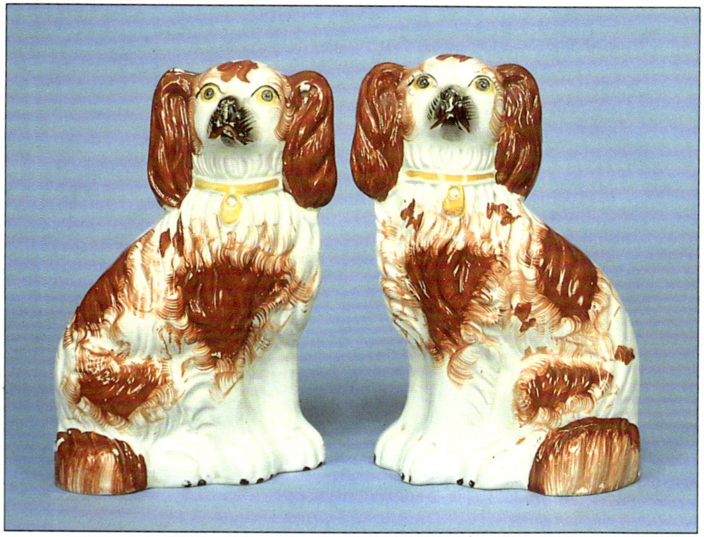

*Figure 28.*

*Figure 28.* Sporting yellow collars.
Circa 1865
Height 7¼ inches

*Figure 29.* A pair of No. 1 dogs in white with gilt decoration (see Figure 22 page 86).
Circa 1850
Height 12½ inches

*Figure 30.* "Wide-Eyed and Bushy-Tailed"
Circa 1860
Height 12 inches

*Figure 31.* Head to toe in lustre.
Circa 1870
Height 10½ inches

*Figure 32.* "Is it dinner time yet?"
Circa 1865
Height 9¾ inches

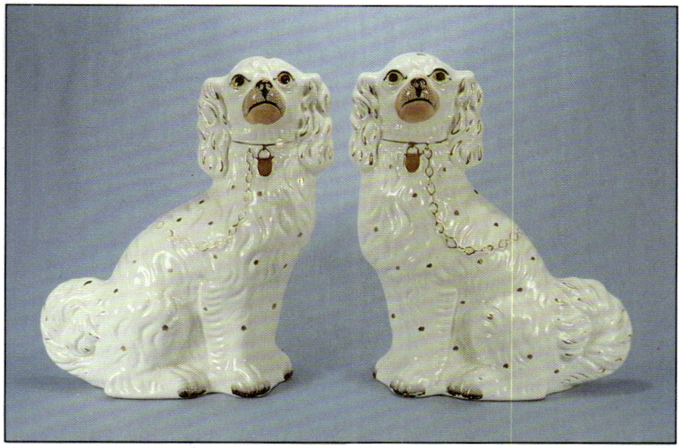

*Figure 29.*

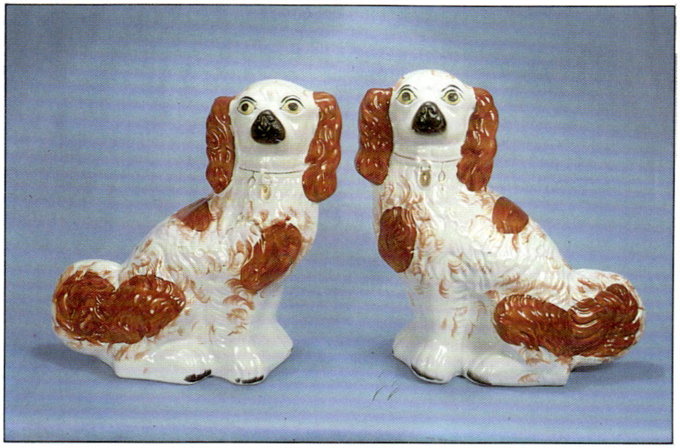

*Figure 30.*

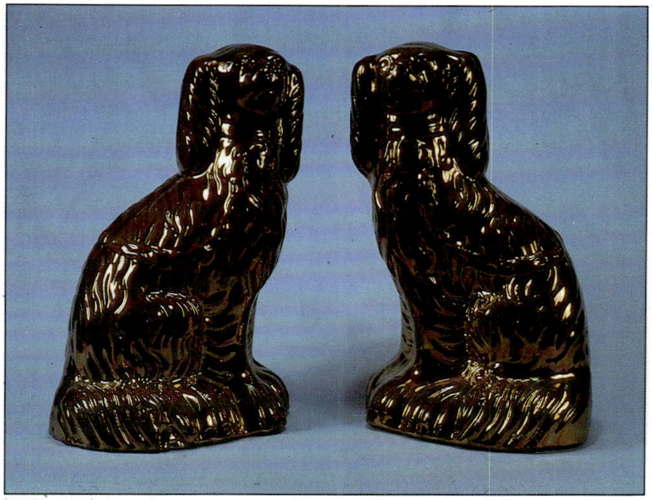

*Figure 31.*

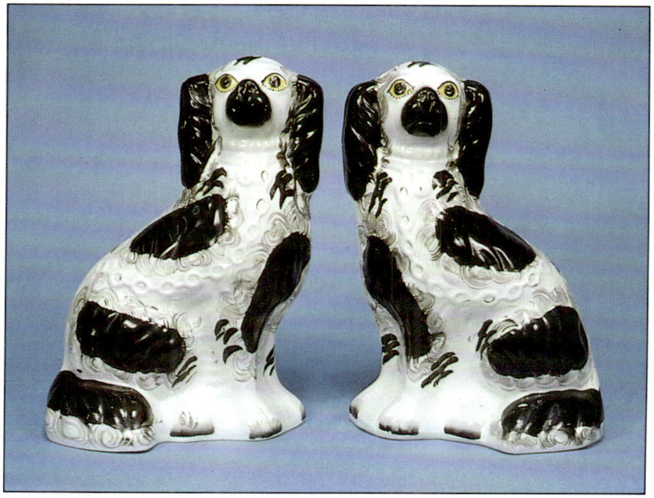

*Figure 32.*

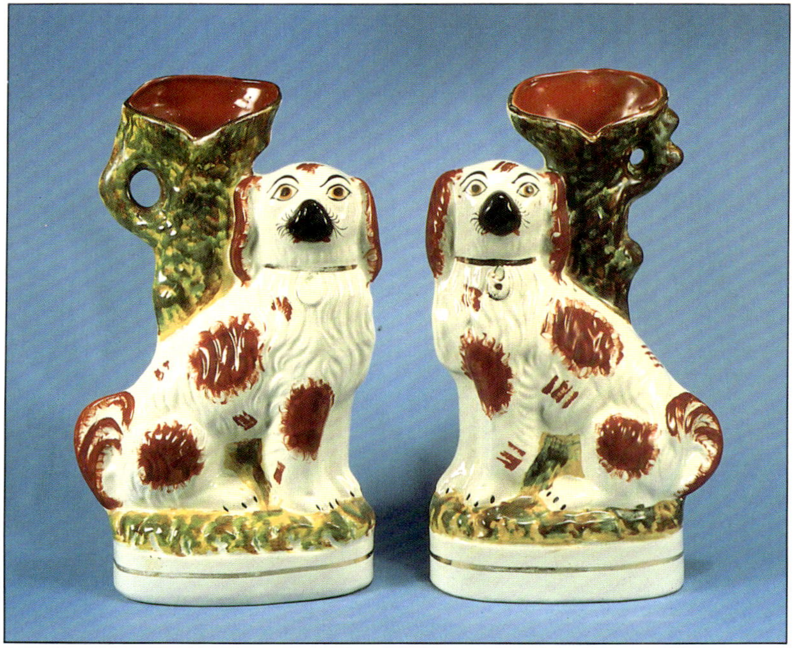

*Figure 33.*

*Figure 33.* The only model of Comforter Spaniels which support large spill vases.
Spill vases were used to hold long spills of rolled paper to light additional fires or pipes etc., from an already lit fireplace. In those early days matches were expensive.
Spill vases were not intended to hold flowers (unless dried) as the unglazed interiors do not hold water.
Circa 1880
Height 13 inches

*Figure 34.* A small pair of chunky Spaniels.
Circa 1850
Height 7¼ inches

*Figure 35.* "We may be plain but we do have an appealing look"
Circa 1865
Height 10¼ inches

*Figure 36.* "Somebody loves us!"
Circa 1890
Height 14¾ inches

*Figure 37.* Porcellaneous bodied.
Circa 1850
Height 5½ inches

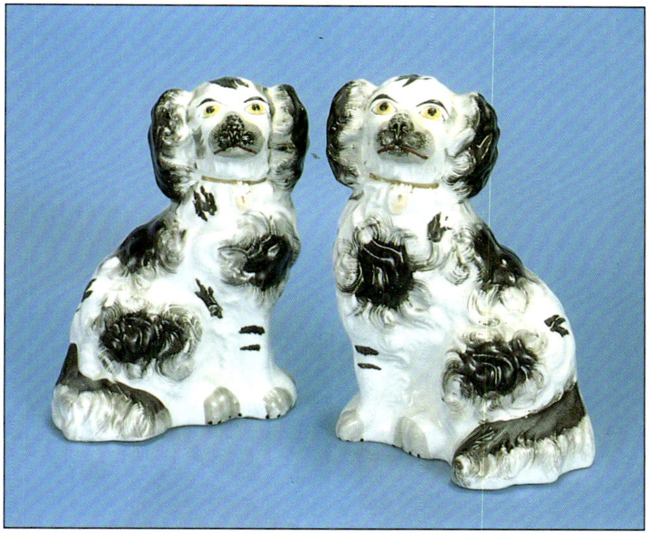

*Figure 34.*

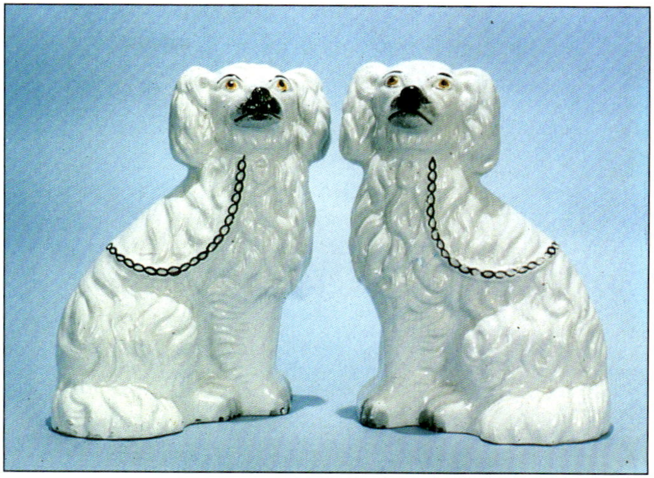

*Figure 35.*

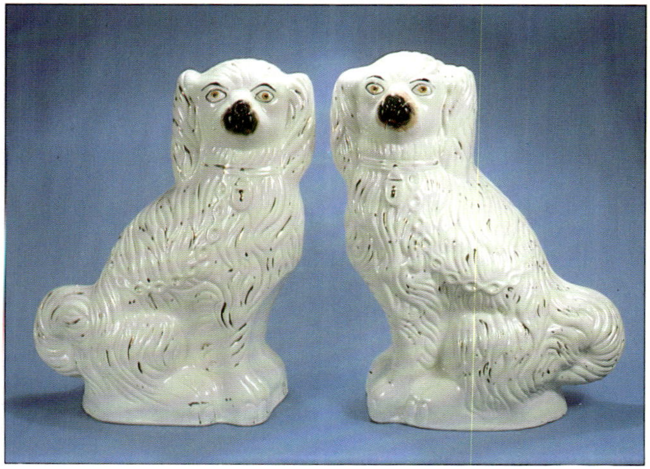

*Figure 36.*

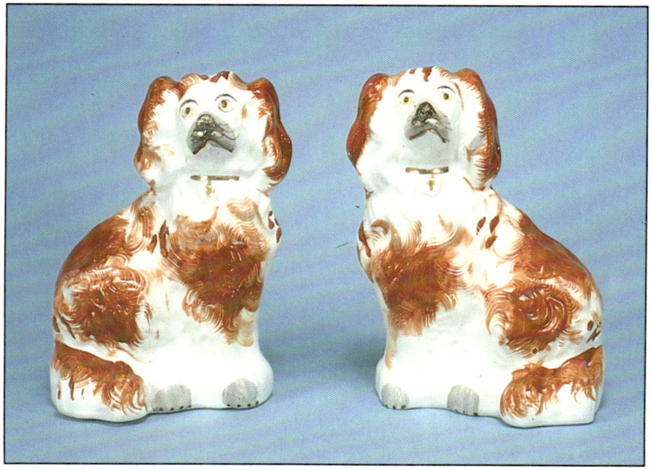

*Figure 37.*

# *Spaniels with separate legs*

*The use of an extra mould to add to a separate front leg added a pleasing extra touch of realism and dimension to the simplest form of two-piece Comforter Spaniel.*

*Due to the additional labour (and cost) they entailed, these models appear to have been made in fewer numbers than their more familiar counterparts.*

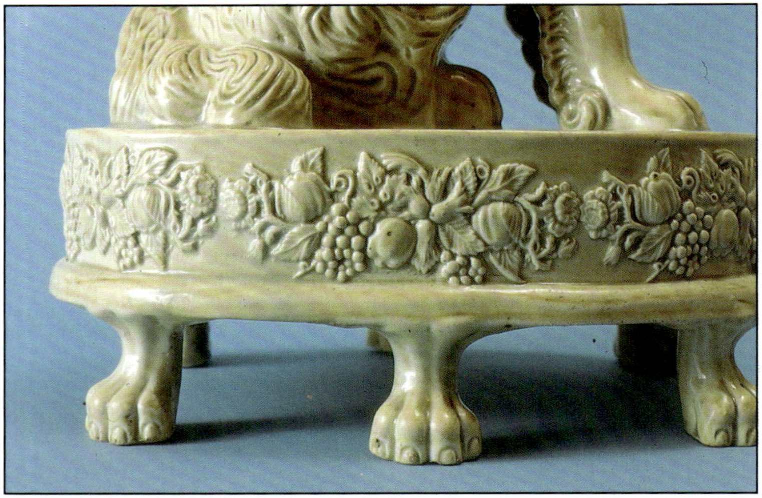

*Figure 38.*

*Figure 38.* Detail of base from Figure 39.

*Figure 39.* "High Society"
A magnificent pair of buff-coloured Spaniels with separate legs sitting on large oval bases decorated with fruit and vines.
The bases supported on paw feet.
Salt-glazed stoneware.
Extremely rare.
Circa 1835
Height 14¾ inches

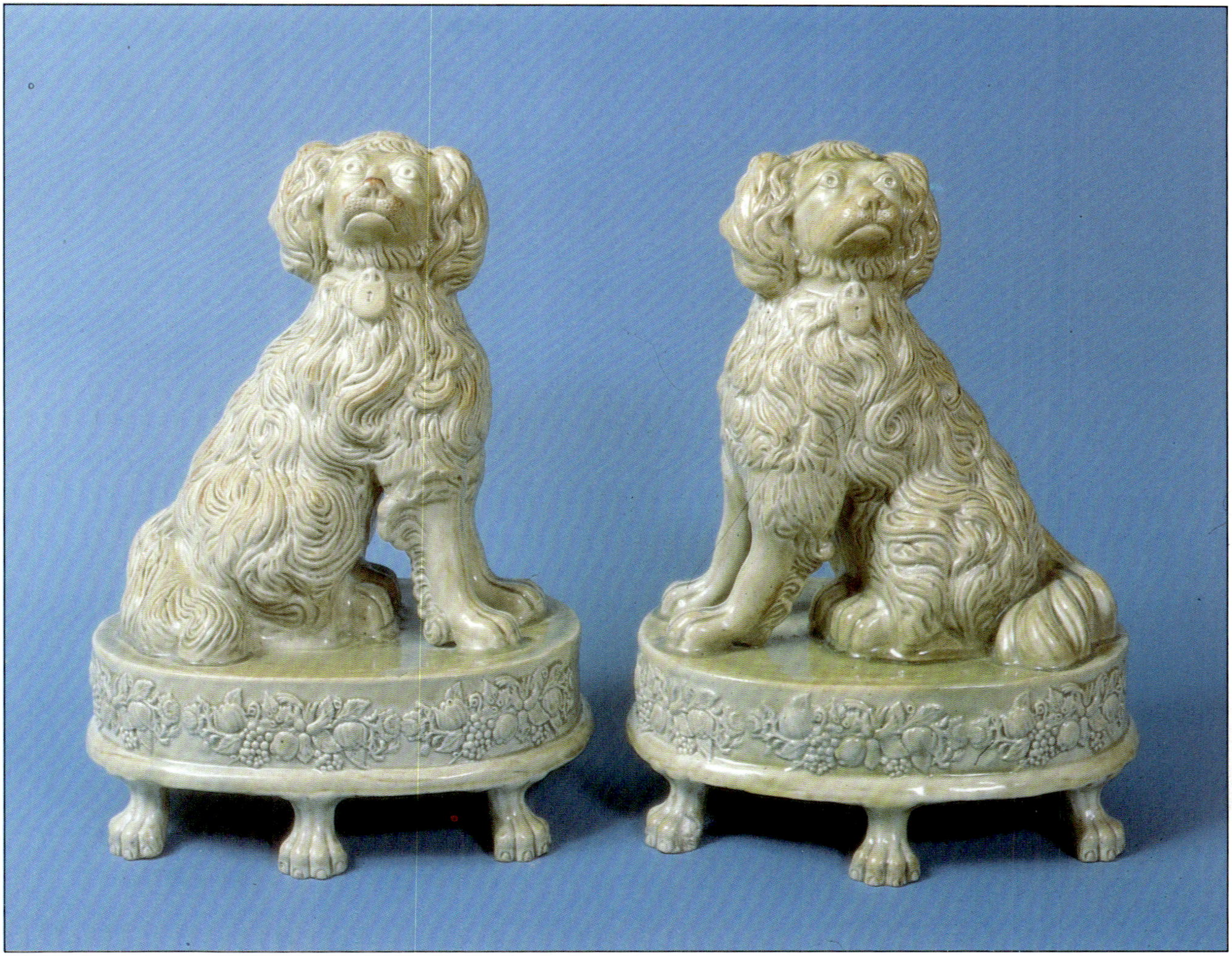

*Figure 39.*

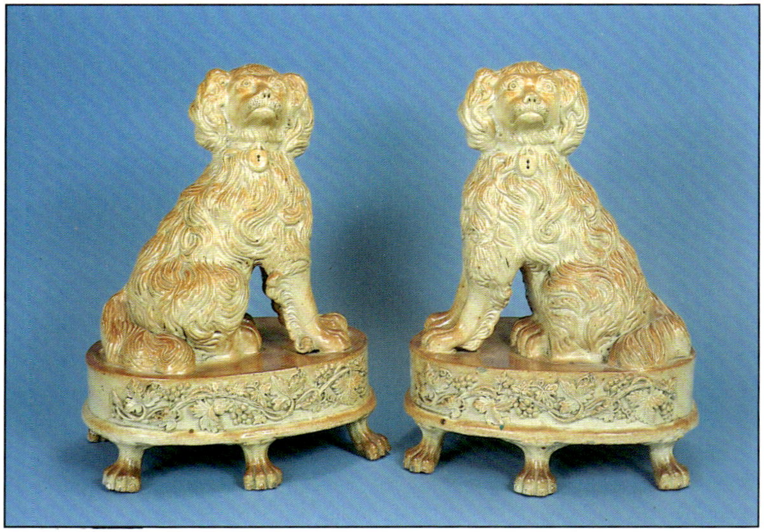

*Figure 40.*

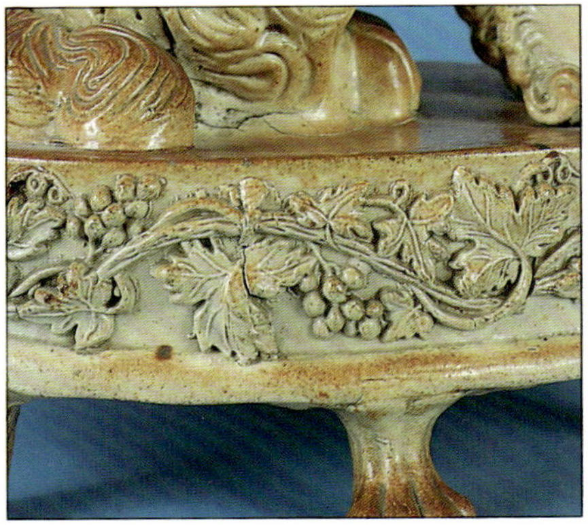

*Figure 41.*

*Figure 40.* As Figure 39. Finished in a pleasing honey colour. The base design minus extra fruit.
Circa 1835
Height 14¾ inches

*Figure 41.* Detail of base from Figure 40.

*Figure 42.* The same exciting model as Figure 39 and 40 used here, minus their bases. They still retain great individuality.
Circa 1845
Height 12 inches

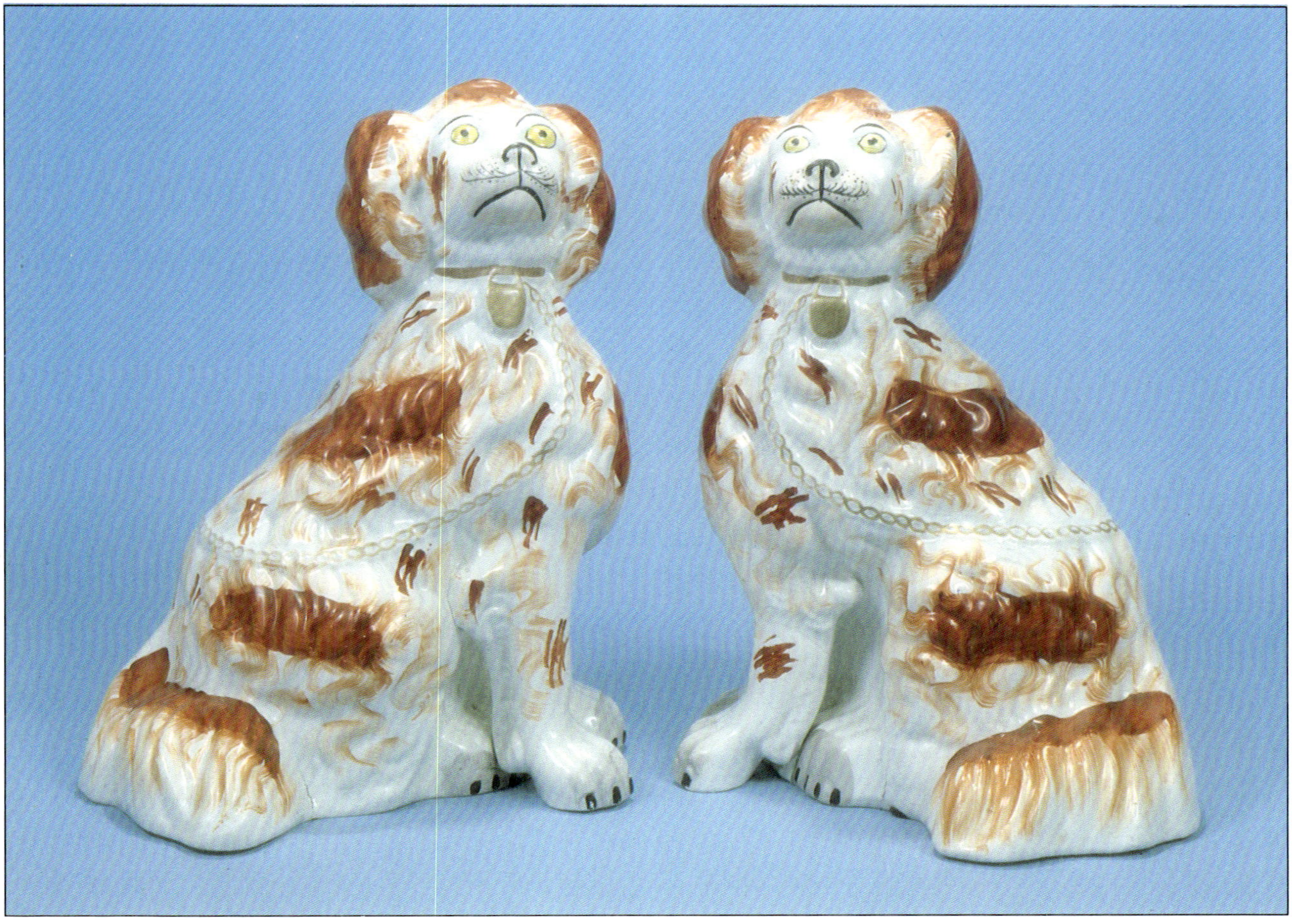

*Figure 42.*

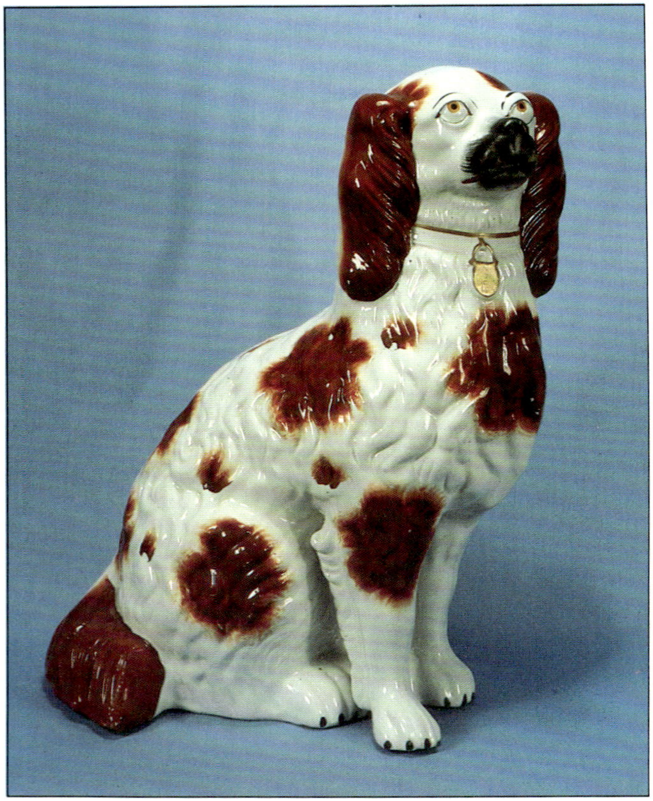

Figure 43.

Figure 43. A large mantelpiece would be needed to place such a pair. They would probably be more at home sitting each side of the hearth.
Circa 1850
Height 15 inches

Figure 44. The same model as Figure 45. Produced at a later date with lustre decoration.
Circa 1890
Height 9½ inches

Figure 45. A pleasing, popular model with fine feathered painting.
Circa 1850
Height 9½ inches

Figure 46. Centre-Partings!
With bright gold decoration.
Circa 1865
Height 12¼ inches

Figure 47. Both front legs separate and a porcellaneous body dressed in liver and white.
Circa 1845
Height 5½ inches

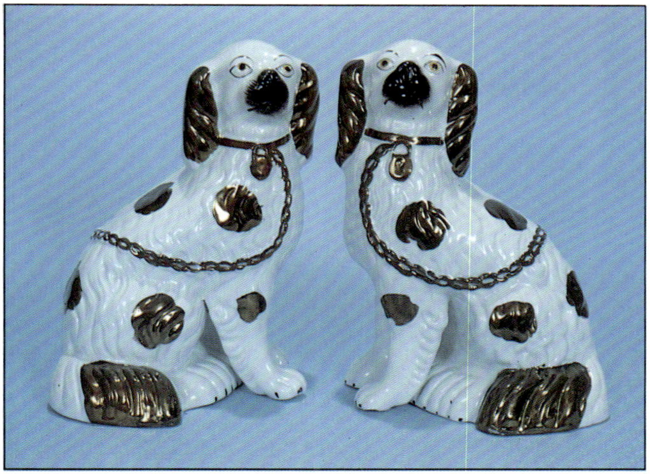
Figure 44.

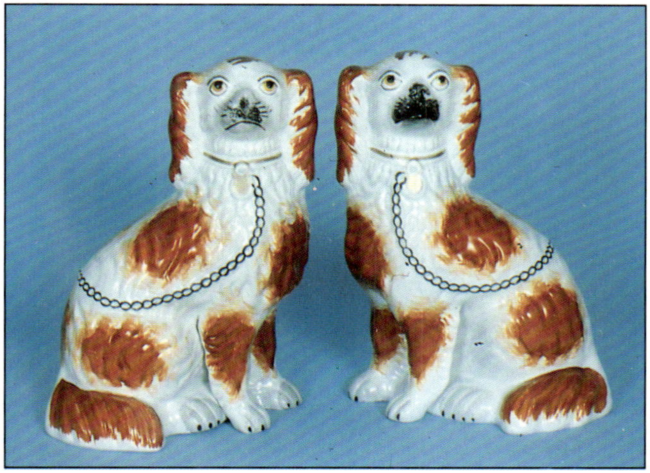
Figure 45.

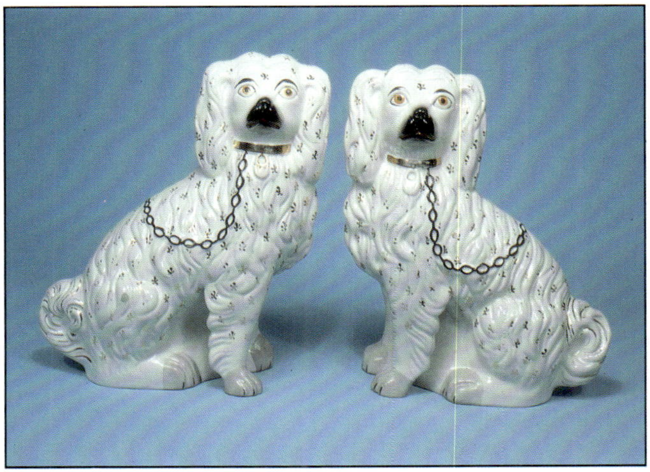
Figure 46.

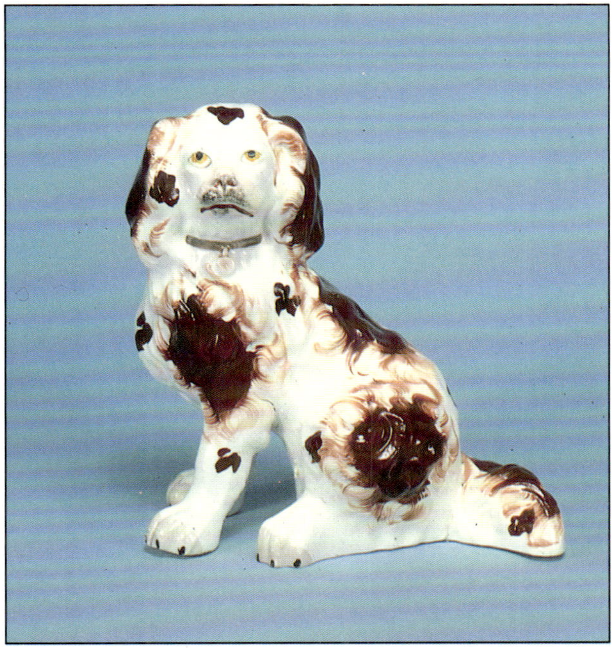
Figure 47.

# *Disraeli Spaniels*

*Benjamin Disraeli who served Queen Victoria as a brilliant Prime Minister was also a great dandy and paid special attention to his hair, always sporting a carefully groomed central forehead curl.*

*Consequently the affectionate name "Disraeli" has endeared itself to this particular model amongst dealers and collectors as a means of identification when searching for this rare model.*

*Figure 48.* Blue-Eyed and Bushy-Tailed, with pale pink noses.
Smart enough to win First Prize at any dog show.
Circa 1850
Height 10 inches

*Figure 49.* Model as in Figure 48, with black and white patches.
Circa 1850
Height 10 inches

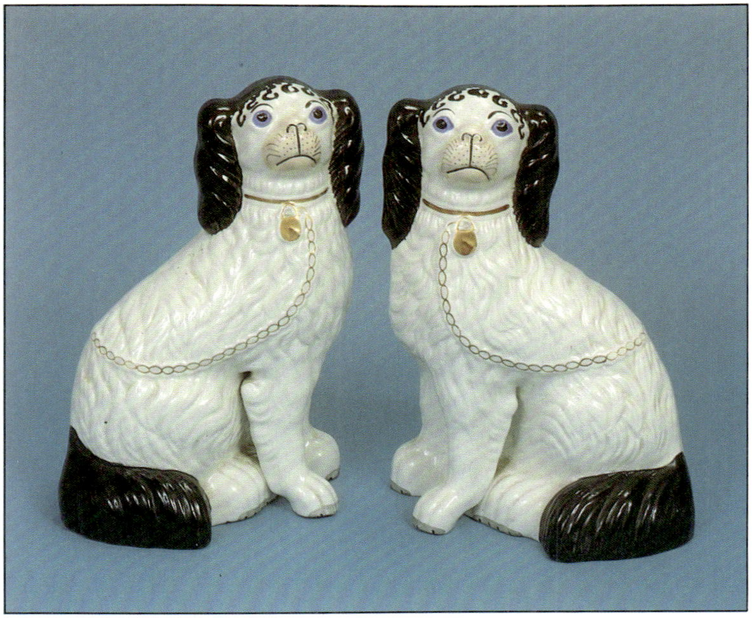

*Figure 48.*

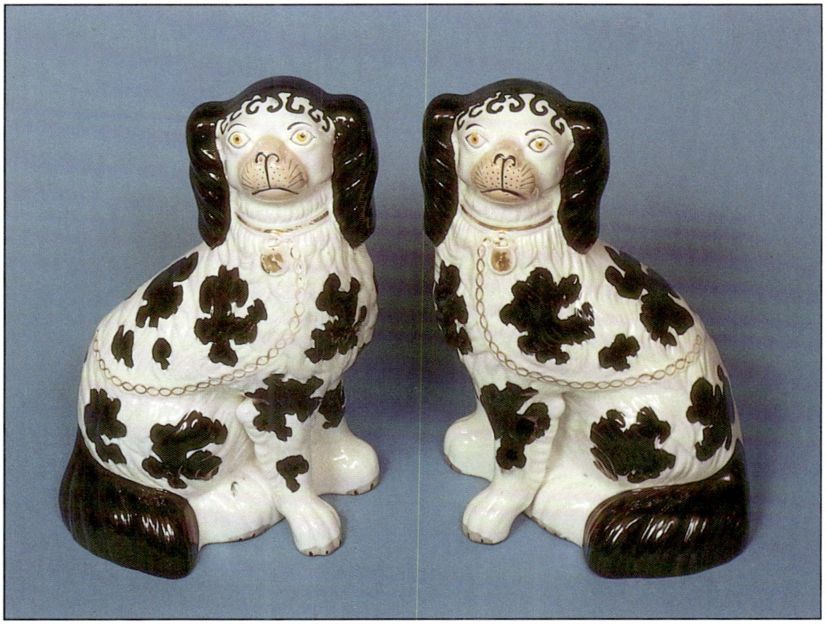

*Figure 49.*

# *Flower Basket Spaniels*

*Although there are several variations and must have been produced in some quantity, their added charm makes them very desirable to collectors, entitling all of them to be considered "rare" in today's market-place.*

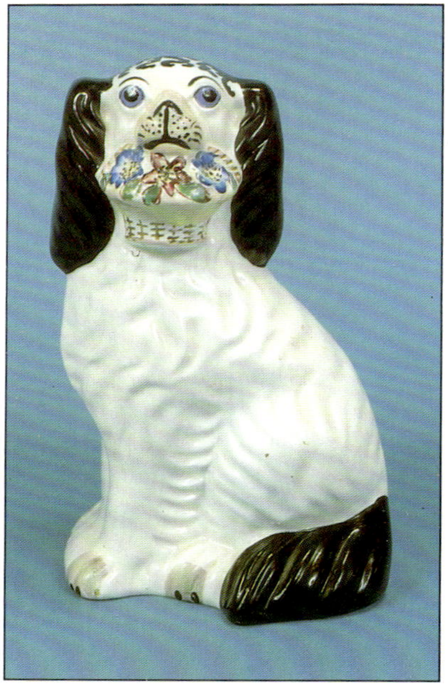

*Figure 51.*

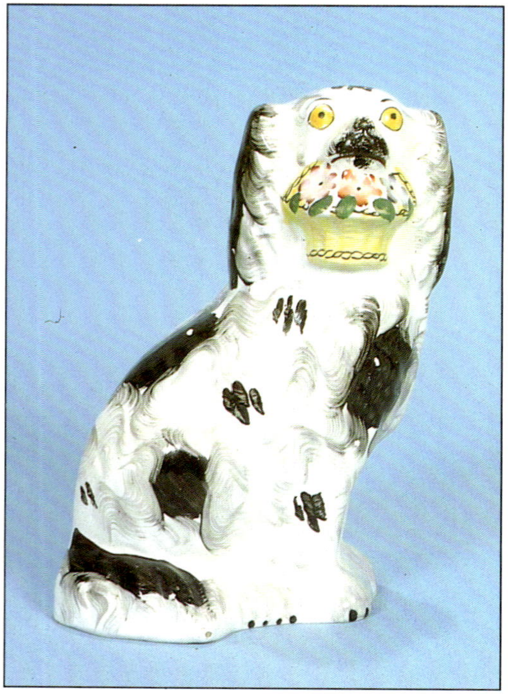

*Figure 50.*

*Figure 50.* Circa 1850
Height 7¾ inches

*Figure 51.* Circa 1850
Height 7¾ inches

*Figure 52.* Circa 1855
Height 8 inches

*Figure 53.* Circa 1850
Height 8 inches

*Figure 54.* Circa 1850
Height 5 inches

*Figure 55.* Circa 1850
Height 8 inches

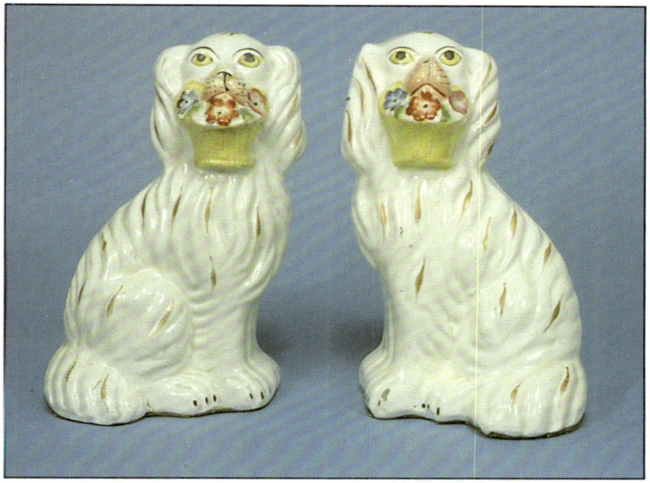

Figure 52.

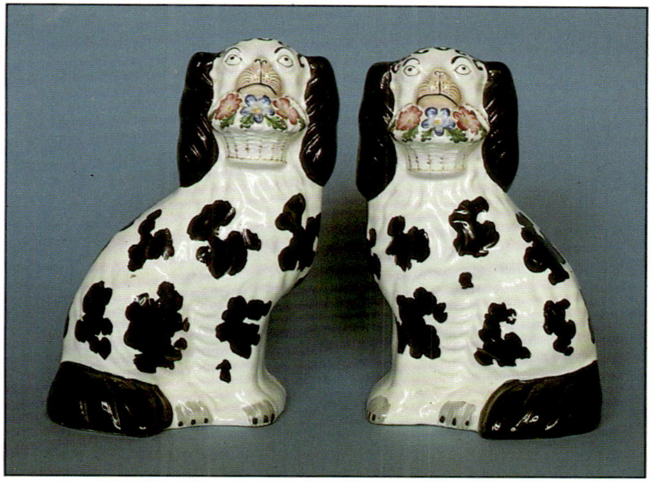

Figure 53.

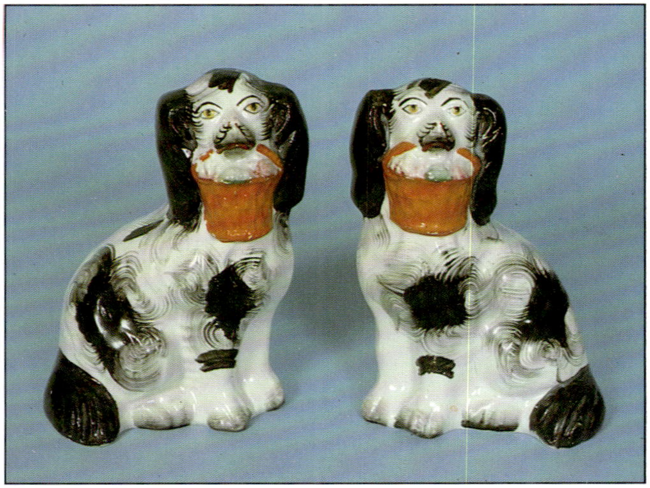

Figure 54.

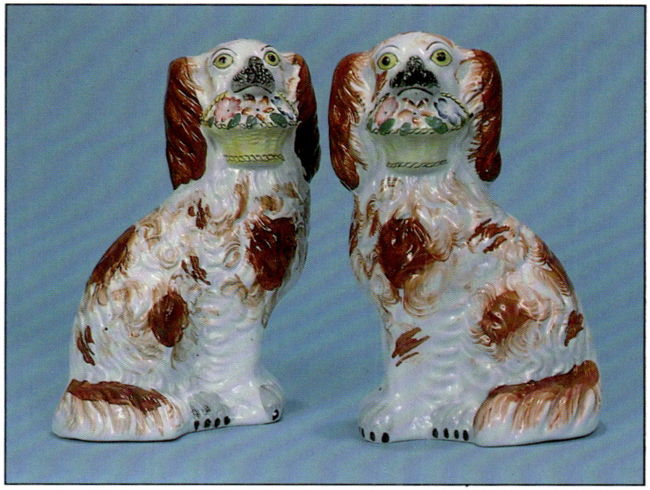

Figure 55.

# *Lying Spaniels*

*Figure 56.* Pair of Spaniels with children sitting on their backs.
Circa 1850
Height 6½ inches, Length 6½ inches

*Figure 57.* "Ménage a trois"
A small pair of Spaniels with a single large central Spaniel (one of a pair).
It is a charming way to display these uncommon models.
Circa 1850
Central Spaniel Height 6 inches
Length 8½ inches
Flanking Pair Height 5 inches
Length 7¾ inches

*Figure 58.* Pair of Spaniels painted in rust and white (as central Spaniel in Figure 57).
Circa 1850
Height 6 inches, Length 8½ inches

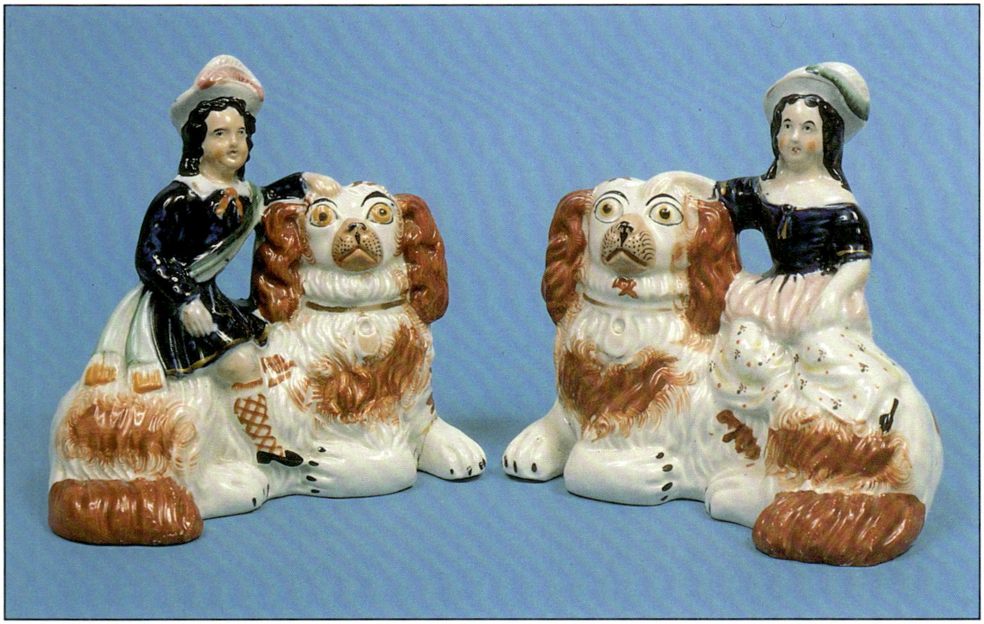

*Figure 56.*

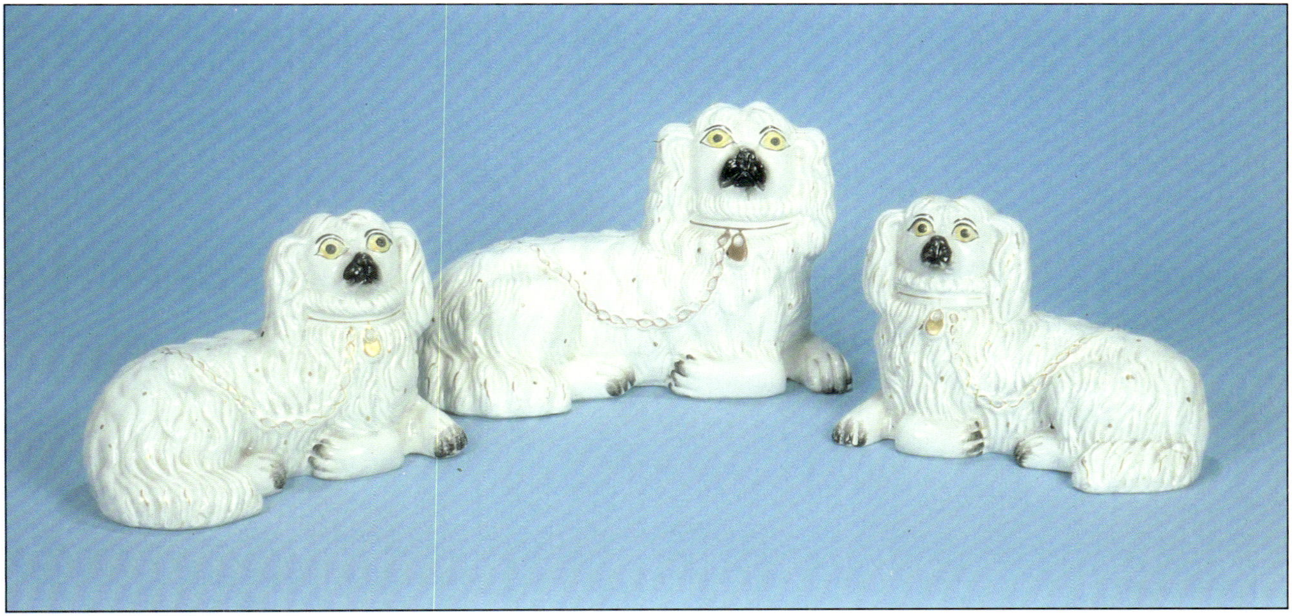
*Figure 57.*

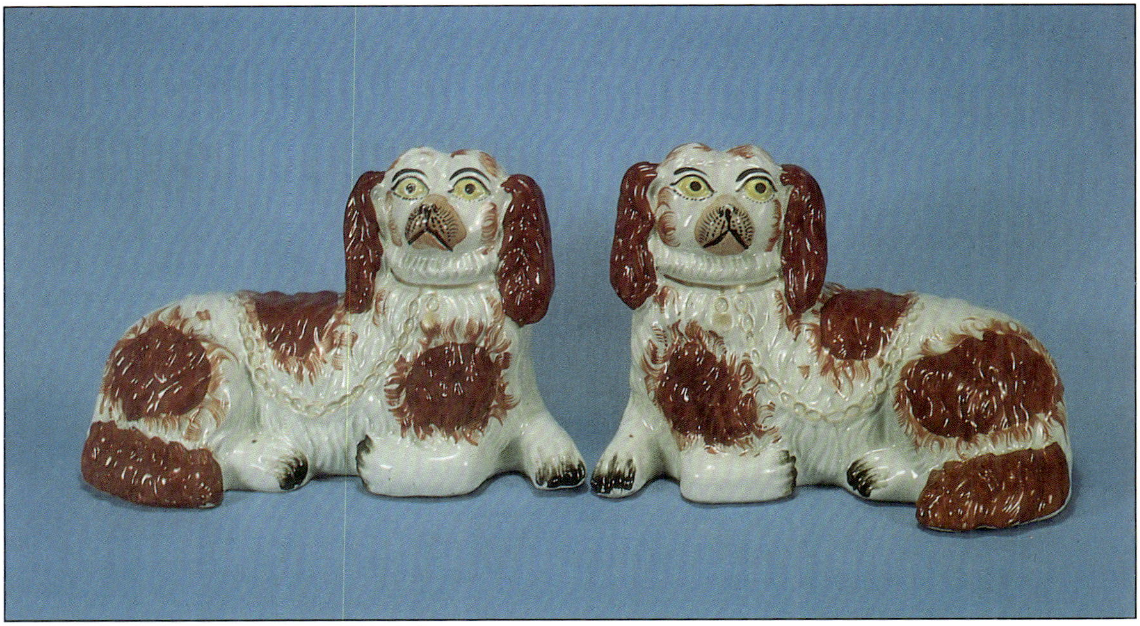
*Figure 58.*

# *Glass-Eyed Spaniels*

*Glass eyes first appeared in children's dolls of the 1830 period, proving an instant success.*

*They soon became invaluable for adding a touch of realism to Berlin wool work pictures depicting birds and animals (including Spaniels), a popular pastime and at its height in the mid 19th century.*

*These earlier uses are possibly responsible for the inexperienced collector's idea that glass-eyed dogs pre-date their less fortunate forebears.*

*The spray painting technique and the sole use of harsh bright gold evident on all the glass-eyed models prove without doubt that even when inserted into earlier models, (i.e. moulds that had been in use for some years), glass-eyed dogs date from no earlier than 1860 (more likely the 1870s, 1880s and later).*

*Perhaps previously considered an unnecessary production expense, they nevertheless helped resurrect a flagging market. Their added charm justifying their desirability today, as it did over a century ago.*

*For other glass-eyed examples see page 20 (Collie) and page 144 (Pugs).*

*Figure 59.* "Royal Comforters".
Glamorous gilded bows present a welcome change from the usual collar and chain on these obviously house-trained charmers.
Circa 1880
Height 13 inches

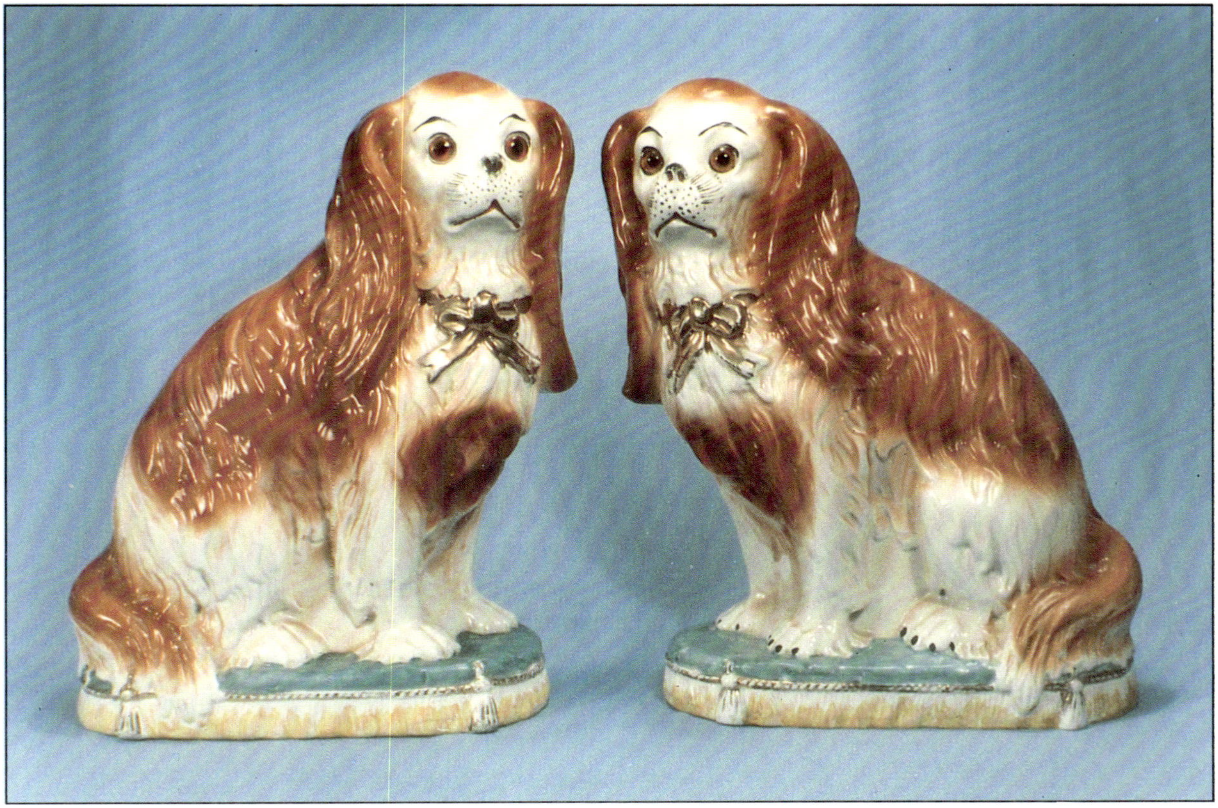

*Figure 59.*

*Figure 60.* An earlier model with separate front legs brought up to date with glass eyes (see Figure 43 page 98).
Circa 1885
Height 15 inches

*Figure 61.* Loads of lavishly gilded feathers make this pair as proud as peacocks.
Circa 1890
Height 11 inches

*Figure 62.* Unusual "apricot" coats on this standard model lend them individuality and status.
Circa 1875
Height 11 inches

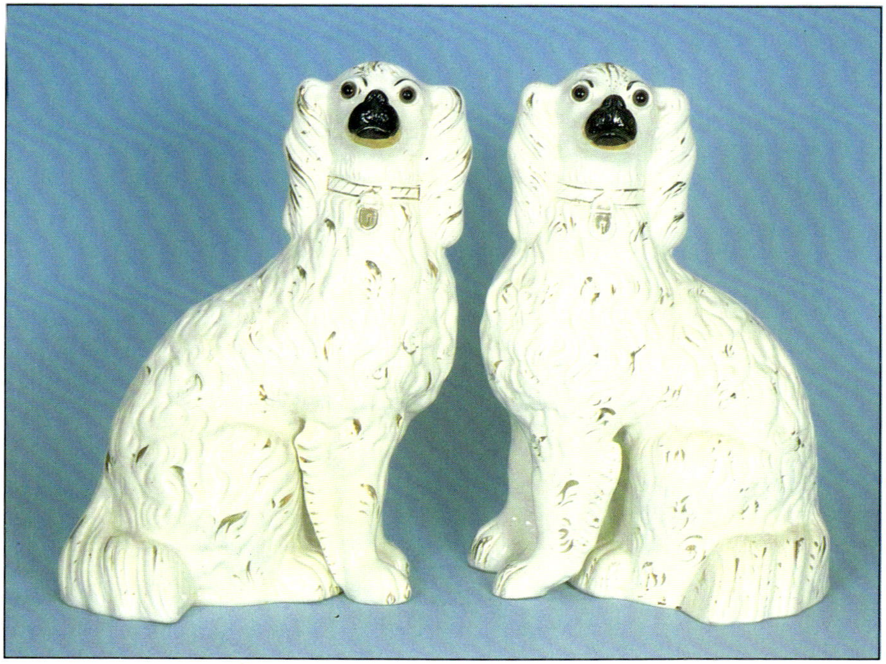

*Figure 60.*

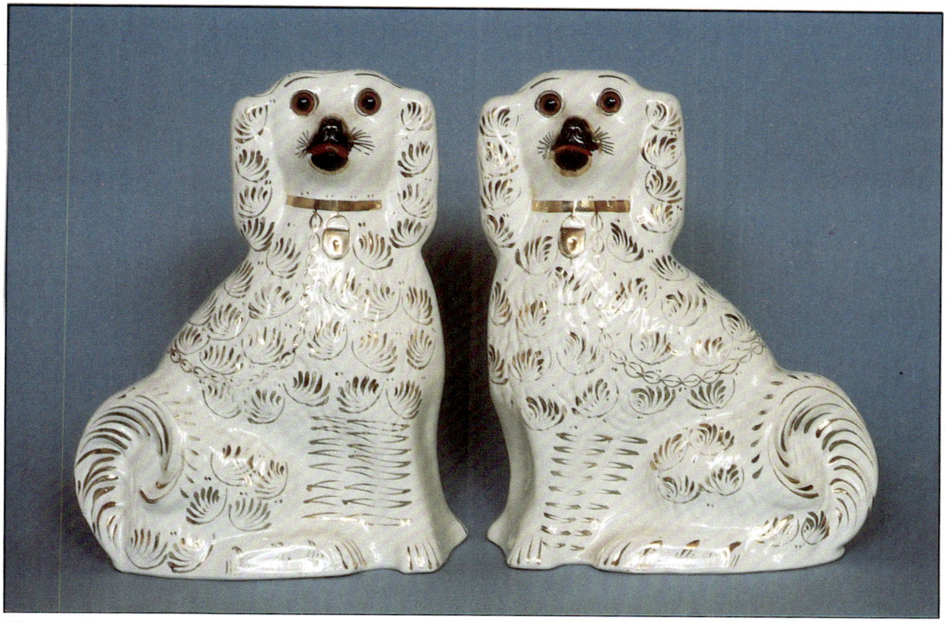

*Figure 61.*

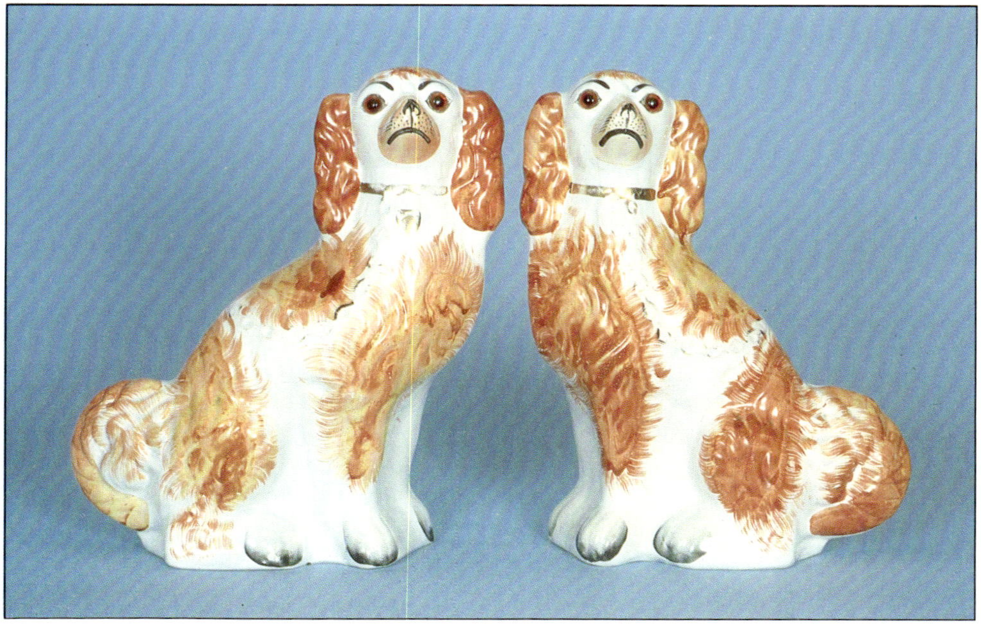

*Figure 62.*

# *Spaniels with children*

*The pairing of children with dogs was obviously a popular subject matter for our potters, with Spaniels predominating.*
*Here are a few examples:*

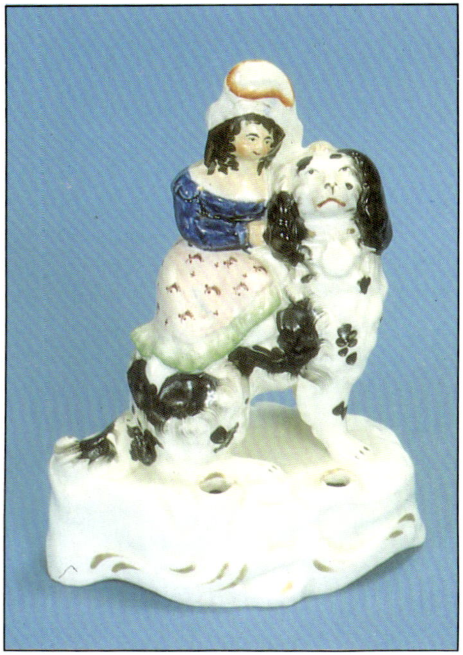

*Figure 63.*

*Figure 64.* Left to Right:
Standing girl holding posy.
Circa 1845
Height 5½ inches

Standing boy with sister sitting on dog.
Circa 1850
Height 7 inches

Girl on lying dog, (miniature).
Circa 1860
Height 3 inches

Girl hugging dog.
Circa 1865
Height 4 inches

Children with begging dog.
Circa 1855
Height 6¼ inches

Young girl sitting on dog's back.
Circa 1865
Height 4 inches

*Figure 63.* A double quill holder
The Princess Royal
with "Dash".
Circa 1850
Height 6 inches

*Figure 65.* Pair of children sitting on dogs, she demurely side-saddle.
Circa 1850
Height 6¾ inches

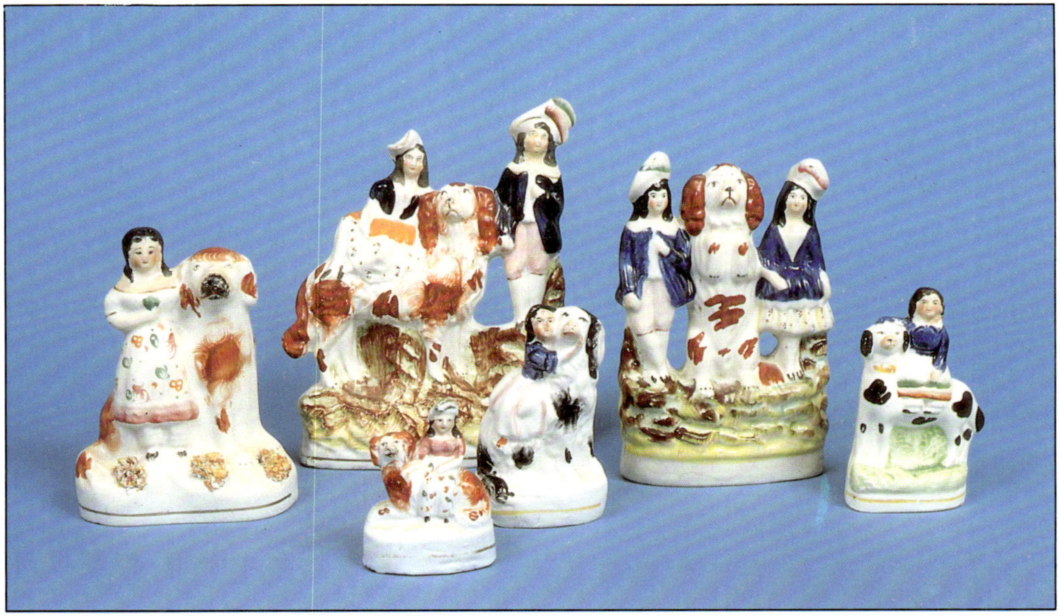

*Figure 64.*

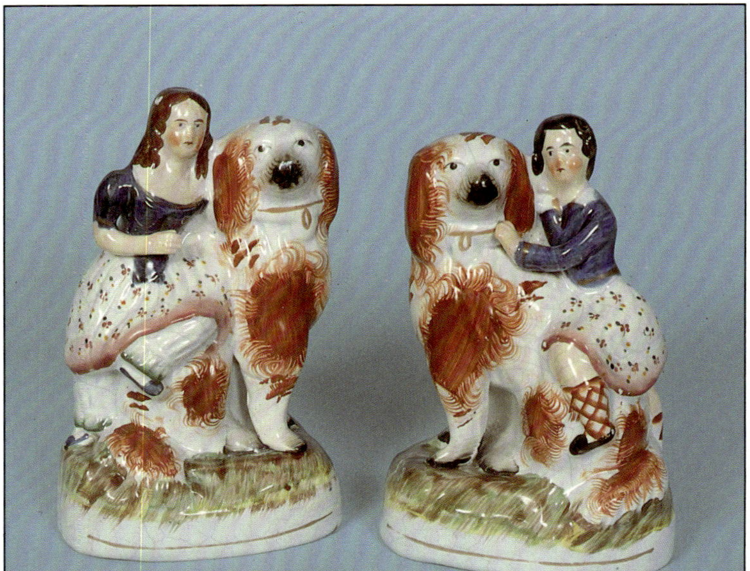

*Figure 65.*

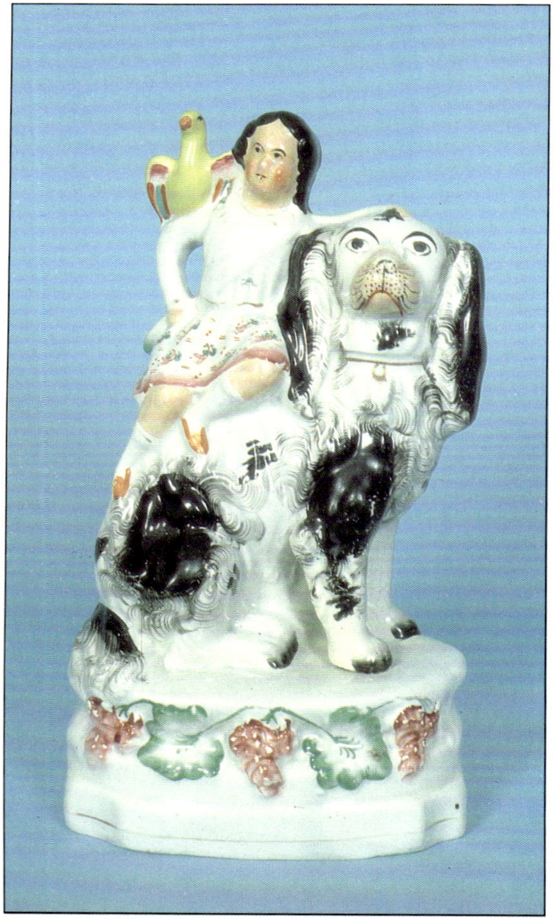

*Figure 66.*

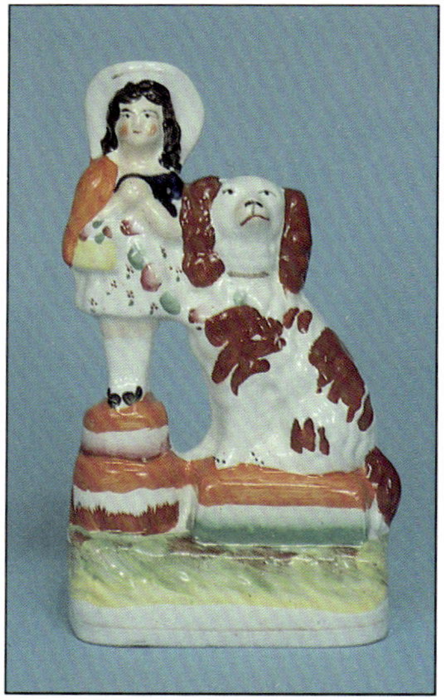

*Figure 67.*

*Figure 66.* "The Best of Friends"
On a raised elaborate base
decorated with grapes.
Circa 1850
Height 10 inches

*Figure 67.* "Tall is Best"
Perched on double cushions, the little girl
is holding her dog by a chain of flowers.
Circa 1855
Height 7¾ inches

*Figure 68.* Looking out at the world distainfully from
a heavily tasselled cushion,
or perhaps annoyed the parrot is out of reach!
Circa 1850
Height 9½ inches

*Figure 69.* A Scottish lass holding a basket of flowers
sitting on a large Spaniel.
Circa 1870
Height 10¾ inches

*Figure 70.* An interesting pair of spill vase groups of
children with dogs and puppies.
The girl is holding the dog's chain while her
boyfriend, definitely in-charge, holds
a tiny whip.
Circa 1850
Height 8½ inches

*Figure 71.* "That parrot pushing in again!"
The trio set upon an unusual footed base.
Circa 1850
Height 8½ inches

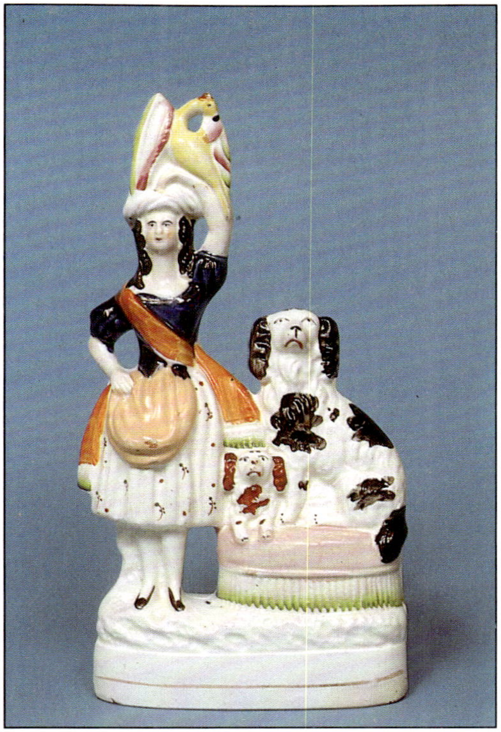
Figure 68.

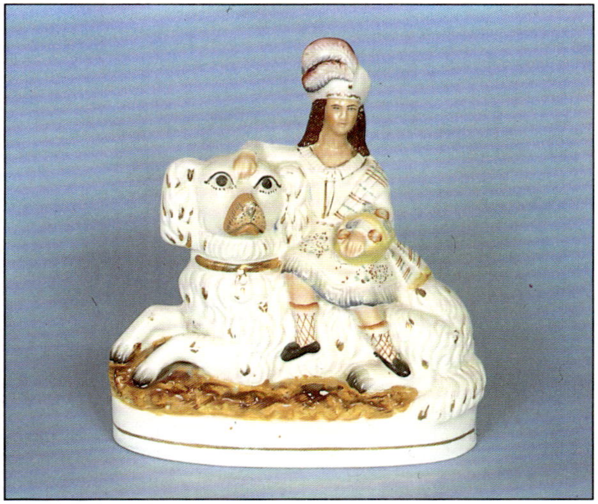
Figure 69.

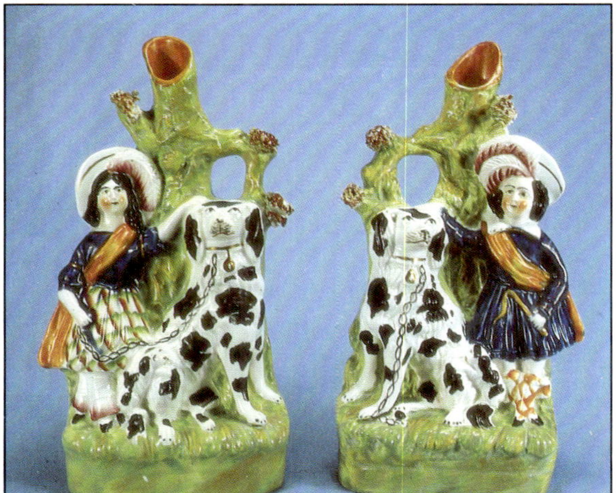
Figure 70.

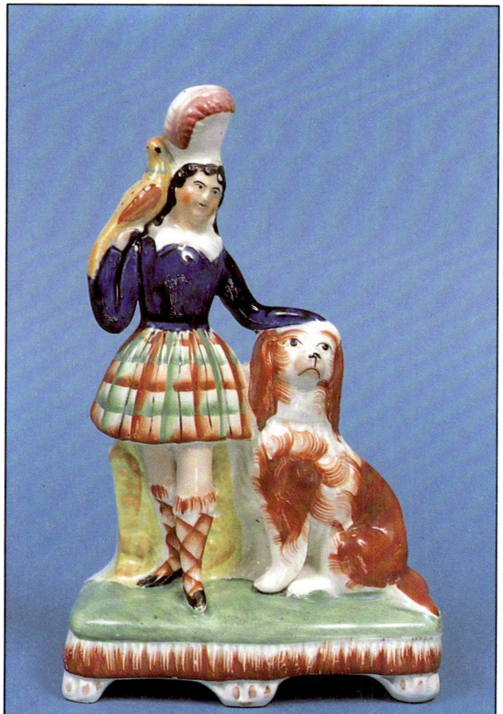
Figure 71.

# Novelty Spaniels

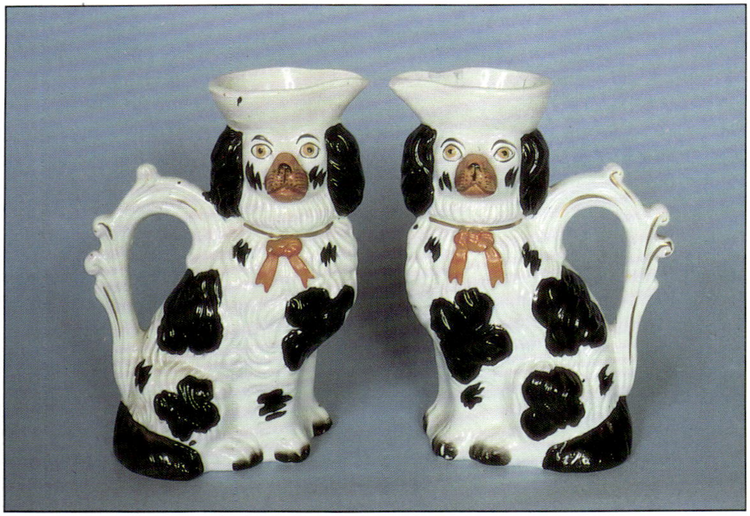

*Figure 72.*

*Figure 72.* Pair of Spaniel jugs with thoughtful handles for thumbs!
Circa 1850
Height 8 inches

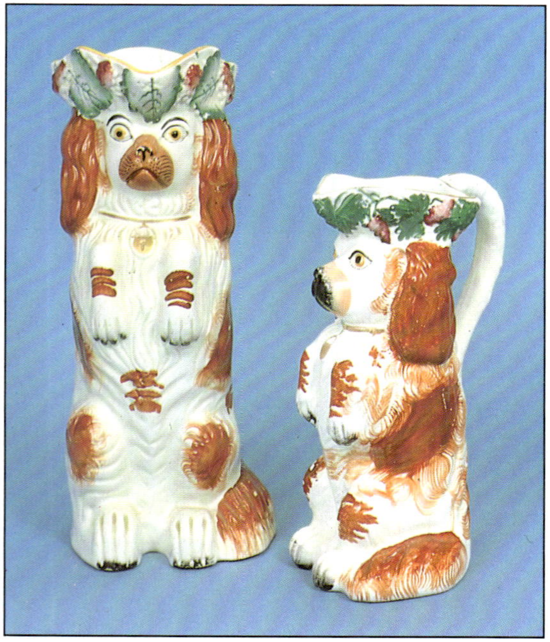

*Figure 73.*

*Figure 73.* Large begging Spaniel jug.
Circa 1855
Height 10 inches
Small begging Spaniel jug.
Circa 1855
Height 7¼ inches

*Figure 74.* A pair of rare sash-window jambs.
Circa 1850
Height 4¼ inches

*Figures 75/76.* A tobacco jar (presently used to house our dog's chocolate drops!)
Circa 1870
Height 5½ inches

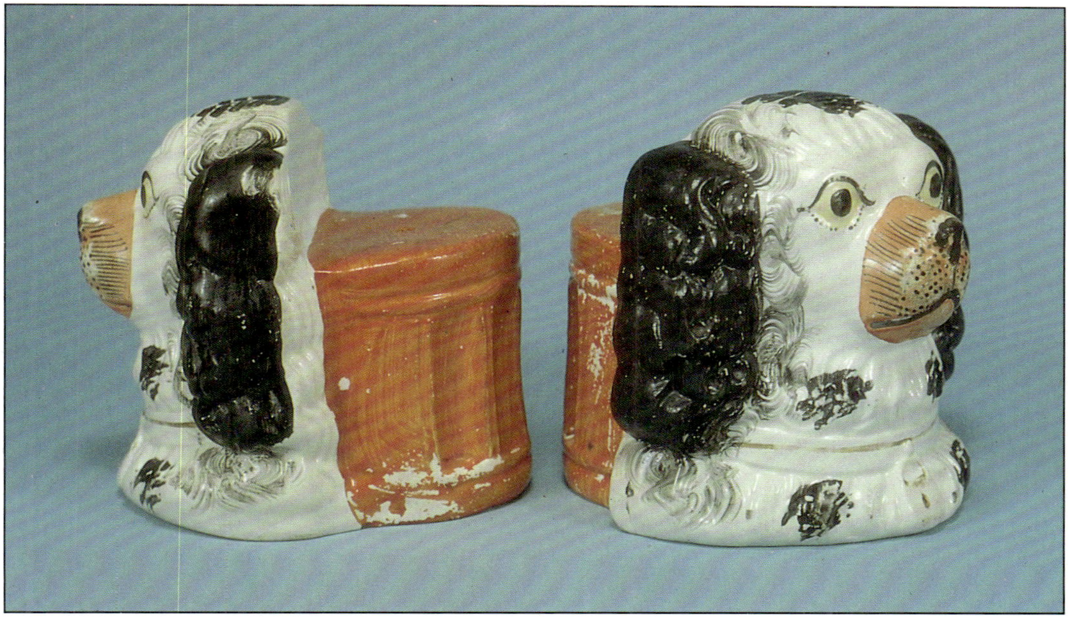

*Figure 74.*

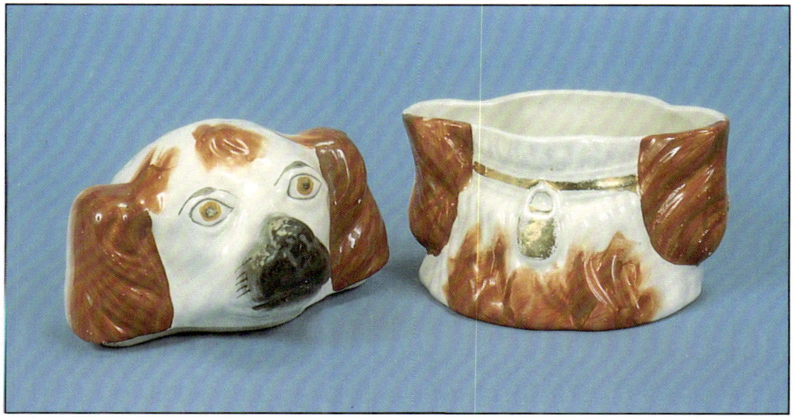

*Figure 75.*

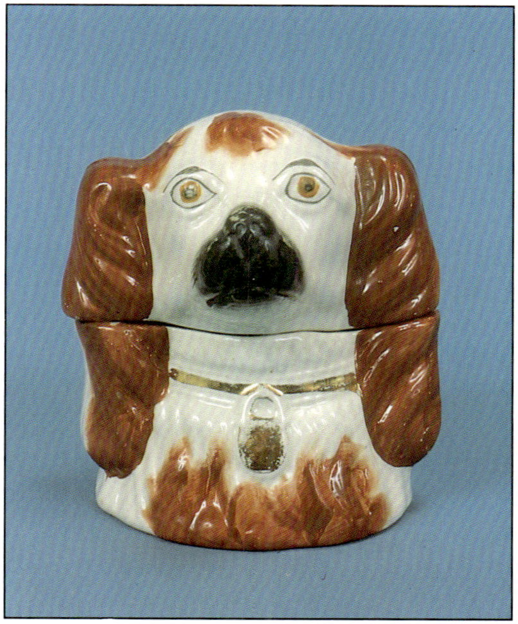

*Figure 76.*

# Little Lion Dog

*A very old breed known all over Europe for over 500 years but very rare today.*
*A lively affectionate character, similar in size to the miniature poodle.*
*The tail was left long with a lion-like tuft of hair at the tip.*

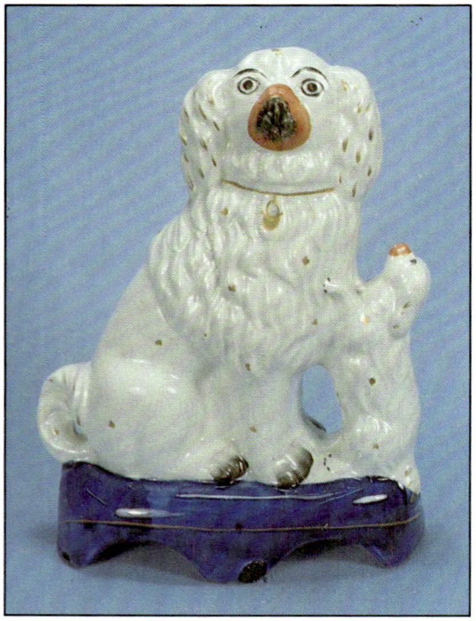

*Figure 1.*

*Figure 1.* Mother and begging pup on blue serpentine base.
Circa 1860
Height 8¼ inches

*Figure 2.* Carrying fruit baskets with black-spotted decoration.
A very rare model.
Circa 1850
Height 11½ inches

*Figure 3.* White and gilt with separate front legs.
Circa 1855
Height 6 inches

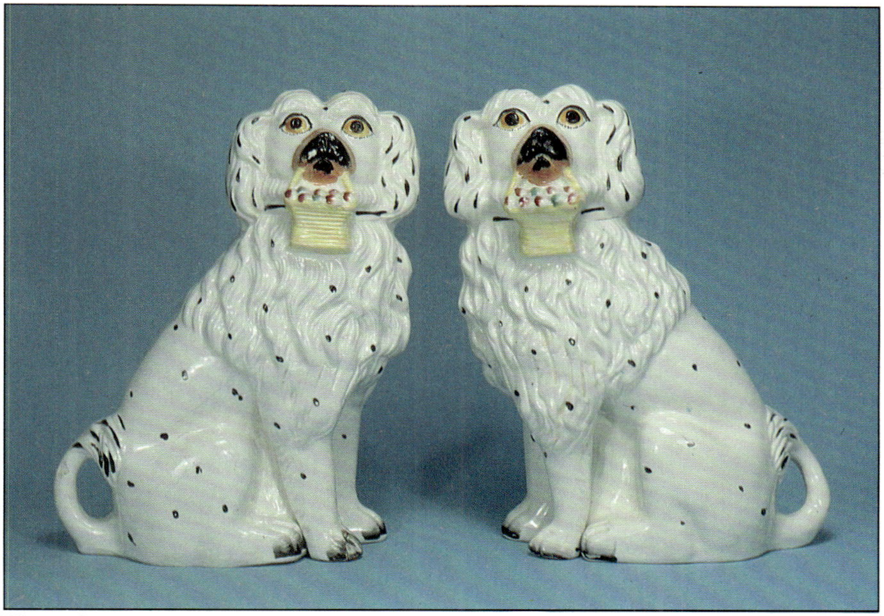
*Figure 2.*

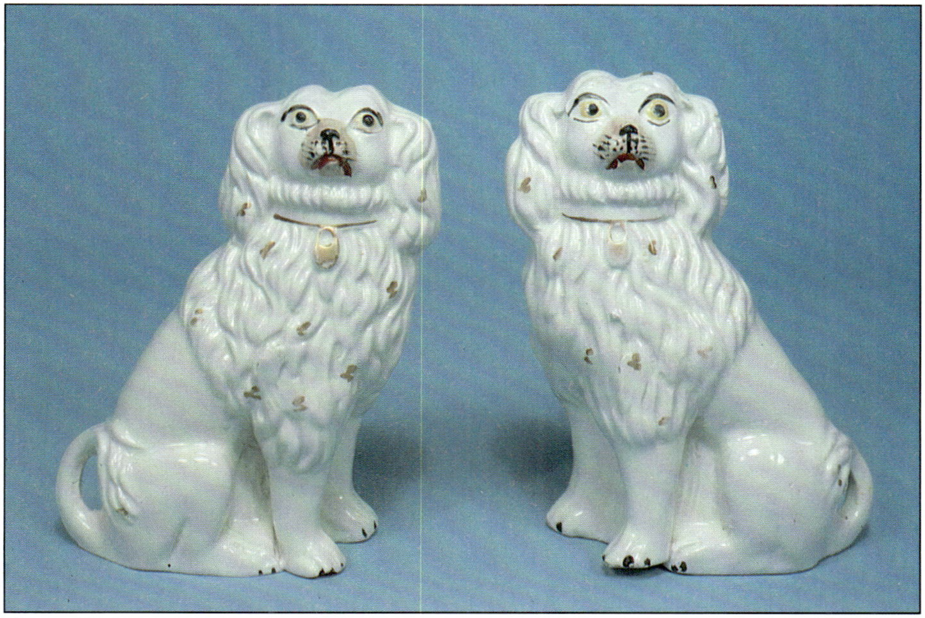
*Figure 3.*

# Lurcher

*A cross-bred dog, usually with Greyhound and Terrier blood. Normally associated with poachers and gypsies.*

*In today's affluent society this fast and intelligent hound has almost died out.*

*Figure 1.* A soulful hound.
This model is very rare and appealing.
Circa 1845
Height 8½ inches

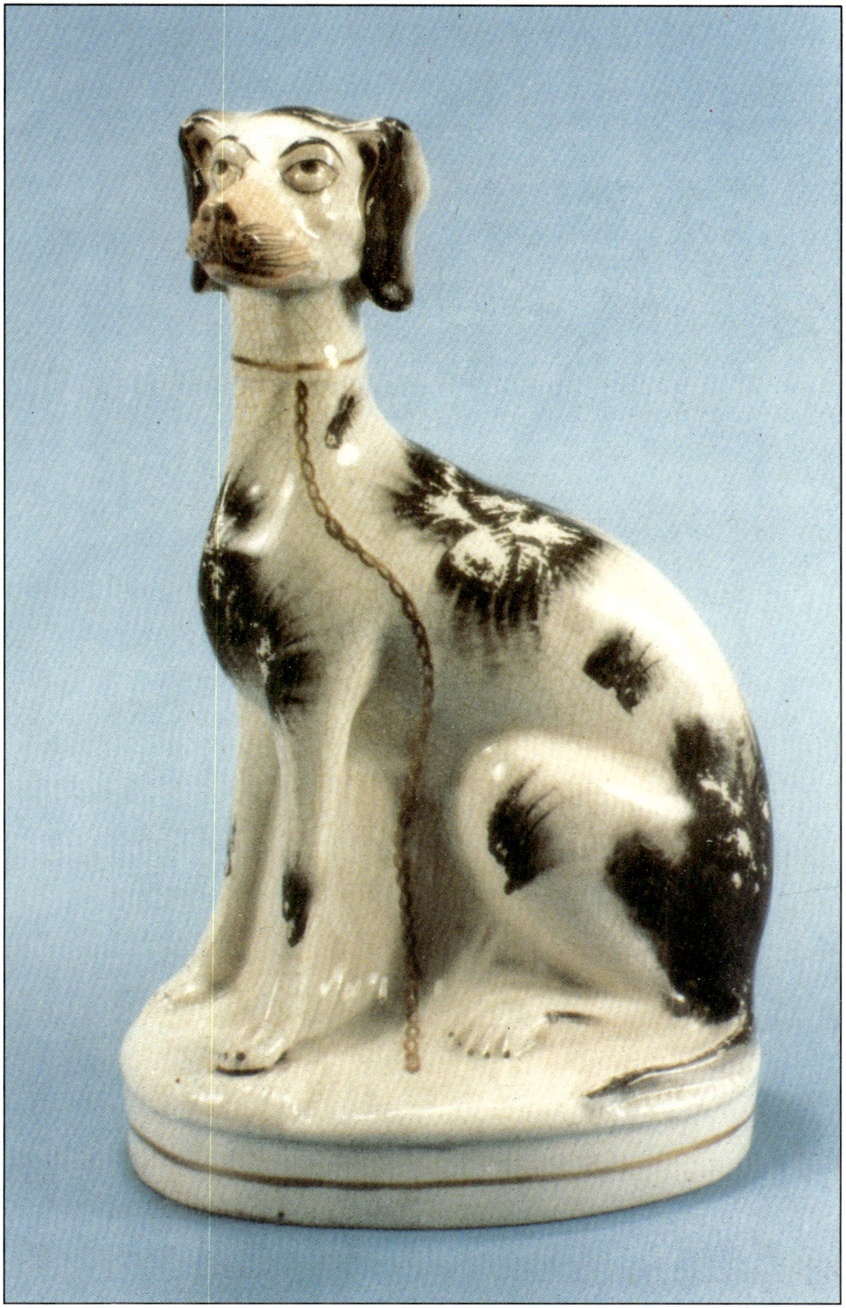

*Figure 1.*

# Maltese

*Said to have originated from the island of Malta, it arrived in England around 1540, and became popular as a lap-dog in the second half of the 19th century.*

*Figure 1.* A red bow and swagged cushion base, no wonder he wears a jaunty air.
Circa 1865
Height 7½ inches

*Figure 2.* "Beg Sir"
Circa 1850
Height 5¼ inches

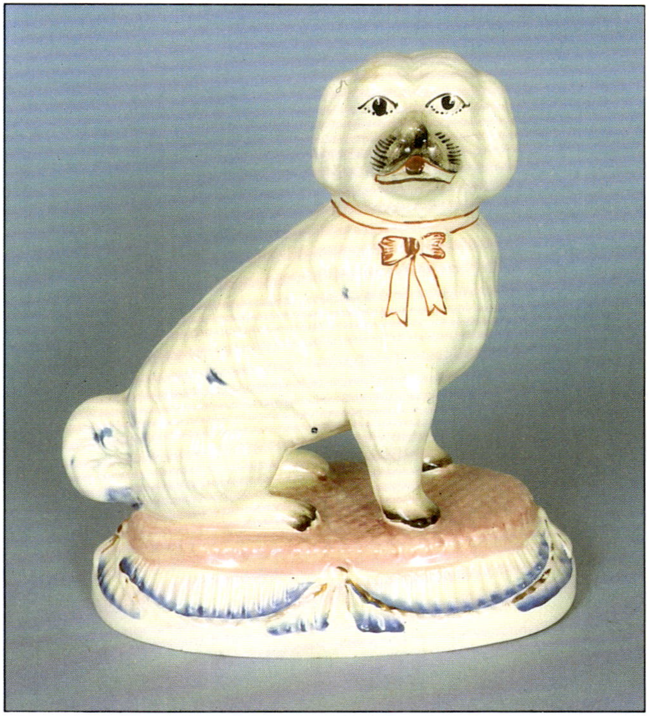

Figure 1.

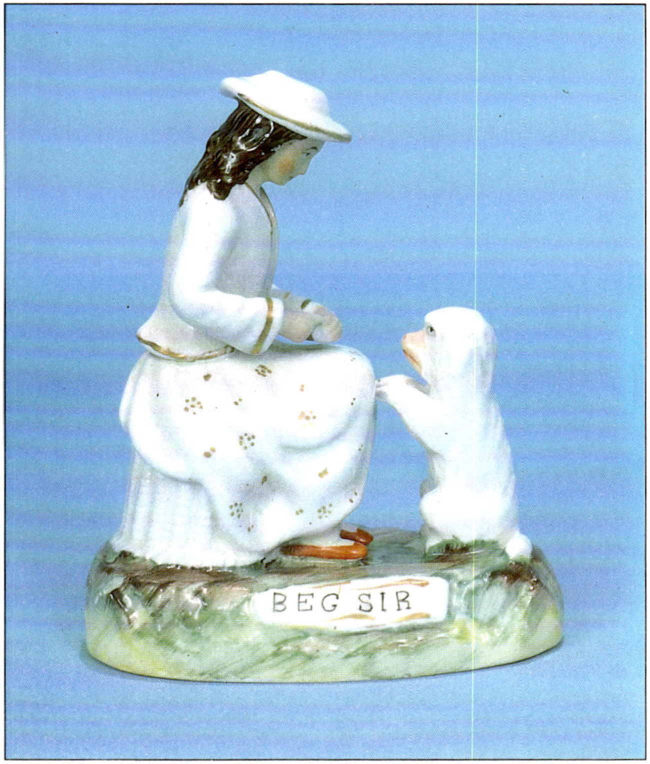


Figure 2.

# Mastiff

*This very large, heavy fighting dog was originally used as a bear-baiter.
Its main use in the 19th century was as an excellent guard-dog.*

*Figure 1.* The only known model of this unmistakable breed.
Circa 1855
Height 6 inches

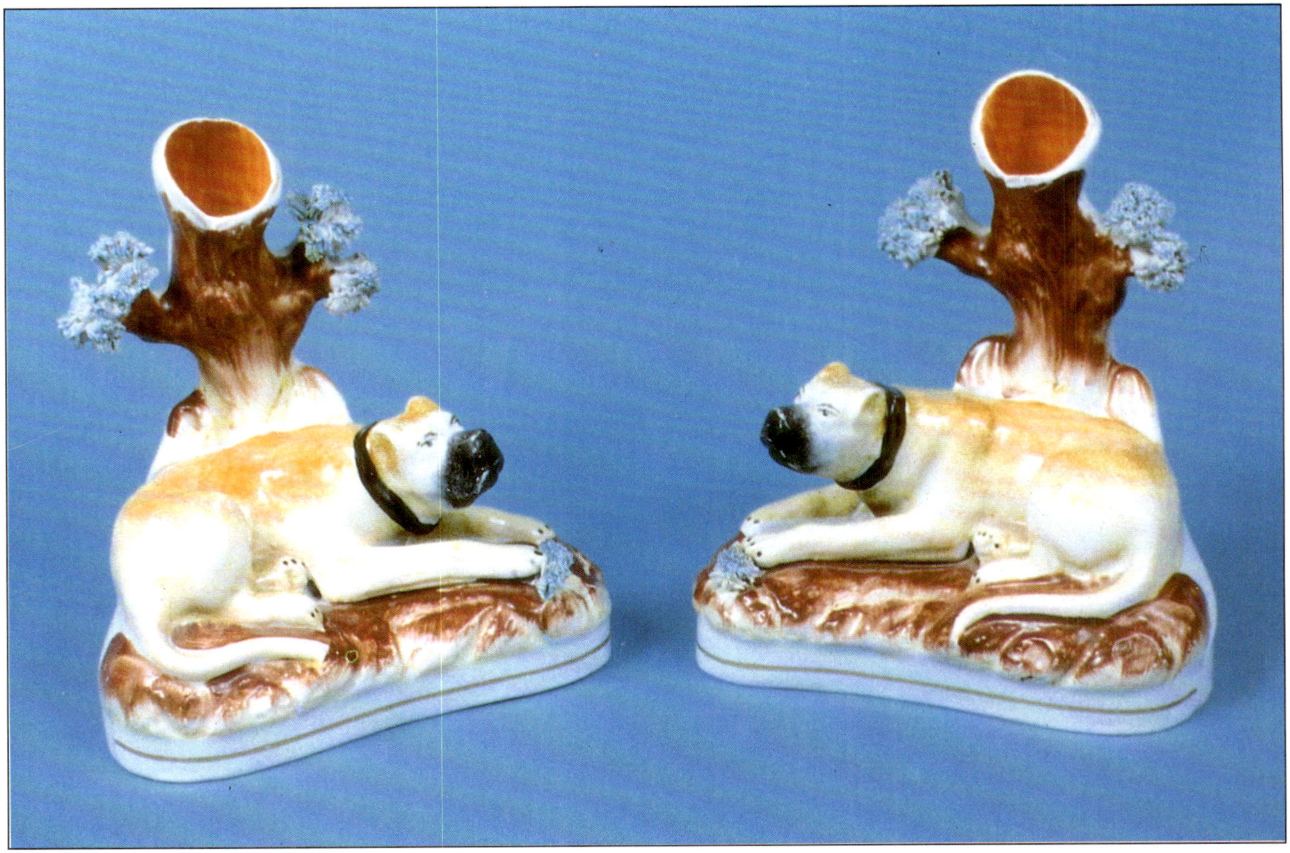

*Figure 1.*

# Newfoundland

*Exceptionally gentle and docile, but gifted with incredible strength, the Newfoundland stands for devotion and courage.*

*During the 19th century this lovable giant became quite a status symbol.*

*Sir Edwin Landseer enhanced its popularity when a black and white Newfoundland featured in his 1838 painting titled* "A Distinguished Member of the Humane Society!"

*The two-colour variety of the breed has since been known as the Landseer.*

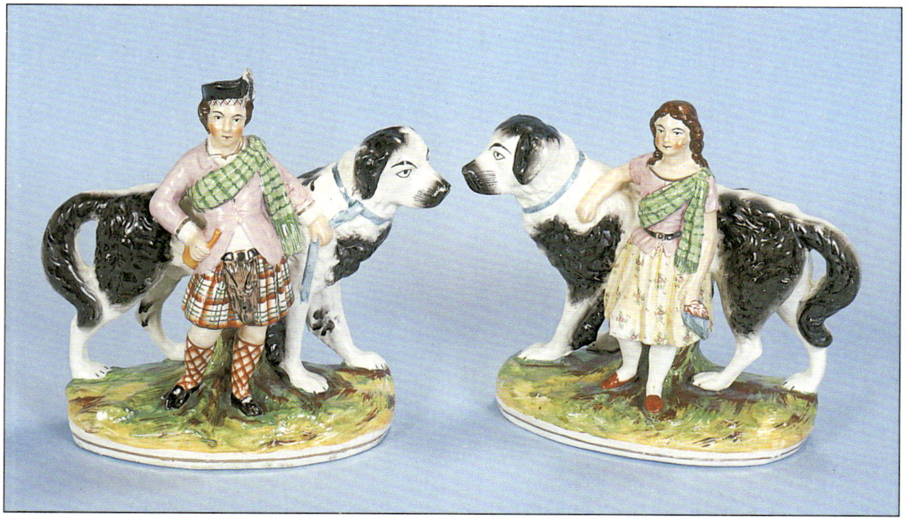

*Figure 1.*

*Figure 1.* A pair of "Landseer" escorting the Prince of Wales and his sister the Princess Royal.
Circa 1870
Height 10½ inches

*Figure 2.* The slight painting variation makes this very rare model worthy of a second appearance.
Circa 1870
Height 9¾ inches

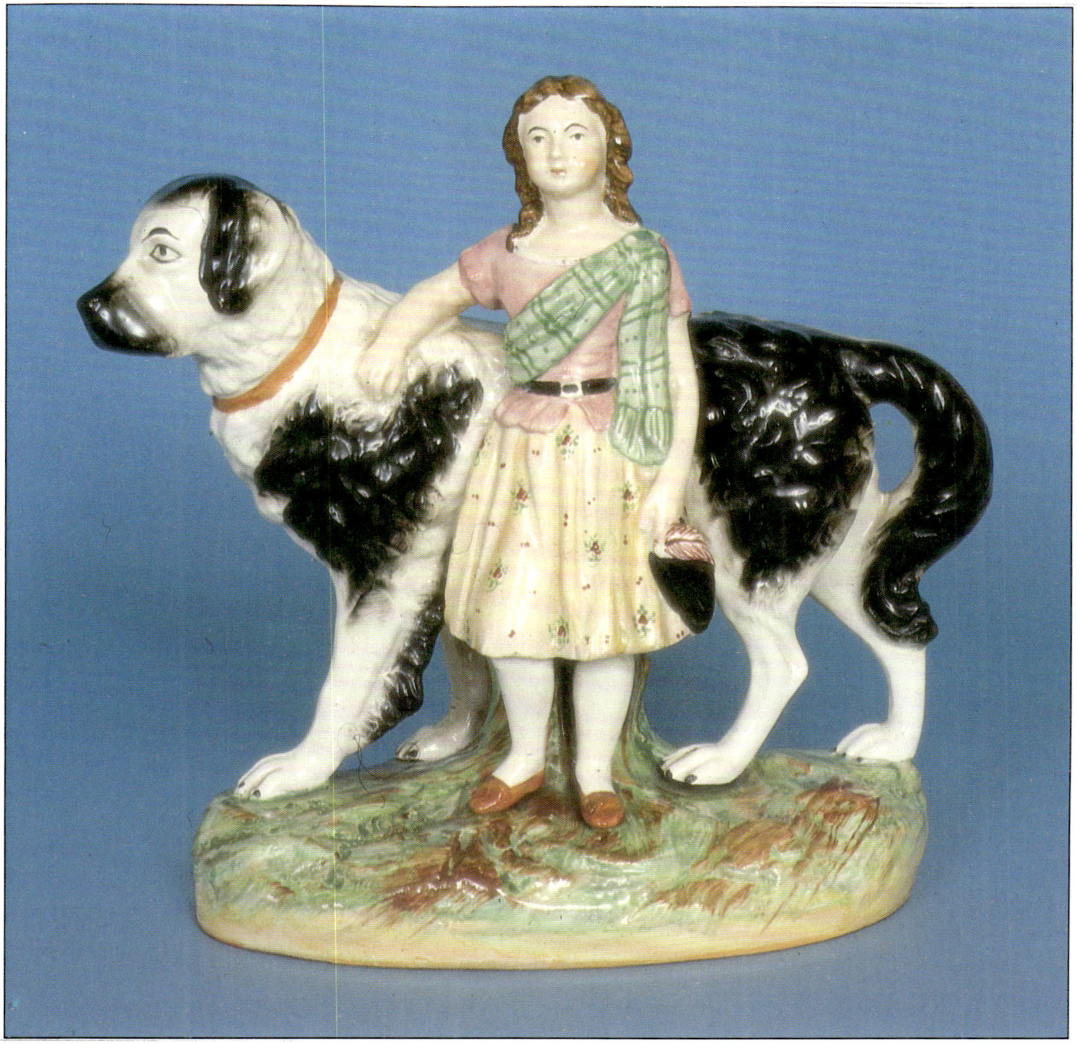

*Figure 1.*

# Otterhound

*The otter was hunted in England for many centuries and was still a normal country pursuit in the early 19th century.*

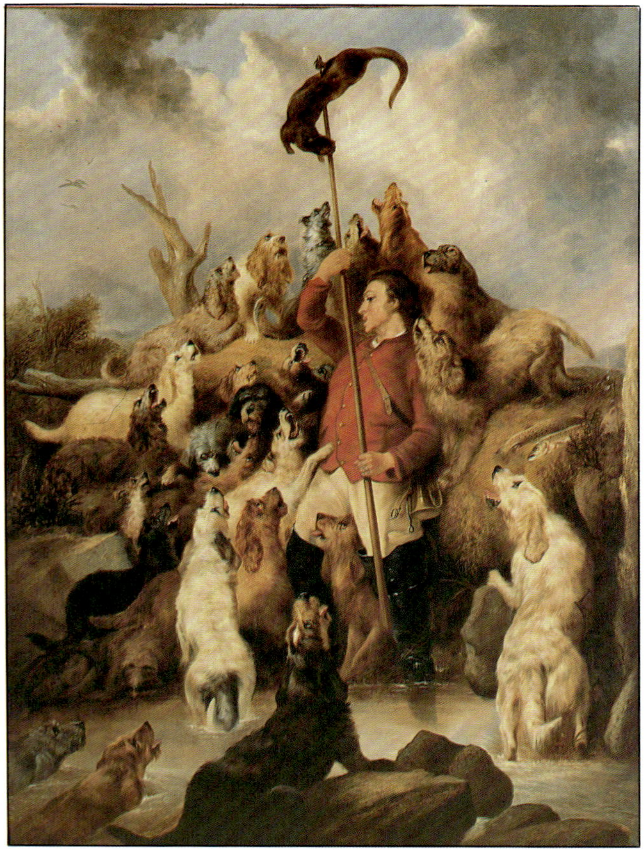

*Figure 1.* "The end of an otter-hunt"
Sir Edwin Landseer, R.A. 1844

Reproduced by kind permission of the Wadsworth Atheneum, Hartford, Connecticut. The Ella Gallup Sumner and Mary Catlin Sumner Collection.
Commissioned by the Earl of Aberdeen, this painful picture attracted much criticism by Landseer's contemporaries which resulted of course in bringing it to the forefront of public attention and the potter's eye. It is obviously the source for this Figure.

*Figure 1.*

*Figure 2.* Now, as then, the subject does not please us, this poor little fish-eating creature is these days so sadly in decline.
As an exercise in the potter's skill, however, it is a wonder of separate moulds and riotous colour.
The gruesome subject obviously attracted only "News of the day" interest, as this Figure is extremely rare.
Circa 1845
Height 16 ¾ inches

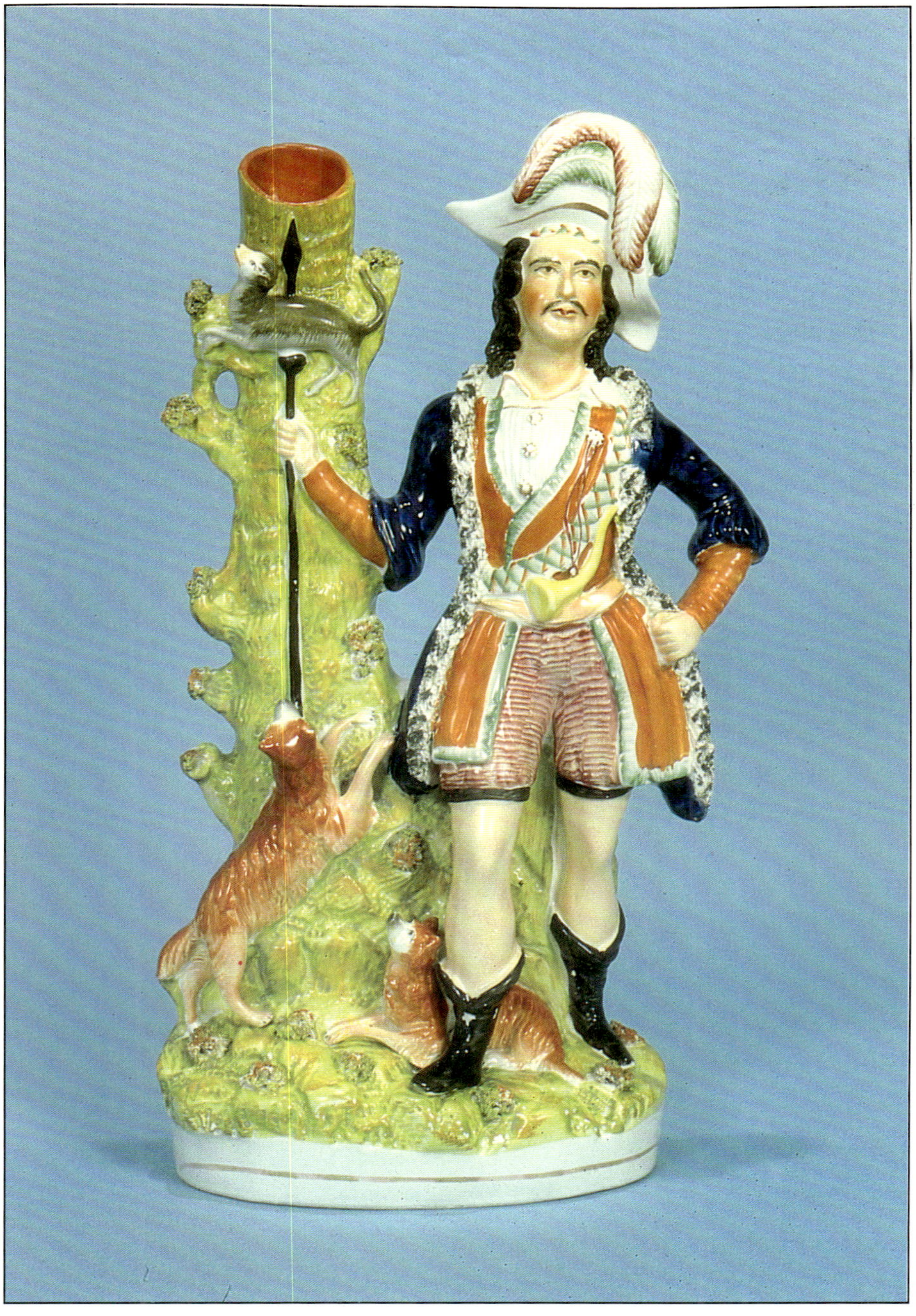

*Figure 2.*

# Pekinese

*Essentially Chinese and confined to the imperial palace for centuries.*

*A few specimens owned by one of the Princesses survived when Peking was overrun by the British in 1860. These dogs were brought to England with Queen Victoria's approval and coupled with their romantic past slowly gained popularity.*

*Figure 1.* "Inscrutable"
Spray painted with black finishing touches by hand and superbly modelled.
They also appear with glass eyes.
Circa 1885
Height 8 inches

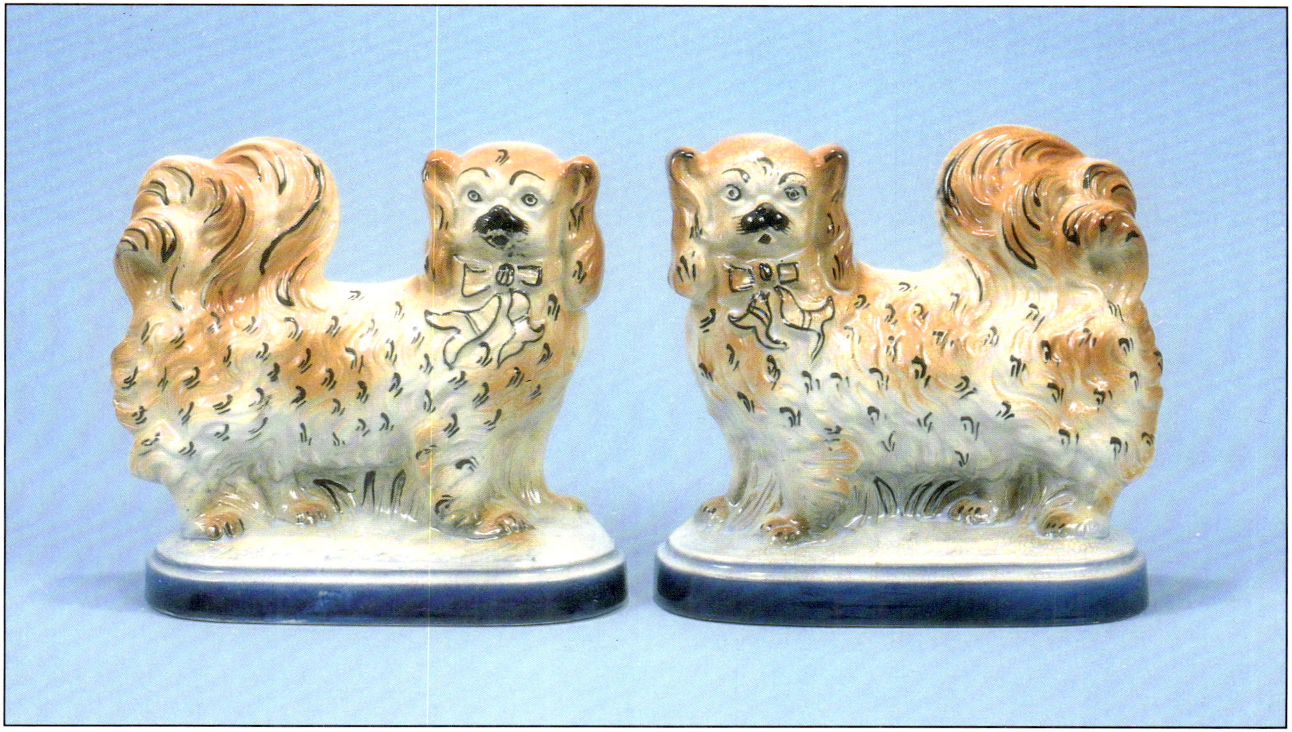

*Figure 1.*

# Pipe–Smoking Dogs

*The new processes of etching and engraving (made more permanent by the process of electrotyping) which came into vogue around 1840, introduced a large and hitherto uninstructed public to the great painters and illustrators of the period. Their art was for the first time, able to be reproduced in large numbers through the pages of the London Illustrated News and other regular periodicals.*

*These popular new printing methods coincided exactly with the latest technical advances of a simpler pottery production. The Staffordshire potters took full advantage of this situation by very often using, as their inspiration for a figure or group, the ready and proven market of this "art in print".*

*Armed with this knowledge I was eventually to discover the "Otter Hunt" (page 126) and in so doing, discover (for myself) the works of Sir Edwin Landseer.*

*Landseer was the most commercially successful of all the 19th century artists, reaching the peak of his powers as the young Queen Victoria ascended the throne. The lovely young Queen and her handsome consort greatly admired his work and secured him a lifetime of royal patronage. With their fondness for animals, particularly dogs, they commissioned several paintings of the palace pets, Prince Albert's favourite Greyhound "Eos", "Islay" a Scots Terrier, the Queen's favourite, a King Charles Spaniel named "Dash" and many others.*

*Becoming enthralled by this fascinating man (whose last great achievement was sculpting the famous lions at the foot of Nelson's Column in Trafalgar Square) I was almost side-tracked but not without a rewarding consolation prize.*

*The juxtaposition of artist and potter is clearly evident in this print taken from the original oil sketch by Landseer titled "A Quiet Pipe" (circa 1829), which he executed whilst preparing for his famous painting "Low Life". Reflecting human feelings and character this humoristic print amused the Victorians, (perhaps even the Queen herself!), and became a best seller.*

*It must be the source that inspired these models of pipe-smoking dogs.*

*No other artist, before or since, has painted dogs in such variety and number. I am sure there must be more source discoveries amongst Landseer's work, still waiting to be made.*

*Figure 1.* Print of "A Quiet Pipe"
Circa 1840
From the Pears Xmas Annual 1907 after the original painting by Landseer.

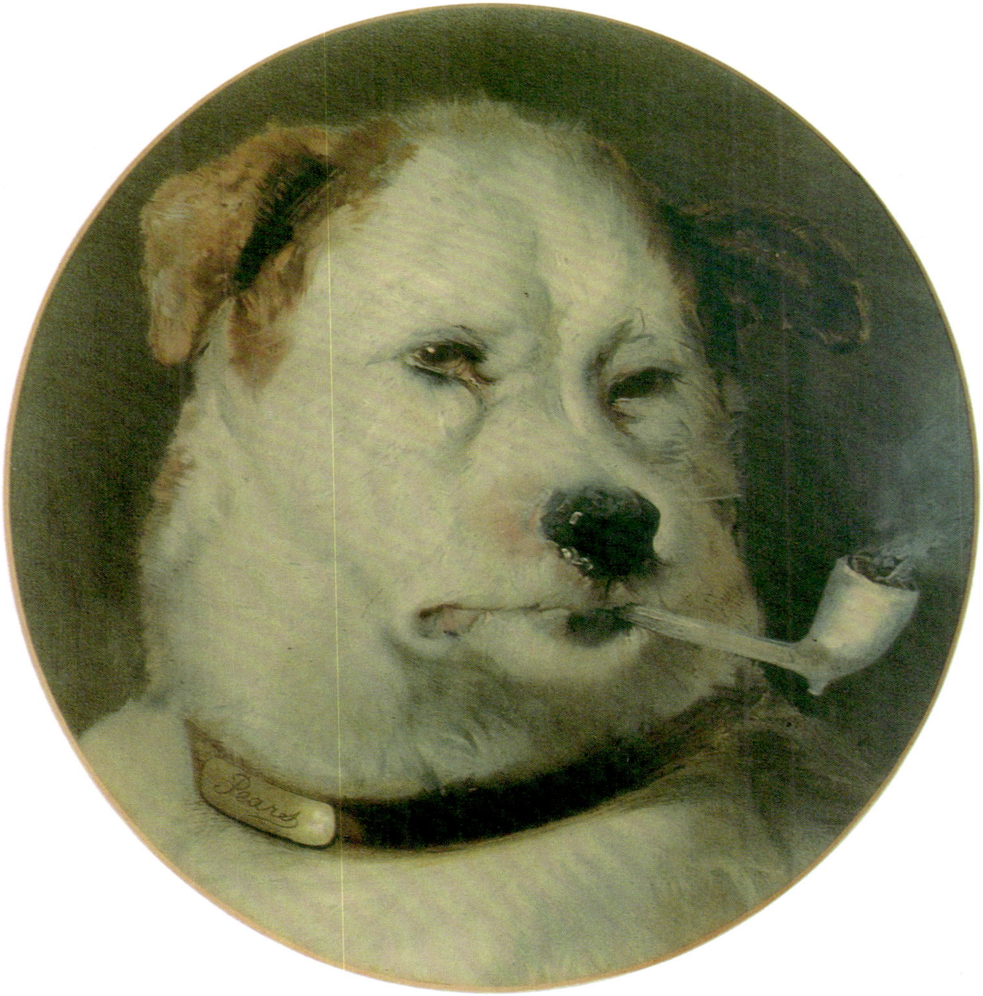


*Figure 1.*

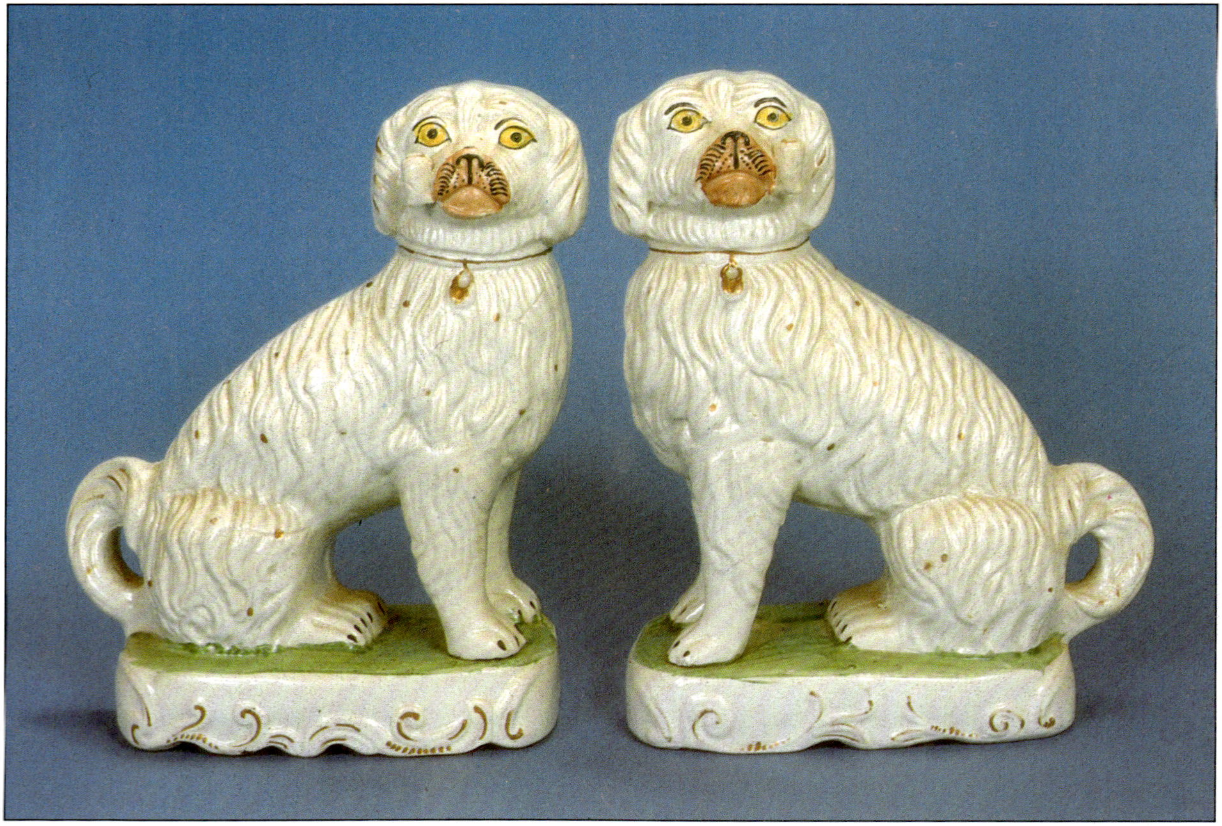

*Figure 2.*

*Figure 2.* Both enjoying a quiet smoke, sitting-up on apple green bases scrolled with gilt.
Circa 1850
Height 10½ inches

*Figure 3.* All the pipe-smoking models are extremely rare but this smaller version does appear occasionally and also with black or red patches.
Circa 1850
Height 8½ inches

*Figures 4/5.* The same model as in Figure 2 with black patches.
Circa 1850
Height 10½ inches

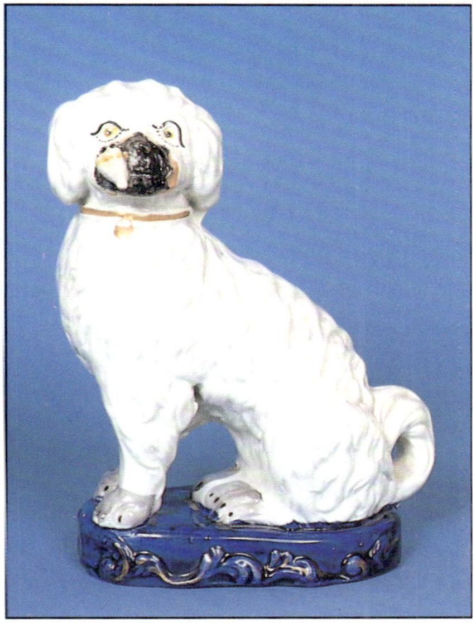

*Figure 3.*

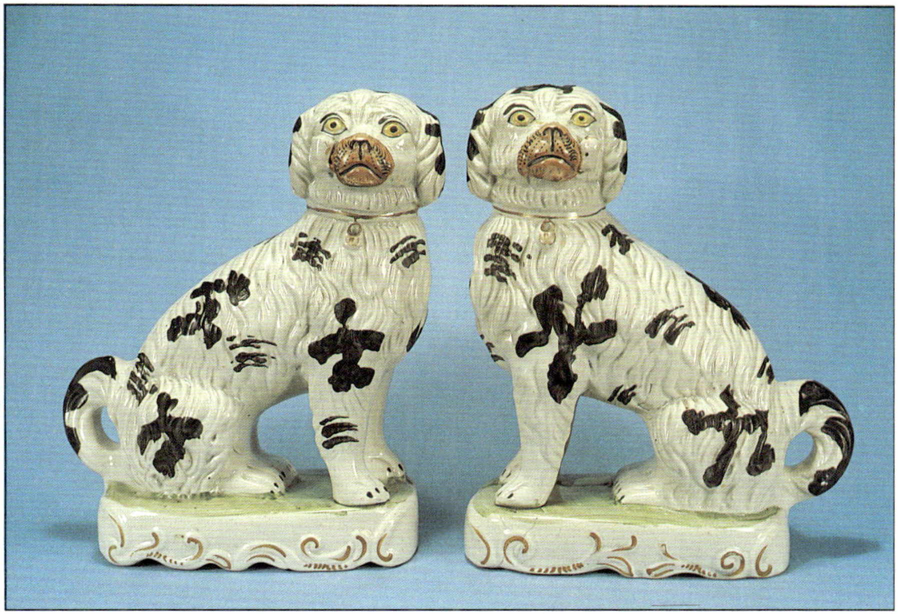

*Figure 4.*

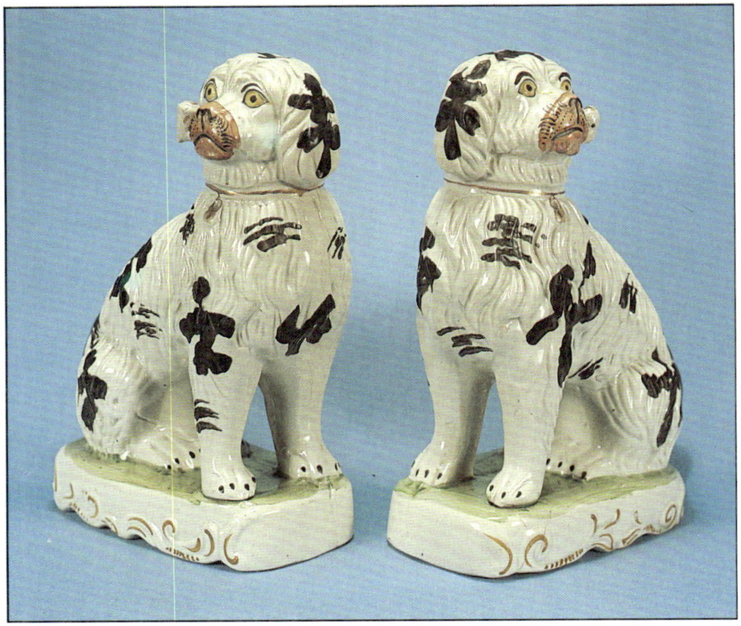

*Figure 5.*

# Pointer

*The Pointer originated in Spain. Famous for its ability to point the bird with its nose, body and tail in a straight line.*

*It was one of the breeds at the first British dog show held in Newcastle in 1859.*

*Figure 1.* Standing on grassy mounds, with three of their four legs separate, this pair are very finely modelled.
Circa 1855
Height 11¼ inches

*Figure 2.* "Pointing the Way"
Spill vase.
Circa 1855
Height 6¼ inches

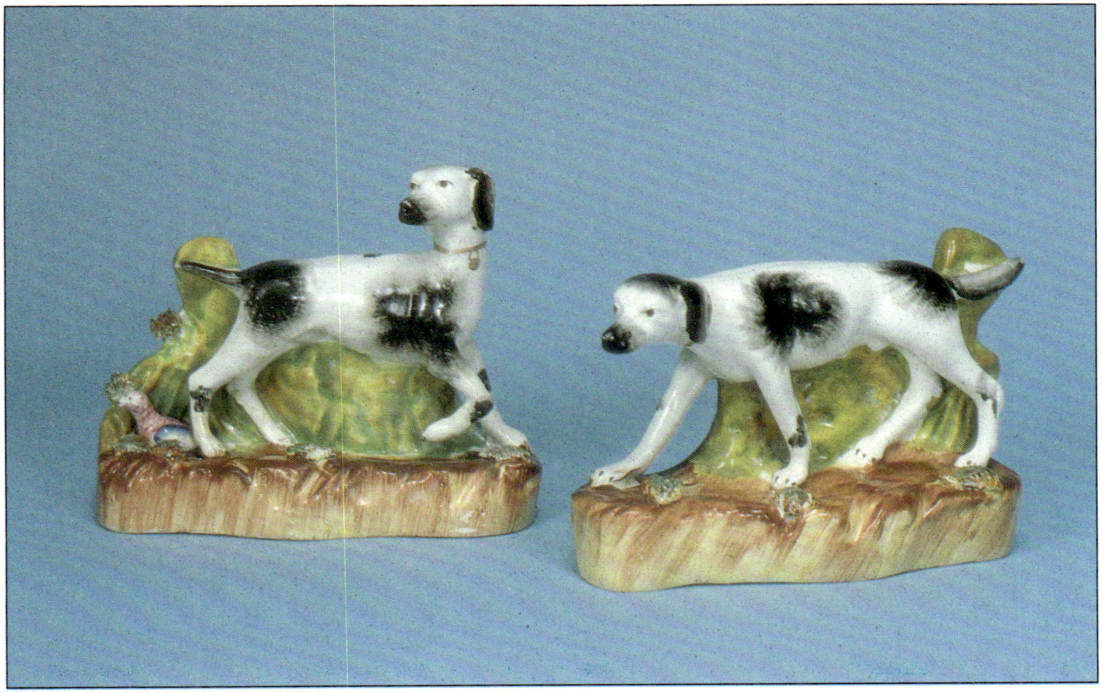

*Figure 1.*

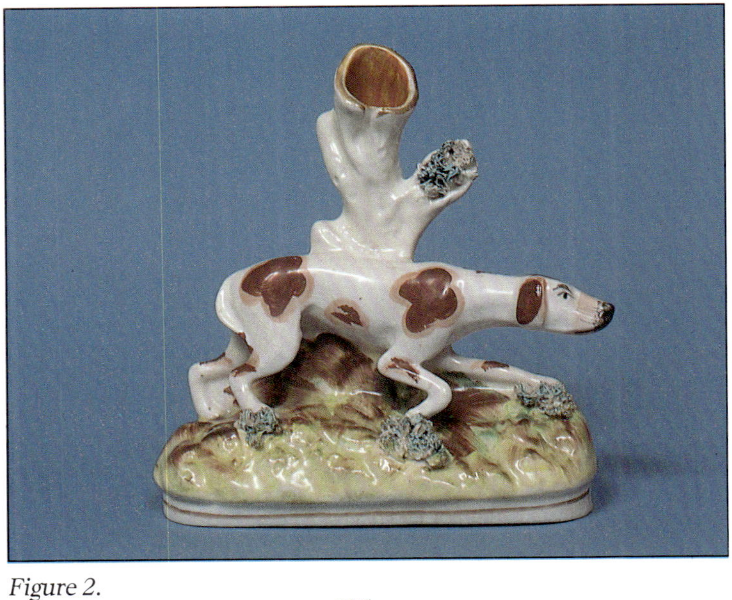

*Figure 2.*

# Poodle

*Known on the continent as a Water Spaniel, hence its name, derived from the German word "puddeln" – to splash water.*

*The smaller breed made a fashionable pet throughout the 19th century.*

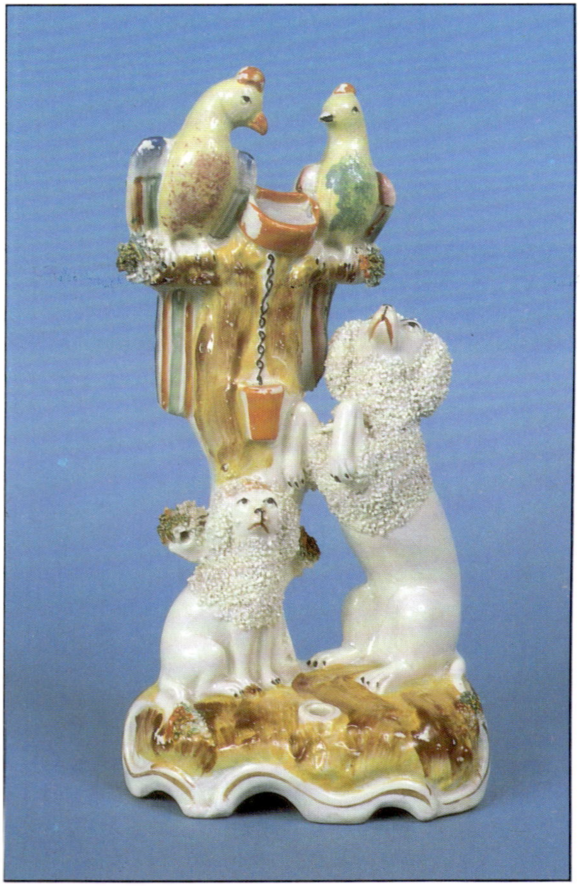

*Figure 1.*

*Figure 1.* An attractive quill holder group.
No amount of pleading will entice these parrots off their perch!
Circa 1850
Height 10 inches

*Figure 2.* "The Three Graces"
This clock group centrepiece is also found with three Spaniels or two Spaniels and a Poodle in the centre.
Circa 1855
Height 7½ inches

*Figure 3.* "Well son, you have got me over a barrel"
Circa 1860
Height 5¼ inches

*Figure 4.* "Uneasy friends!"
Circa 1850
Height 3¾ inches

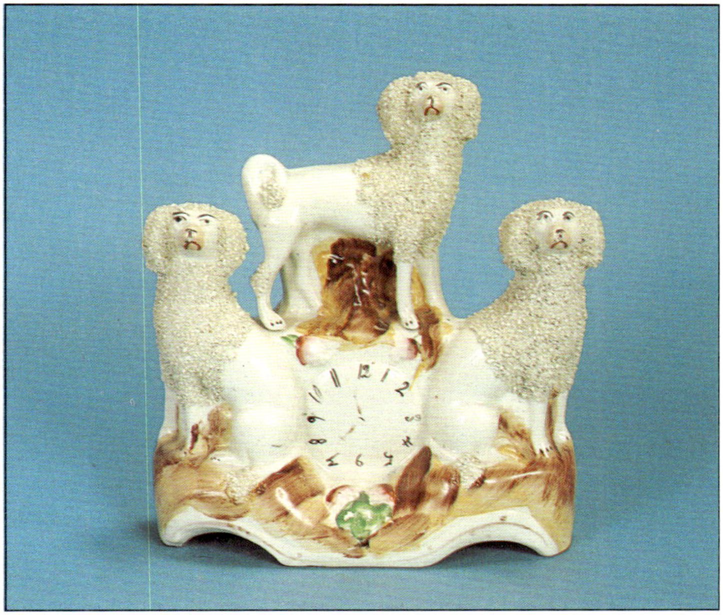

*Figure 2.*

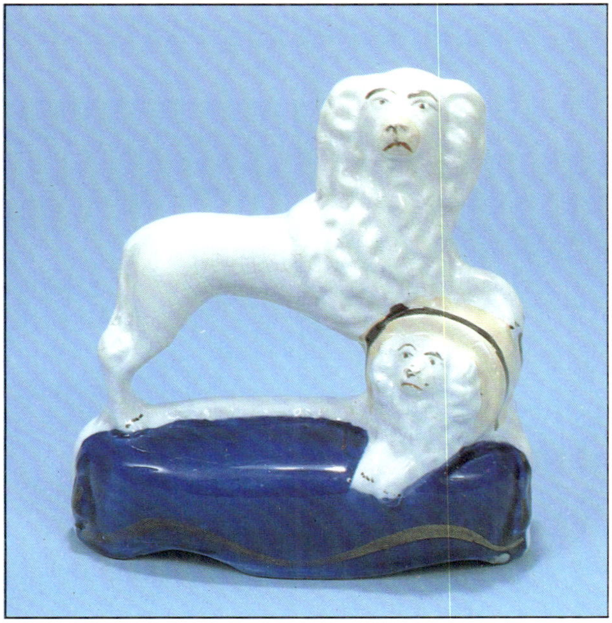

*Figure 3.*

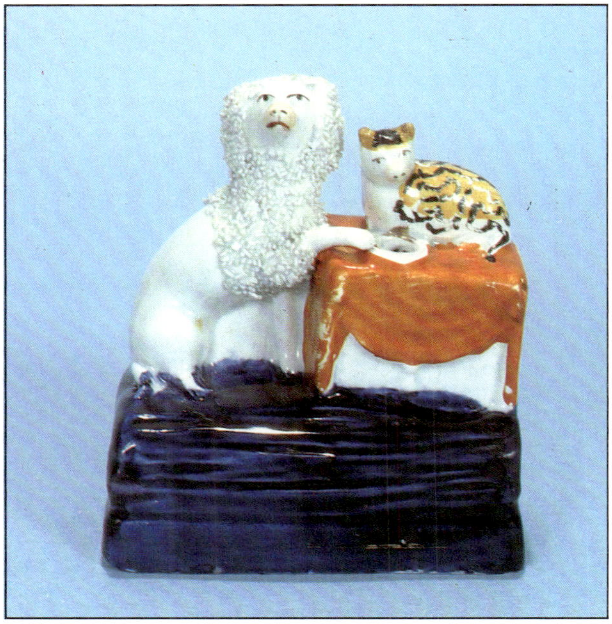

*Figure 4.*

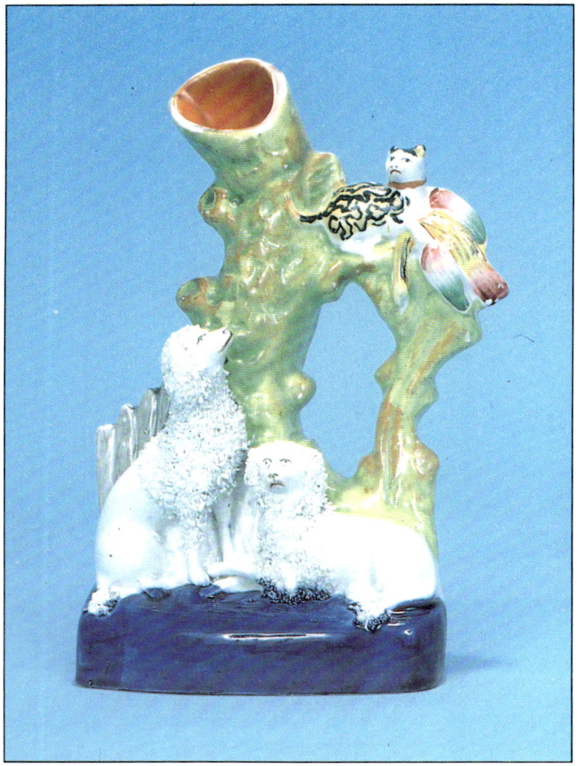

Figure 5.

*Figure 5.* "Cat's Cradle"
Circa 1850
Height 7½ inches

*Figure 6.* "Woolly and Wonderful"
Circa 1845
Height 6¾ inches

*Figure 7.* Chunky and rounded with separate front legs.
Circa 1855
Height 5½ inches

*Figure 8.* A standard pair representative of several similar models.
Circa 1870
Height 9½ inches

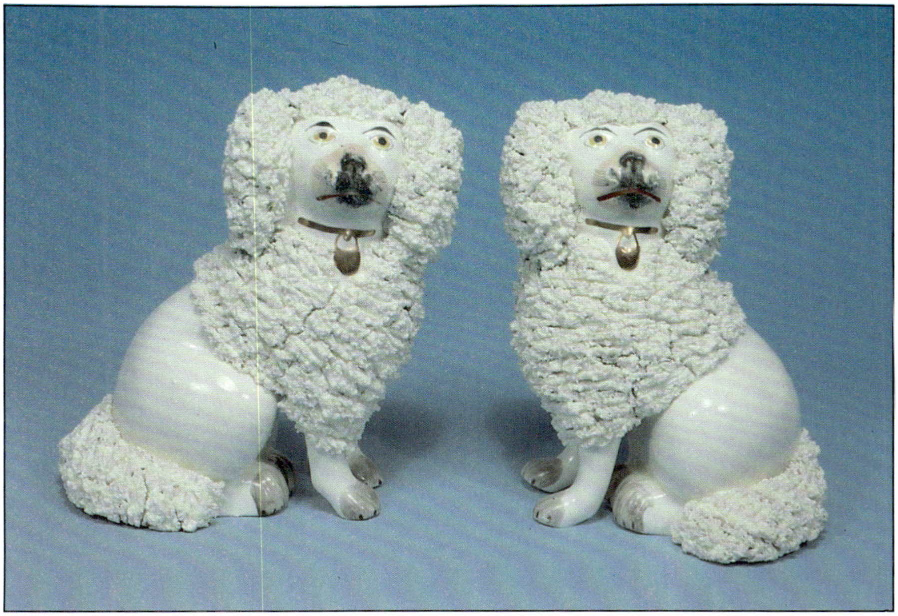

*Figure 6.*

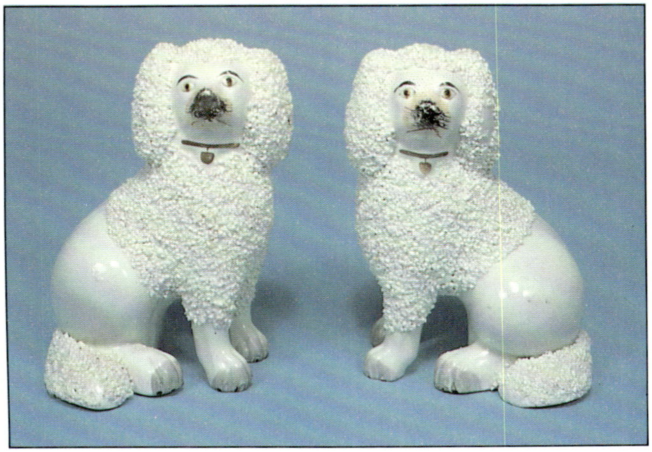

*Figure 7.*

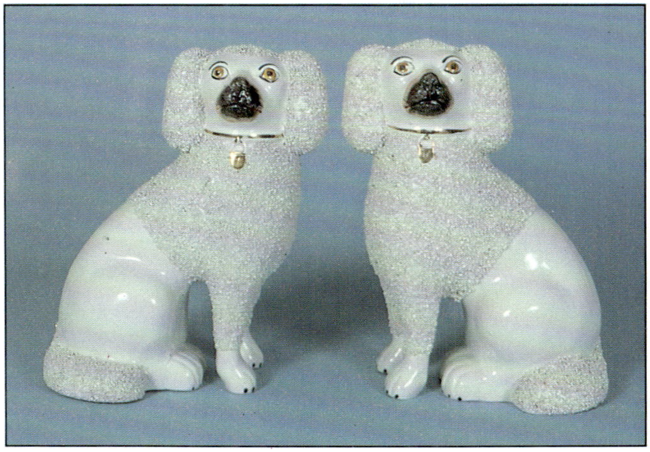

*Figure 8.*

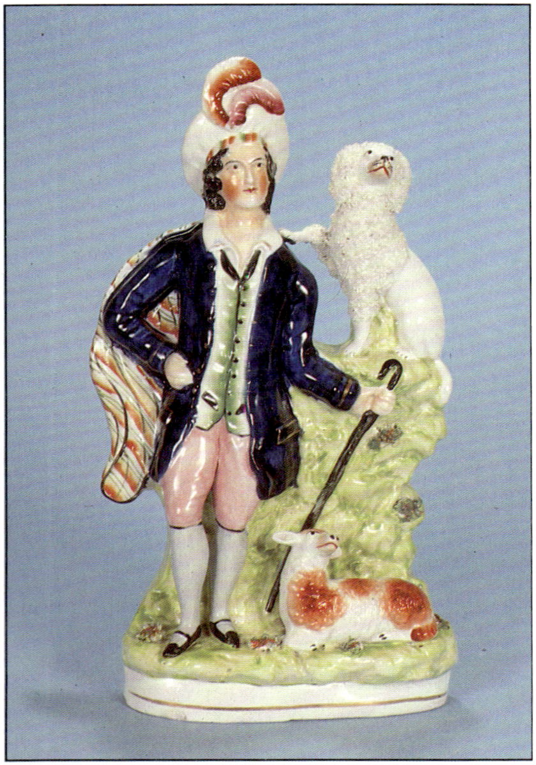

*Figure 9.*

*Figure 9.* "The Masquerade"
An interesting if somewhat odd combination of a shepherd with a lamb and a poodle posing as a sheepdog.
It nevertheless all adds up to pure delight.
Circa 1845
Height 13½ inches

*Figure 10.* A pair of kennelled poodles.
Spill groups.
Circa 1855
Height 8 inches

*Figure 11.* Poodles with puppies, looking dignified by parenthood.
Circa 1850
Height 8 inches

*Figure 12.* "Hey junior, watch you don't fall!"
A delightful study of motherhood.
Circa 1840
Height 5½ inches

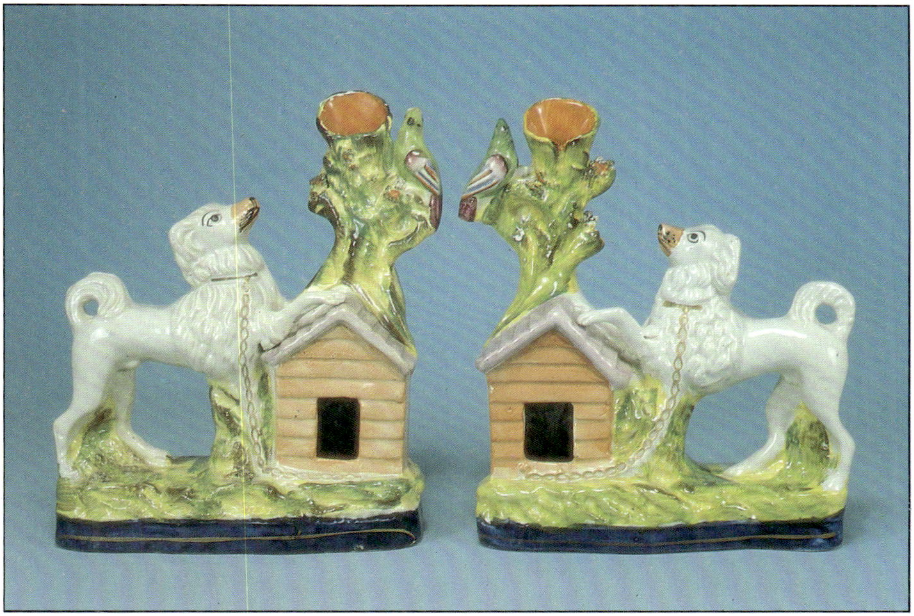

Figure 10.

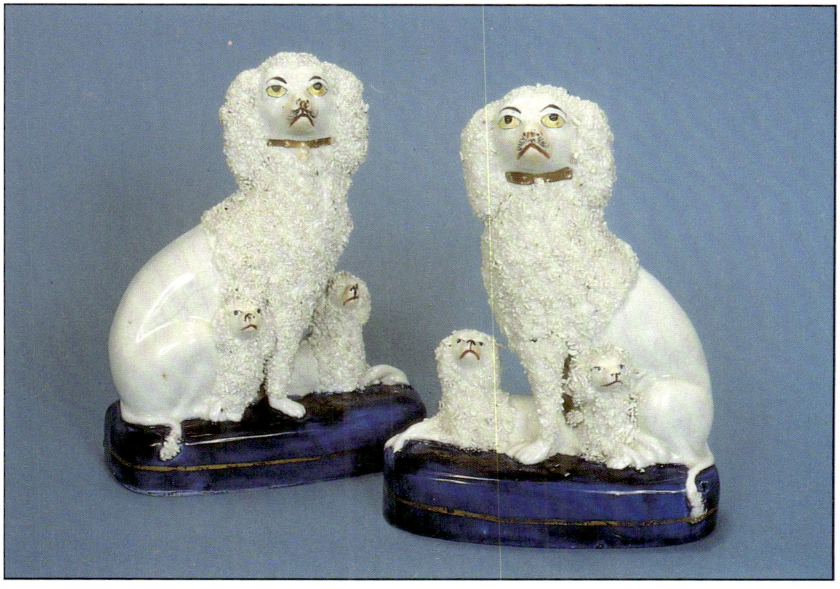

Figure 11.

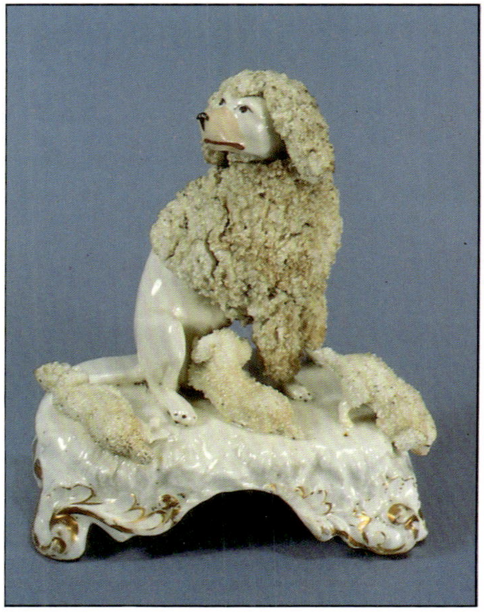

Figure 12.

# Production Method and Gilding

## Production Method

*The manufacture of a Staffordshire dog begins with a modeller sculpting his creation free-hand in oiled clay.*

*From the modeller's figure a mould is made in plaster-of-paris. This is known as the master-mould from which further working moulds could also be taken.*

*The moulds were made in two halves, a front and back. Wet clay is then pressed into each half. The halves are then secured together by binding and liquid clay brushed along the inside seams through the open bottom. This is then placed on a shelf in a warm room until the clay has dried to the touch.*

*The hollow figure could then be removed from the mould for final hand finishing and sealed at the bottom with a flat piece of clay as a base.*

*A small hole would be punctured, usually in this base piece or at the back of the figure to allow the expanding air to escape during the firing.*

*The figure removed from the kiln after firing is then ready for painting and glazing before its second and final firing that hardens the glaze and secures the colours.*

# *Gilding*

*Gilded decoration was used on the earliest of Staffordshire dogs right through until the end of the 19th century and it is an important clue to dating.*

*There were two types of gilding that of "best gold" and "bright gold".*

*Best gold was a gold powder which was applied with a borax–flux and required firing to "fix" in place. It was used exclusively up until 1860 when bright gold was first introduced.*

*Bright gold, in an already liquid form, was applied by brush after the final firing. Its simplicity of use made it extremely popular.*

*Best gold continued to be used until the end of the century, but much more sparingly, whereas no figure painted in bright gold pre-dates 1860.*

# Pugs

*Originally from China, the breed was already in Europe in the 16th century and especially favoured in the Netherlands.*

*When William and Mary came to the English throne in 1789 their Pugs came with them, but they only became popular towards the end of the 19th century.*

*Figure 1.* A standing model of a Staffordshire Pug.
Circa 1890
Height 5½ inches

*Figure 2.* These handsome glass-eyed devils are thoughtfully modelled with heavy loose folds of fur lying around their gilt collars and the spray painting has been no less skilfully applied.
(Glass eyes see page 106).
Circa 1880
Height 12 inches

*Figure 3.* Completely separate legs and black muzzles.
Circa 1875
Height 10¾ inches

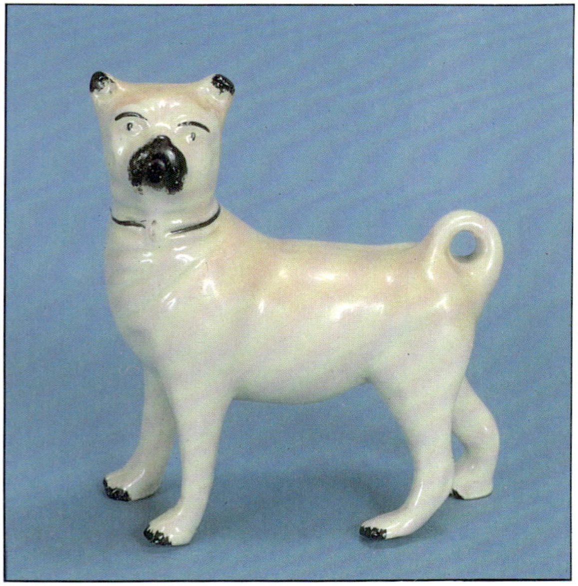

*Figure 1.*

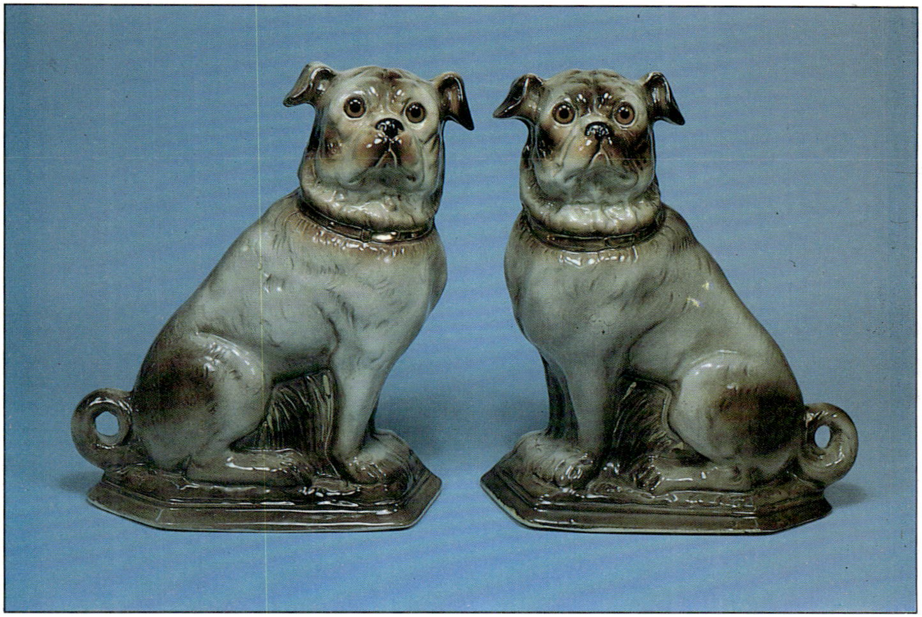
*Figure 2.*

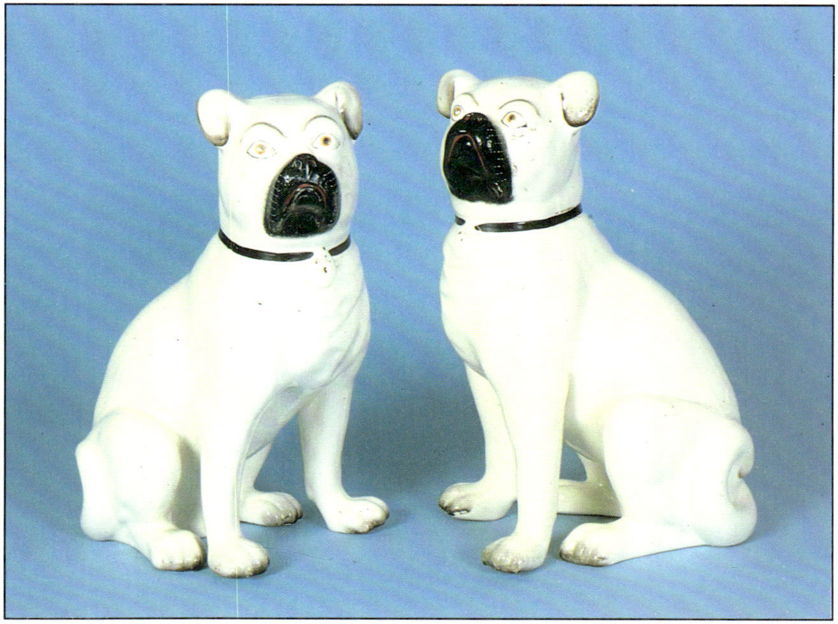
*Figure 3.*

# Q

# Reproductions

*"Where there is a demand there is always a supply", could be the faker's motto. Reproductions of worthwhile antiques with an eye to profit have been with us for centuries. Staffordshire dogs have not escaped this unsavoury trade, without the necessity of forging a specific factory mark they have become a seemingly easy target.*

*As clever as many of these "fakes" are, it is simply impossible to reproduce the combination of correct clay formula, 19th century colour palette and consistency of glaze without the "repro" becoming more expensive than the original (which rather defeats the object).*

*Written "Pointers" only serve to encourage the forger to try harder and a new collector might expect to be fooled once or even twice by these abominations (a small price to pay for knowledge) but with handling and appreciation of the genuine article arrives experience, the only sure way to defeat the faker.*

*Figure 1.* An assortment of reproduction models.

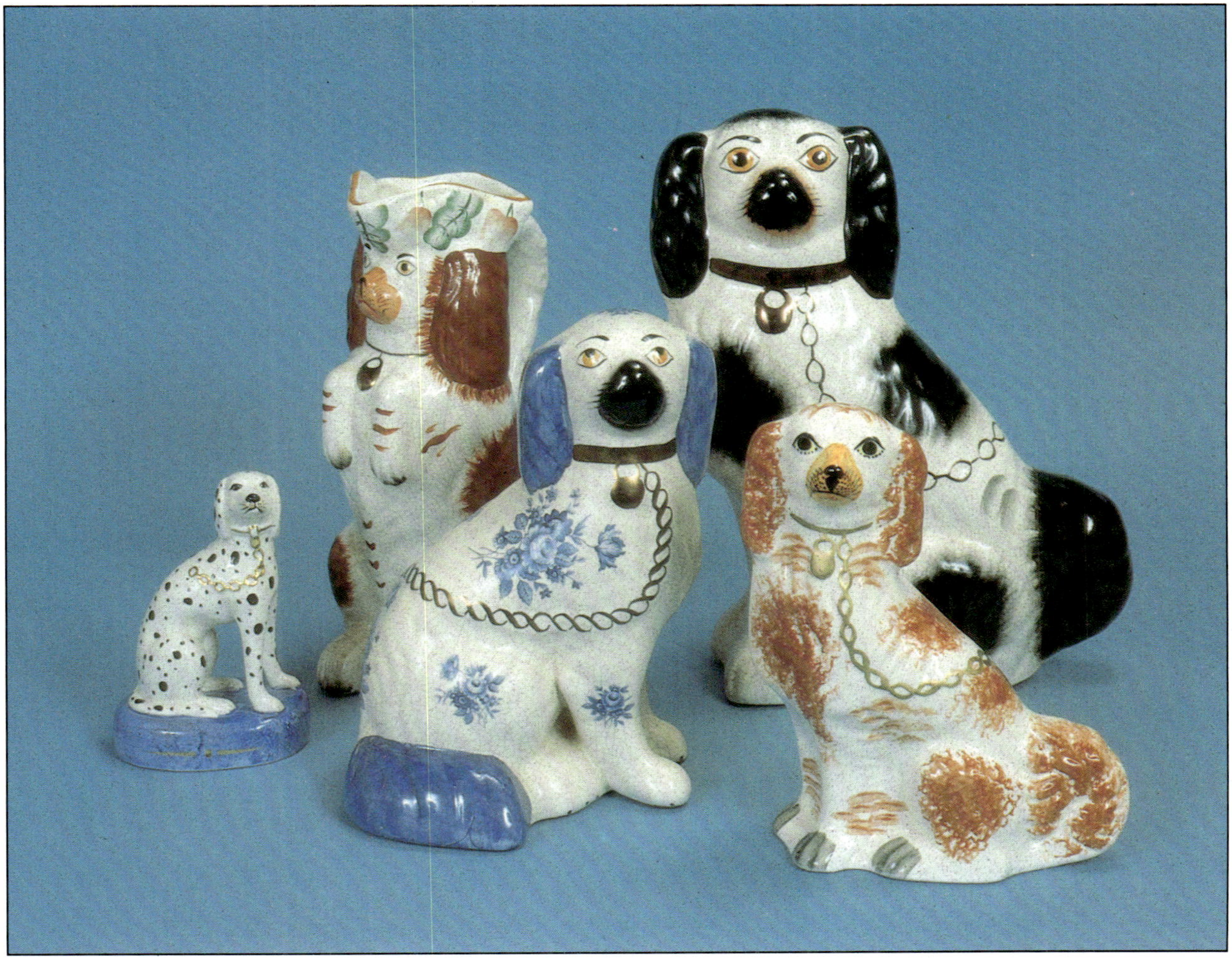

*Figure 1.*

# Saluki

*With a bloodline that has remained pure throughout the ages the Saluki is probably the oldest extant breed of domesticated dog and is believed to have originated in Syria.*

*Egyptian tomb companion figures and paintings bear witness to the fact that this beautiful dog with the almond shaped eyes and the strangely sad expression has been admired in North Africa for thousands of years.*

*A brilliant desert hunter, bred to hunt with falcons to course gazelle and desert fox, it can race at great speed over the most inhospitable terrain.*

*Figure 1.* "The Mystery of the East"
It was questionable whether or not this model should be catalogued under "S" for Saluki.
The first puppies of the breed only arrived in Britain in 1895 but the evidence before one's eyes appears unmistakable.
Could one of our Staffordshire potters have possibly experienced reincarnation?
Circa 1845
Height 9 inches

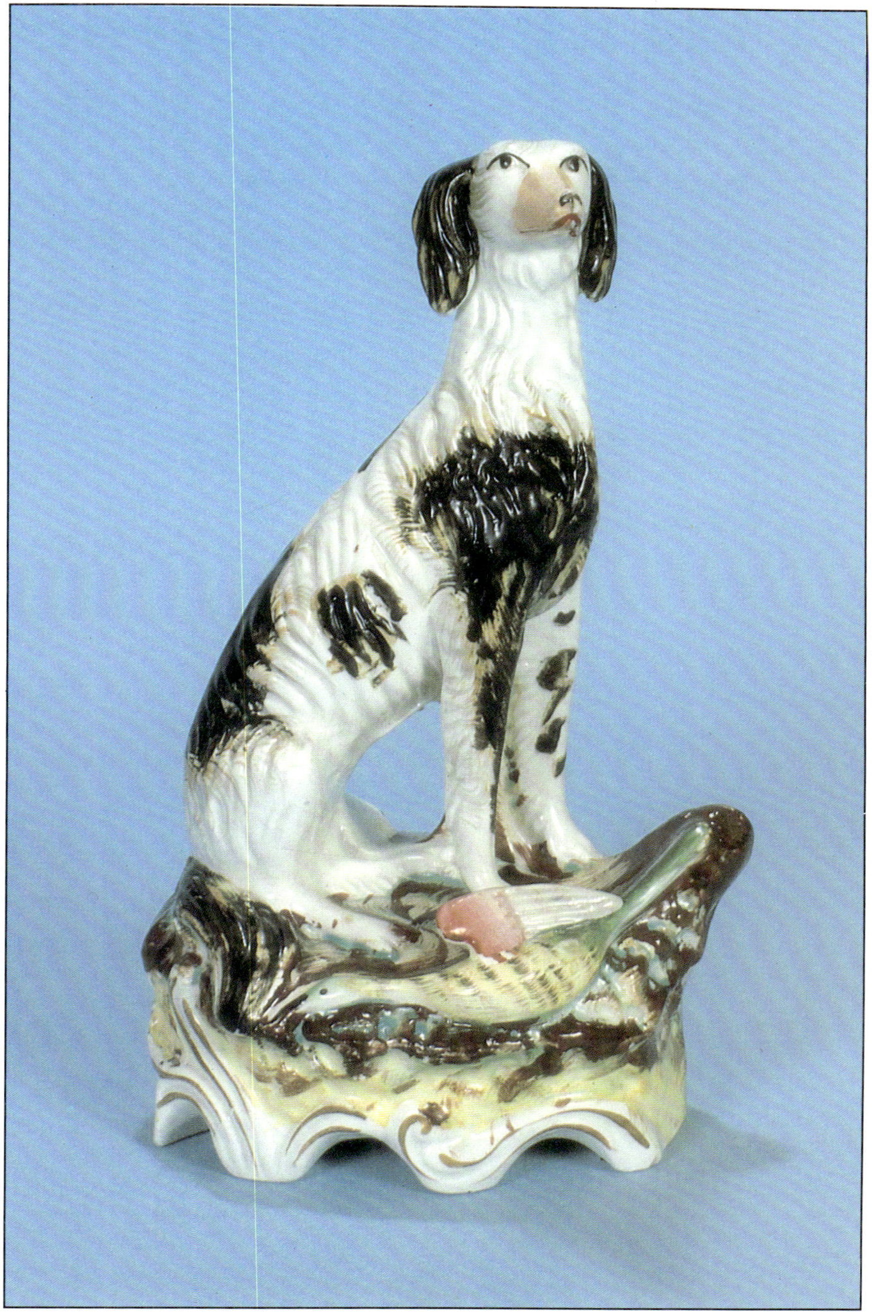

*Figure 1.*

# S t. Bernard

*With its long history of rescue work in the Swiss Alps going back 200 years, this noble breed has a special appeal. Its benevolent expression and docile character makes it a charming companion dog. Cheerful and loyal it even submits to the teasing of children and was certainly a great favourite with Queen Victoria's offspring.*

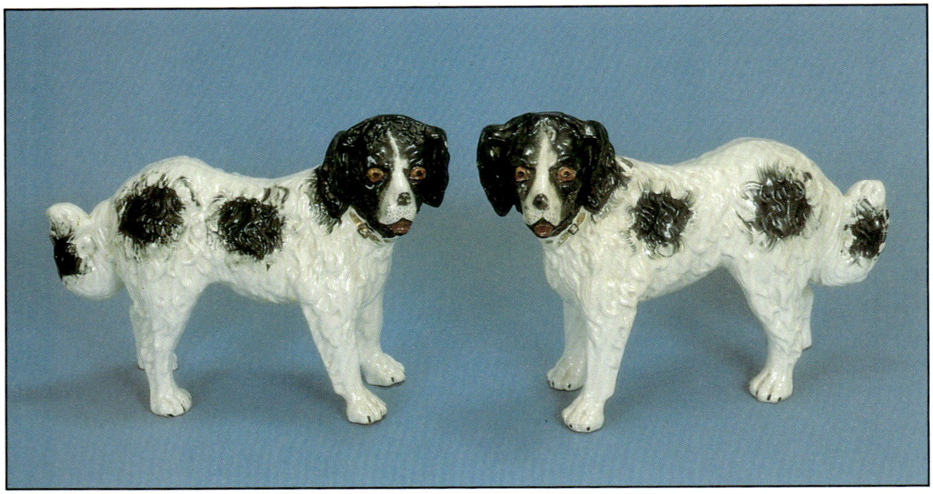

*Figure 1.*

*Figure 1.* This naturalistic stance without a base or spill support only occurs in models towards the end of the century.
Circa 1885
Height 10 inches,
Length 14½ inches

*Figure 2.* "Hairs to the throne"
Carrying the royal children on their backs, both models appear in various colourings, but the model in Figure 3 is subtly different.
Circa 1848
Height 8½ inches

*Figure 3.* This finer model has the benefit of separate arm moulds.
Circa 1848
Height 8½ inches

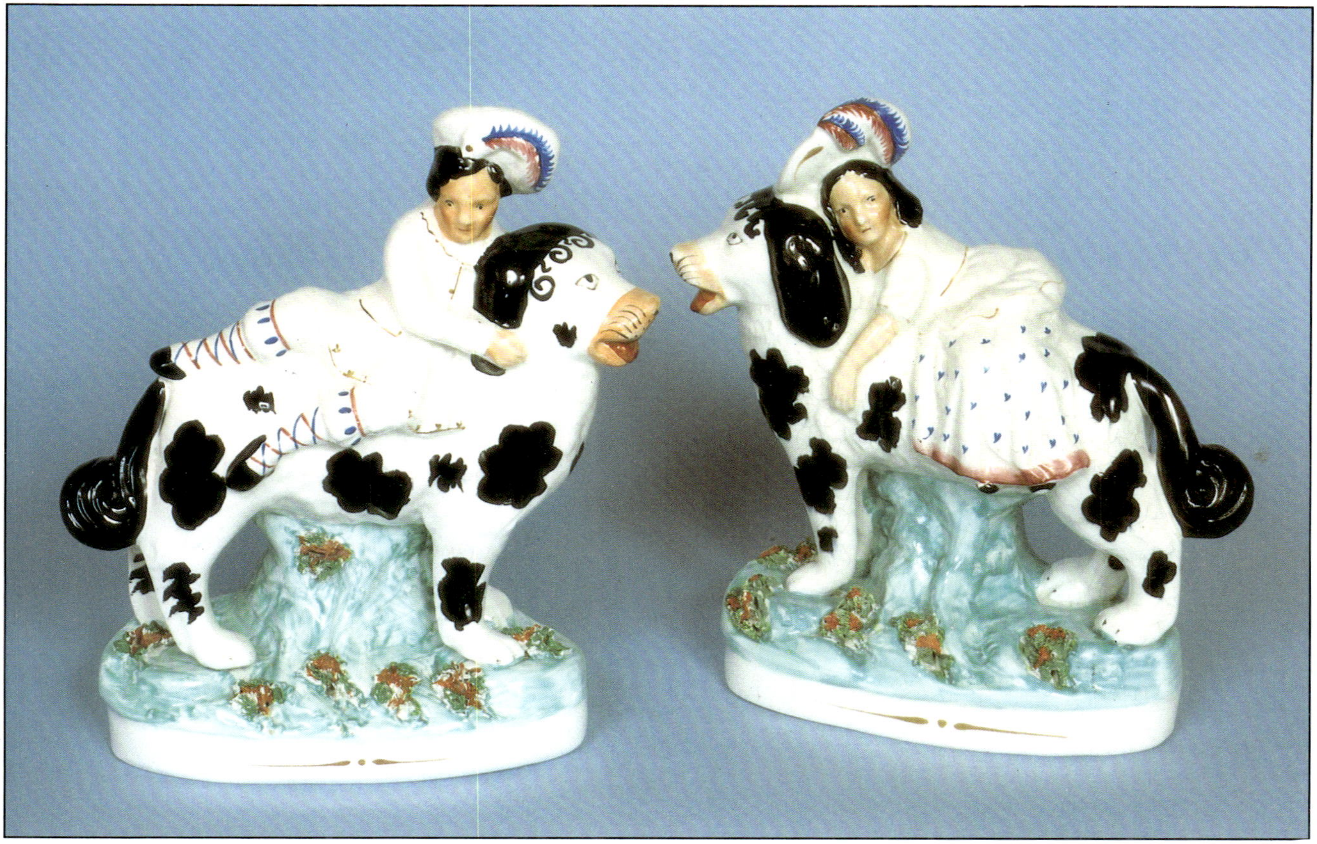

*Figure 2.*

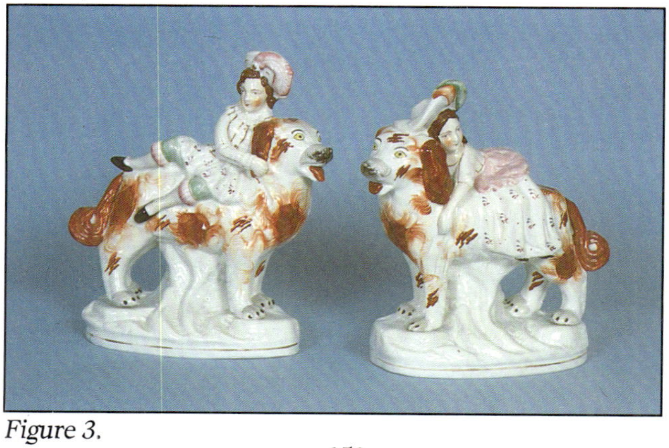

*Figure 3.*

# Staffordshire Bull Terrier

*It is a sad fact of history that the baiting and tormenting of animals has always been a popular pastime of the human race.*

*Bull-baiting, which set dogs against bulls, required a dog with a wide stance, a barrel-chest and a massive jaw and was one of those pastimes, inappropriately called "sport", that was finally abolished in 1835.*

*Public opinion was very much to thank for this piece of legislation. Moral distaste would no longer allow models of any such offenders onto the mantelpiece of the Victorian sitting-room.*

*Without a market value it is not surprising there are no models of Staffordshire Bull Terriers or Bulldogs potted after this date of 1835.*

*Only in fairly modern times when the breeds had been transformed into more peaceable companions do they reappear.*

*Figure 1.* Bull-baiting group made by Obadiah Sherratt. Recorded as working 1815–1846.
Little is known of this pre-Victorian potter's background. Sherratt's figures are never marked.
Pieces are traditionally ascribed to this potter due to their distinctive style.
Circa 1830
Height 10 inches, Length 13½ inches

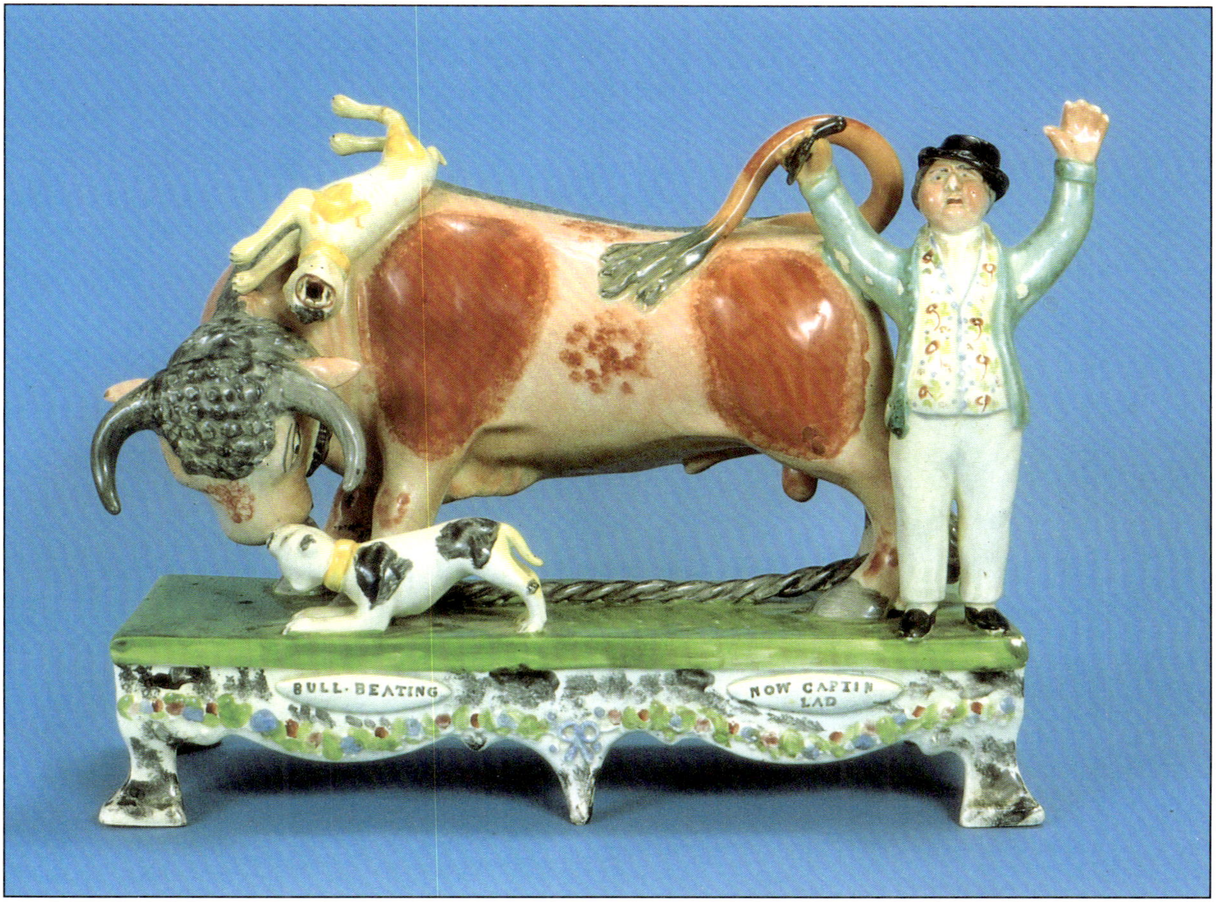


*Figure 1.*

# Terrier

*A small working dog developed in Scotland.*
*Used in the 19th century to rout out badgers and foxes from their dens.*

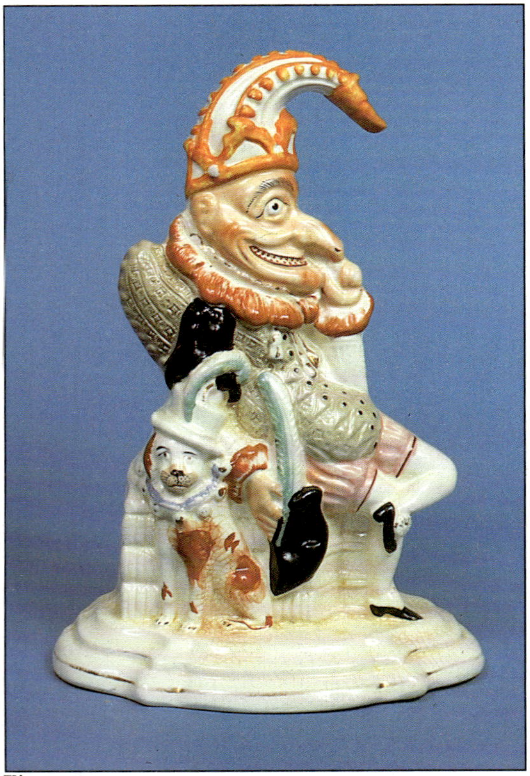

*Figure 1.*

*Figure 1.* Mr. Punch with his dog "Toby".
Modelled in exactly the same vein as cast-iron door stops of the period.
Possibly it may have been intended for such use.
The idea seems improbable bearing in mind its clay composition but would explain (with breakage allowed for) its rarity today.
Circa 1875
Height 11½ inches

*Figure 2.* In a naturalistic brindle colouring.
Circa 1855
Height 9½ inches

*Figure 3.* The same model in fanciful colouring.
Note the waving puppy in the right-hand model.
Circa 1855
Height 9½ inches

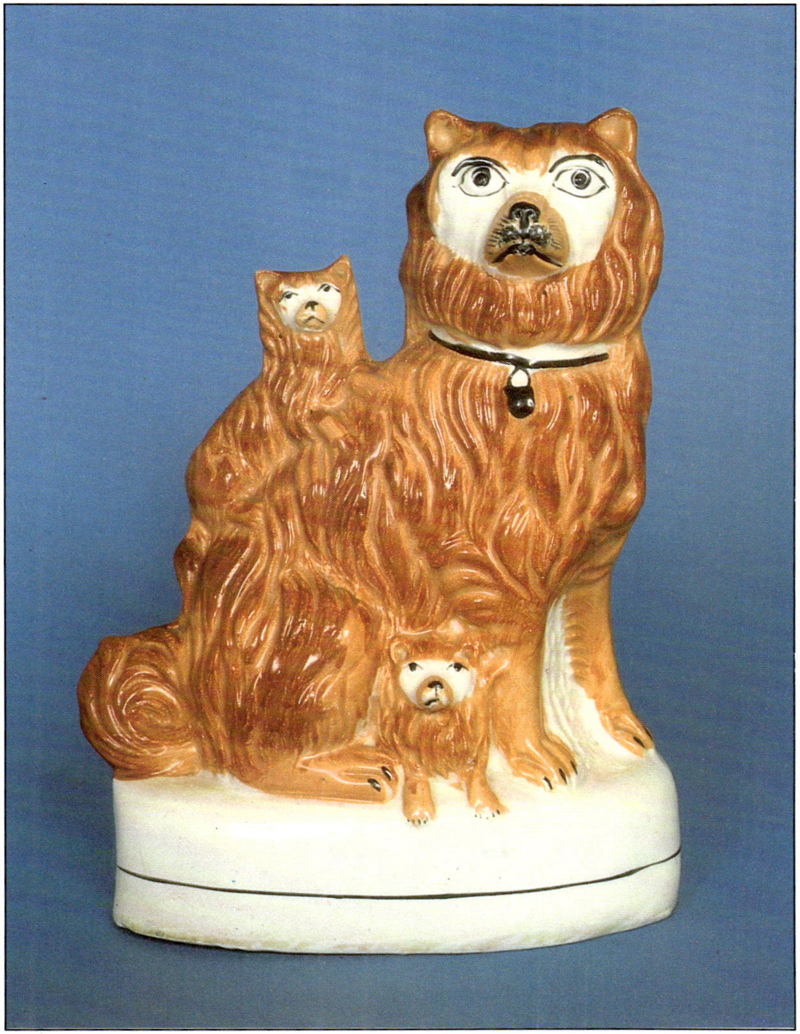

Figure 2.

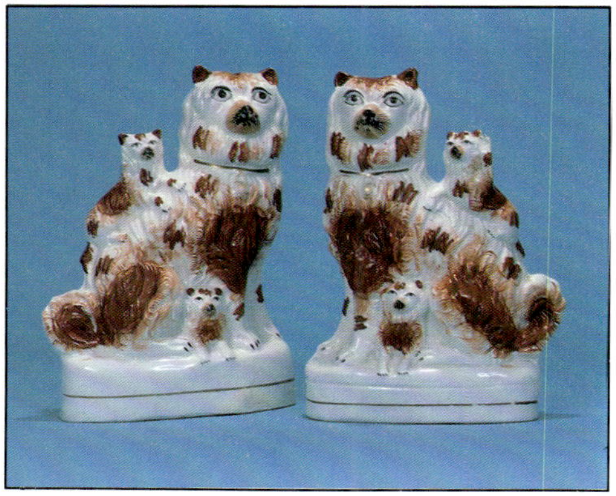

Figure 3.

# Un–Comforter Dogs

*Clearly they are not of the same pedigree!*

*Photography however is a poor substitute for handling the "animal" in order to define the differences of modelling, painting and date which separate "The Good", "The Bad" and "The Ugly".*

*Figure 1.* Left to Right
"The Good"
Well modelled and thoughtfully painted.
Circa 1850

"The Bad"
A modern reproduction.

"The Ugly"
Lack of definition in both modelling and brushwork.
Circa 1880

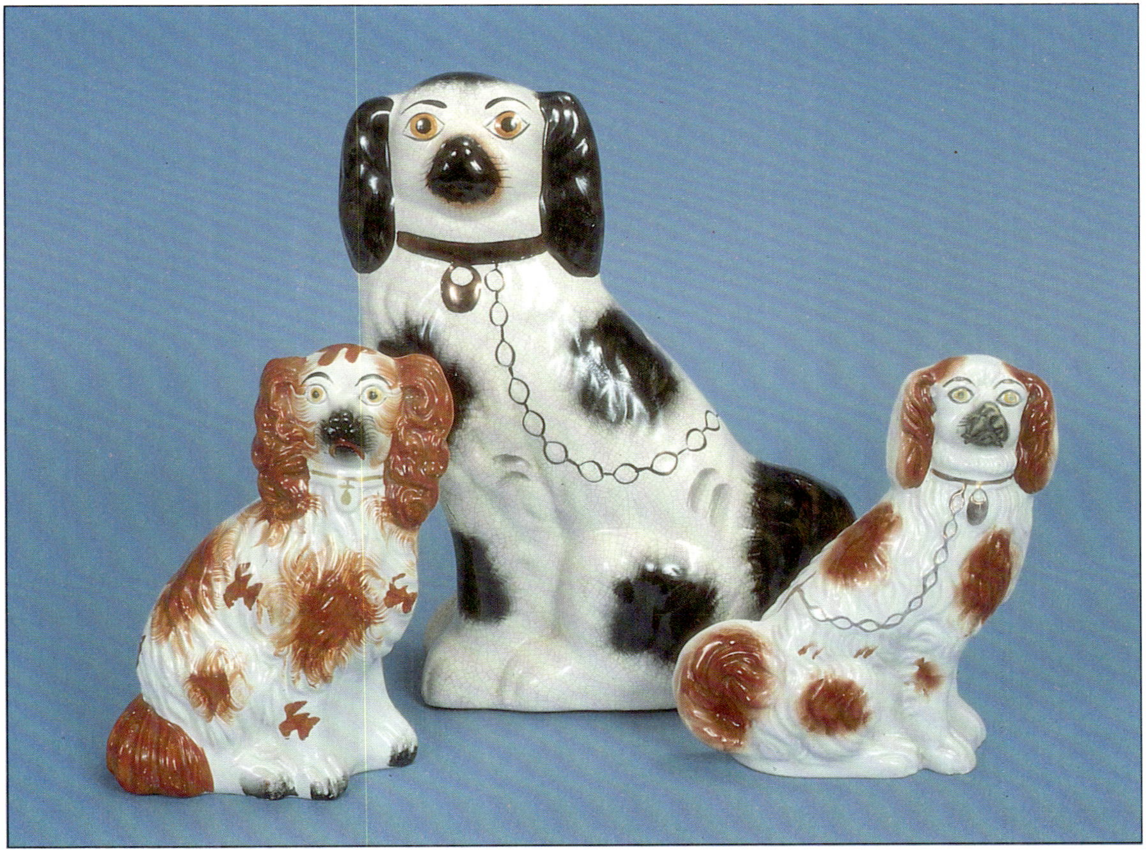

*Figure 1.*

# Value and Pricing

*Attractiveness, quality, condition and rarity are the four key points which determine the market value.*

- *ATTRACTIVENESS is often governed by opinion, rarity can make a piece appear attractive to some collectors, but looking at a model from an aesthetic point of view is the surest guide. If a model is unattractive it must qualify on at least two of the other points otherwise the odds against it are almost unassailable.*
- *QUALITY is easier to understand, fine modelling and delicate brushwork speak for themselves.*
- *CONDITION and restoration should also be taken into account while perfect is obviously "best", limited restoration in an otherwise well modelled and attractive figure is acceptable. After all we are dealing with a pottery medium that has a history of over a 100 years.*
- *RARITY has a more subtle face. A model may be rare due to its limited production, conversely, it is rare to find an early version in good condition of a model that was common and produced over a long period. If the latter is also attractive it has scored three stars out of four on our point system and will attract a better price than a very rare but crudely modelled figure of limited production.*

*"Difficult is it not?", but with love and understanding a practised eye will learn to judge. The satisfaction of achieving the right combination of these four points, will, when correctly judged make today's price into tomorrow's bargain.*

*Figure 1.* "The Losers"
No points can be awarded for their crude modelling, slap-dash painting or attractiveness,
only their rarity of model scores a final place. Judges' decision: 1 point.
Circa 1870
Height 5¼ inches

*Figure 2.* Left
"The Runners-up"
An attractive model and in good condition this pair lose out on quality, rarity and heavy-handed brushwork.
Judges' decision: 2 points.
Circa 1890
Height 4 inches

Right
"The Winners"
Attractive, fine quality and perfect condition, with fine brushwork and a bonus point for their rarity due to desirability.
Judges' decision: 4 points.
Circa 1845
Height 4¼ inches

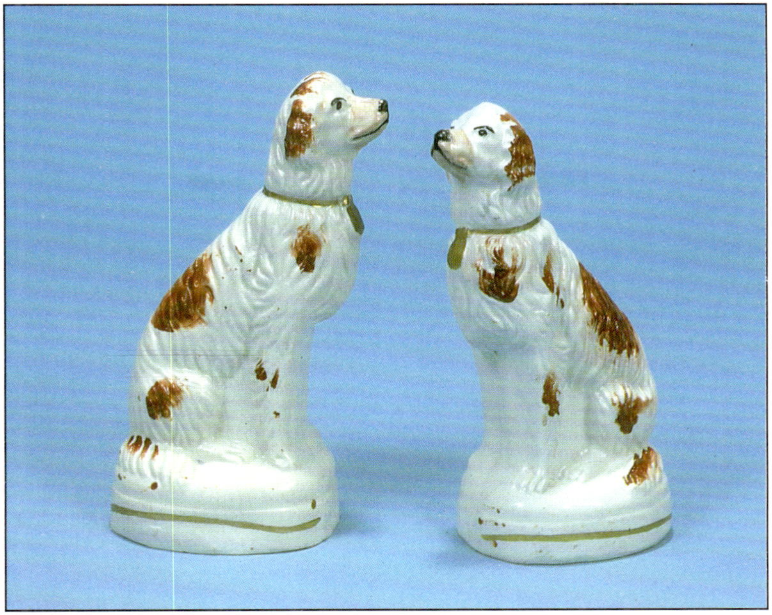

*Figure 1.*

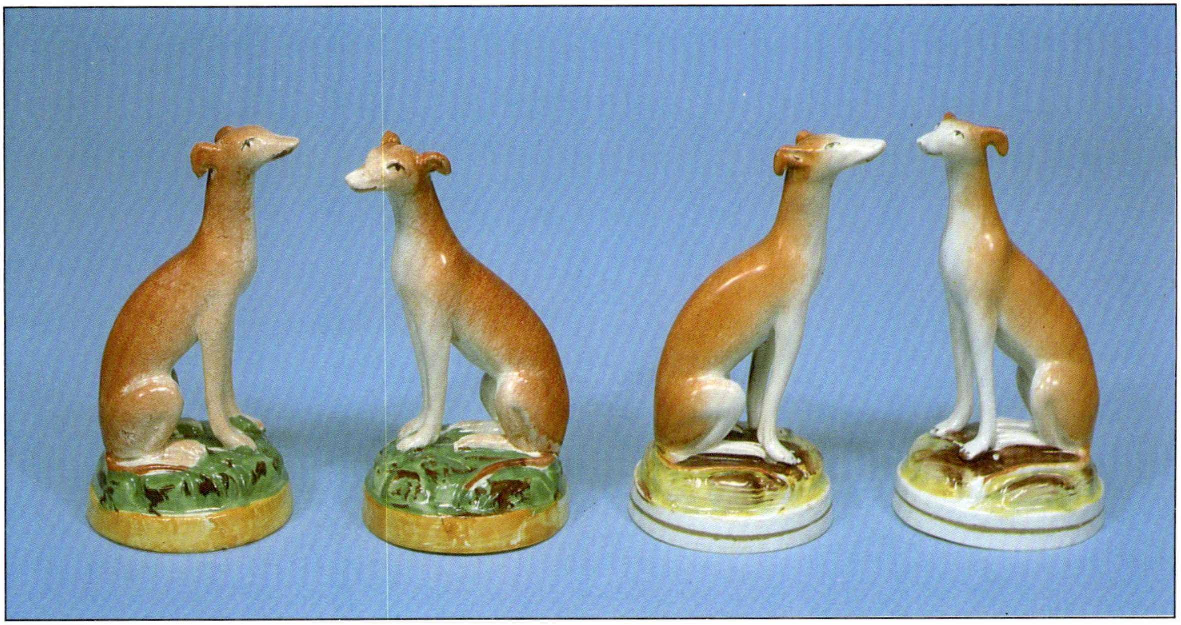

*Figure 2.*

# Welsh Springer Spaniel

*Smaller than its English cousin and called the "Tarfgi" in ancient Wales. Distinguished by its low set ears.*

*A good worker in water as well as on land.*

*Figure 1.* "On the Scent"
This dramatic model has a very striking appearance which is full of expression and action.
Circa 1850
Height 7 inches

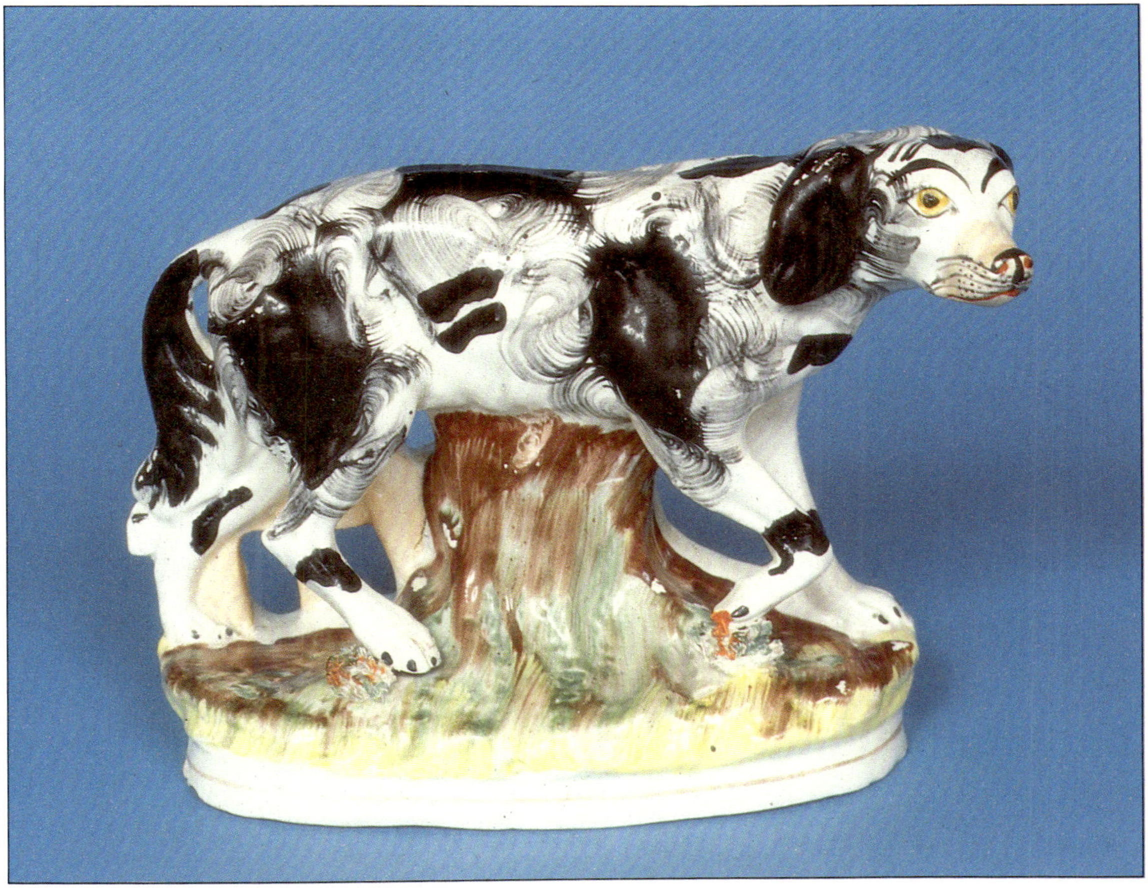

*Figure 1.*

# Whippet

*The Whippet is essentially English but is not really a very old breed.*

*Cross-bred from the Greyhound, the Italian Greyhound and the Manchester Terrier, the Whippet was developed by Northern miners only during the last quarter of the 19th century.*

*It was little known outside the Northern counties and only recognised as a breed in the 1890s.*

*In fact they were considered of little value until they attracted the attention of "modern" pet lovers early this century and have since become one of the most universally popular of today's breeds.*

*Figure 1.* Late, rather heavy painting but fine slender separate legs come to their rescue.
Circa 1890
Height 8¼ inches

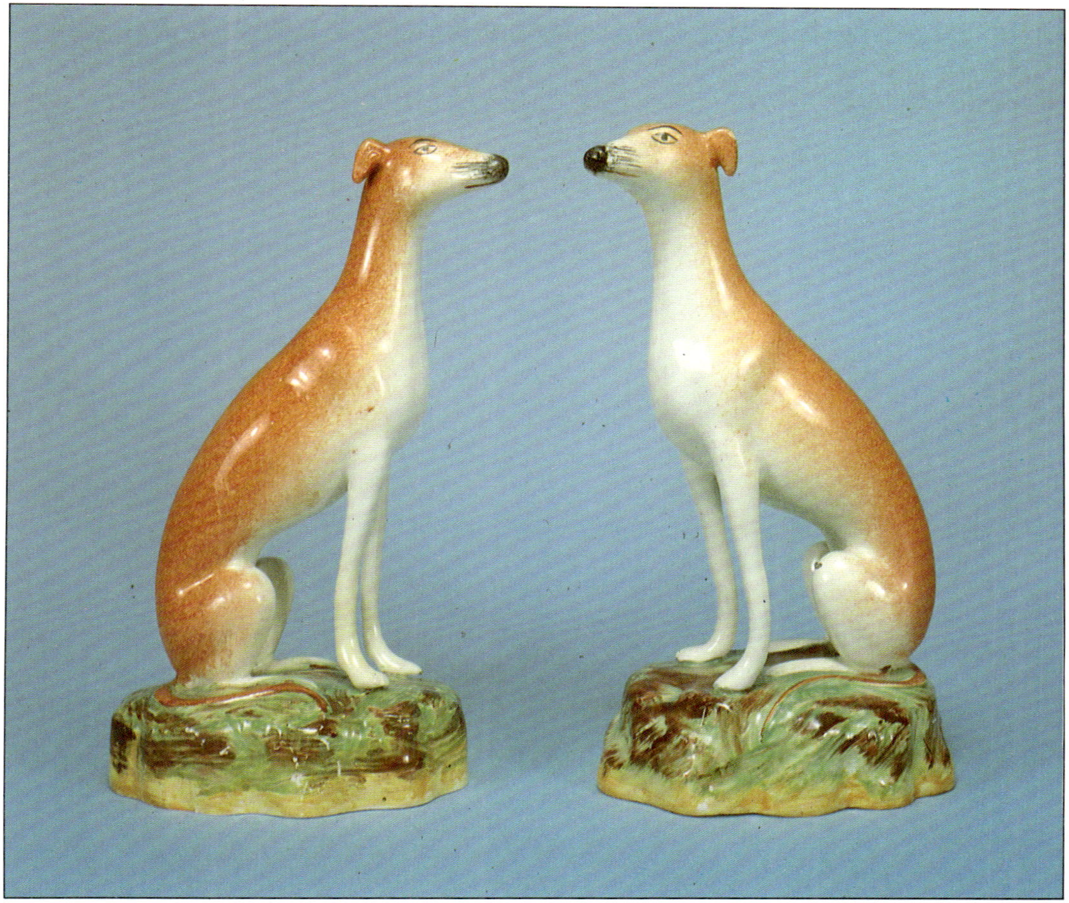

*Figure 1.*

# Mistaken Identity

*Perhaps the impossibility of judging true breed size in the world of ceramics and considering the recognised popularity of the breed today, probably accounts for the false assumption, made by many collectors and dealers alike, that a Greyhound is a "Whippet".*

*Taking the lateness of the breeds introduction as against all the considered early pointers of colour-palette, brushwork and fine modelling which are displayed in the majority of models, it is clear we are in fact looking at Greyhounds or Italian Greyhounds and very rarely in truth, at "Whippets".*

*I have therefore endeavoured to categorise these three distinct breeds into their correct categories, offering them (hopefully) a return to their true identity.* *(See Greyhound page 40 and Italian Greyhound page 64.)*

*Figure 2.* An extremely elegant and unusual pair of black "Jackfield-type" whippets with gilded stars on their breasts.
Circa 1885
Height 6½ inches

*Figure 3.* Reclining cross legged on grassy bases.
Circa 1900
Height 2½ inches

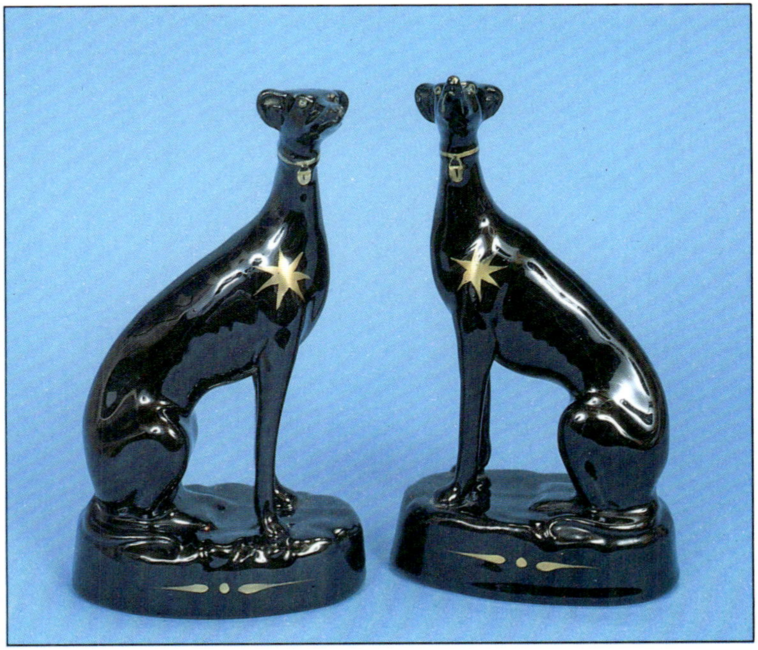

*Figure 2.*

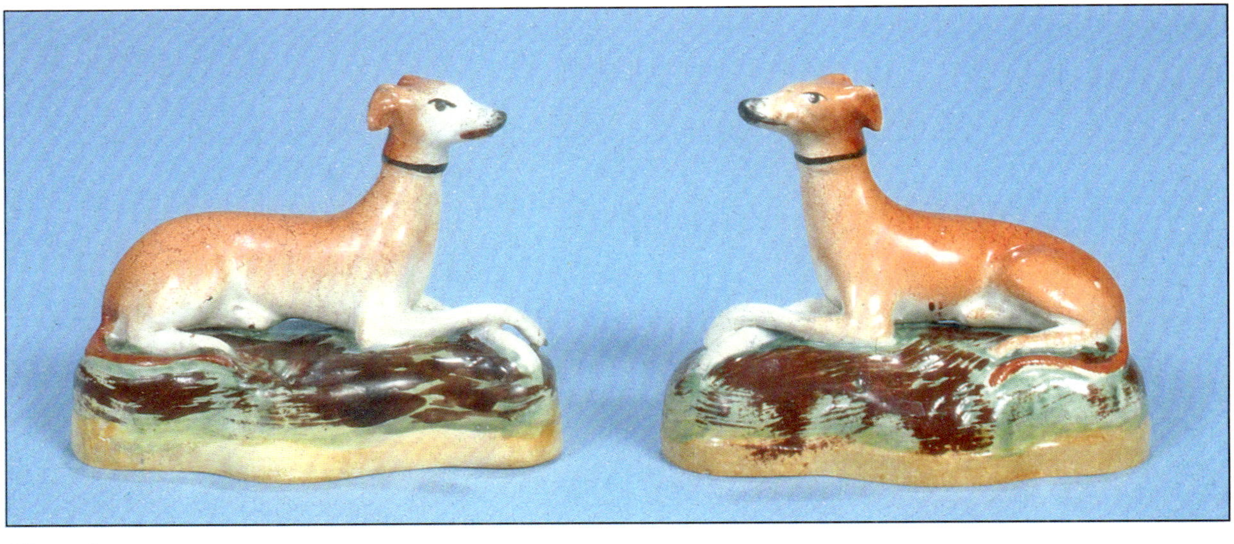

*Figure 3.*

X

Y

Z . . . . . .

# *Tail's End*

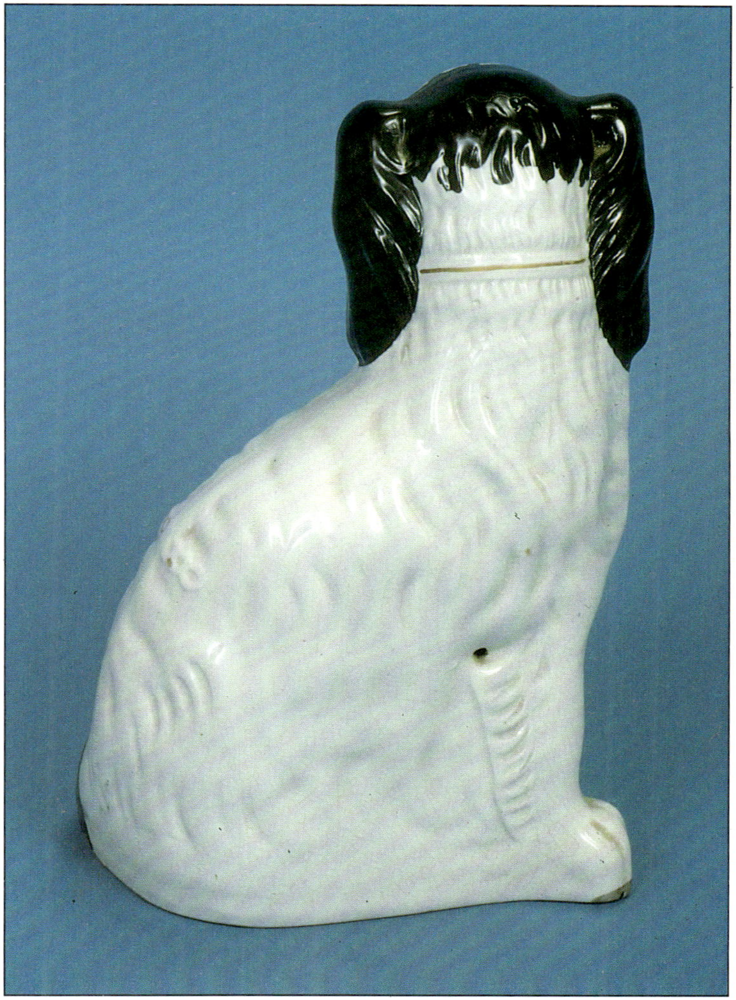

“Disraeli” dog on page 101 Figure 48.
Viewed from the back.

# Index